This story is true, but the names have been changed to protect the privacy and rights of the individuals outlined herein.

All scriptural references and quotations are from the *King James Version* of the Bible.

ISBN: 9780615474618

7th Edition Revised: October 2014

You might find redundancy in some of the scriptures referenced within this story. However, *repetition is the mother of all learning* (Thomas of Aquino, circa 1264).

Muscle and a Shovel

A raw, gritty, true story about finding the Truth in a world drowning in religious confusion.

Michael J. Shank

"The Matrix is a system, Neo. That system is our enemy. But when you're inside, you look around. What do you see? Businessmen, teachers, lawyers, carpenters. The very minds of the people we are trying to save. But until we do, these people are still a part of that system and that makes them our enemy. You have to understand, most of these people are not ready to be unplugged. And many of them are so injured, so hopelessly dependent on the system that they will fight to protect it[1]*."*

—Morpheus

"It is easier to believe a lie
one has heard
a thousand times
than to believe a fact
one has never heard before."

–author unknown

Dedicated

This book is dedicated to my wife, Jonetta, who has always remained at my side. Apart from the love of the Lord, her love and support has been the immovable force in my life.

Special Thanks

A very special note of appreciation to that small handful of Christian men and women at DuQuoin, Illinois, who so graciously loved me and believed in me when few others would.

A special thanks goes to my dear brother in Christ, Dan Webb. This book would have never come to fruition had it not been for Dan's deep love and tireless encouragement.

An additional note of heartfelt gratitude goes to Jeanie Fisher, Jason Fisher, and the Dexter family for their time and attention in offering the necessary feedback to make the book the best it could be.

And to "Randall." Randall, I owe you my eternal life and the eternal lives of my family. You'll never know how much love and respect I have for you. May the Lord continue to bless you richly and without end. I look forward to spending eternity with you.

A Warning with Love

You possess the most priceless possession known to all of humanity – an eternal soul. It is for this reason that I share my story with you, and I share this story out of genuine love and concern for your eternal future.

It is, in my humble opinion, no accident that this book has found its way to your hands. Your existing beliefs are about to be challenged, and your spirit is about to be exercised in ways you may have never considered. I ask only that you remember that it is with Christian love that I share this story with you.

The events in this book happened to me many years ago, and it is my hope that these events will serve as a gift to you.

You will only obtain the blessings though if you are able to read this story from beginning to end. However, please let me warn you. This story is going to anger, frustrate, and agitate your mind and spirit beyond description. It is going to challenge your existing beliefs and may turn your world upside down.

This is not for the weak-minded, nor is it for those who have their sensibilities easily offended. Some who start this story will not be able to finish it due to the emotional reactions it tends to incite.

If you are offended by what you find in the following pages, I ask that you forgive me. My intention is not to offend you but to share something powerful with you.

Will you have the courage, the heart, and the honesty of character to finish this story to the end? I pray that you will have that honest and good heart described by Jesus (Luke 8:15).

May our God and Father bless you richly with wisdom and a love for the Truth.

Last Chance

"This is your last chance. After this there is no turning back. You take the blue pill, the story ends, you wake up in your bed and believe whatever you want to believe. You take the red pill, you stay in Wonderland and I show how deep the rabbit-hole goes[1]*."*

—Morpheus

Friend, I'm about to show you…

Chapter 1
Top of the Steps

March 15, 1988: 12:45 a.m.

"What are three, white faces doing in this part of 'Nashvull' at this time a' night?" That is the way native Nashvillians pronounce the city's name. The Metro-Nashville officer stood at my driver's side window shining the beam from a long Magnum flashlight in my face.

There we were my wife, my best friend, Larry, in the back seat and me. I had pulled our black Pontiac Grand Am[1] to the side of the road at the corner Herman Street and 16th. We were only a few hundred yards from Fisk University's campus. Larry had been trying to get us to our location, but we were lost.

I was searching for the words as I squinted to see the cop through his light. He was the biggest black man I had ever seen – about 7' tall. He could have been a twin to the guy from the movie *The Green Mile*[2]. I bet he played pro-ball. His polished bald head and fire-hydrant sized arms reminded me of the Mr. Clean[3] man.

We had been profiled. Profiled? Yes. Any good cop worth their salt would have done the same. We were out of place in this neighborhood, and the fact that we were driving so slowly made it appear that we might have been looking to buy drugs. I saw the red and blue lights in my rear-view just as we were heading up 16th Avenue North, right across the railroad tracks and a few yards beyond Watkins Park.

Nashvillians call this area of town The West Loop. It was an urban neighborhood comprised mostly of African-American residents. The West Loop was also home to Fisk University, Tennessee State University, and the beloved Meharry Medical College.

Unfortunately, an element of the homeless had disgorged into The West Loop neighborhoods along with the usual accompaniment of drugs. Therefore, three white faces meandering slowly through this part of town at 12:45 a.m. was enough to motivate any alert cop to do a traffic check.

"You'll never believe me," I told the officer.

"Try me." He responded in a deep bass voice that conveyed the unspoken message, "Let's hear what you've got little man. I've heard it all before."

My heart said, "Be honest. Tell him. You've got nothing to lose. Truth has brought you this far, hasn't it?" I might as well give it a shot.

"We're on our way to get baptized!" The giant's eyes widened like someone had mashed his big toe with a drywall hammer.

"Tonight? Where?" he asked with a combination of suspicion and guarded excitement. I told him the name of the church building while shamefully admitting that we were lost. Guys just do not admit that they are lost.

What the cop said next not only blew my mind, it cemented the possibility of something I had long wondered about. Providence. Not Rhode Island's biggest city in the Narragansett Bay estuary, but the providence of God. Providence, in this context, is defined as the foreseeing care and guidance of God or a manifestation of Divine care.

I was never really sold on the concept of Divine providence until I heard the giant cop's response. It was then, upon hearing his words, that the principle was solidified in my mind. The officer's entire demeanor changed. He smiled and said, "I'm a member of *that* church. I actually go to *that* congregation! God must have wanted me to pull you over, because this part of town is not safe this time of night! I'm going to get back into my cruiser, so just follow me, and I'll take you to the building!"

We were speechless. I turned to look at my wife and then to Larry in the back seat. None of us knew what to think or say, but we were beginning to realize that God's fingerprints were on the events that were unfolding that night.

I watched the police officer in my driver's side mirror as he literally ran back to his squad-car. He ripped out around us leaving the red and blue lights on. Nobody back in Eldorado, Illinois, would ever believe this.

We followed the police car with his lights flashing feeling as though we were in some kind of a secret parade following "John Coffey's" twin brother. We drove past Rio Grande Ave, then Ireland Street, past Fisk on our left, then a right on Jackson Street. We continued down a few more blocks and followed him as he pulled into the church building's parking lot. The time was 12:52 a.m.

As we turned into the church's parking lot, Larry said, "Would you take a look at that." My wife, Jonetta (pronounced John–ē–tuh), whispered softly, "Who are they?"

None of us expected to see the elders and deacons standing out there in front of the building. They were all waiting for us to arrive! There they stood, shoulder to shoulder, on that cold March night - in suits and ties!

Those Godly men came to the building for the great event. They left the warmth and comfort of their own homes without hesitation, even wearing suits to demonstrate the dignity and importance of the occasion. We knew that *someone* would be there. I had anticipated two or three people but not a crowd this size.

The officer stepped from his car and greeted the men. It was evident that they all knew one another well. After a lot of smiles, hugs, and handshakes, the huge cop explained what had happened in the minutes prior to our arrival pulling us over, thinking we were buying drugs, and then giving us an escort to the church building because of his concern about our safety.

The giant cop said his goodbyes, killed the emergency lights, and drove off into the dark of the West Loop night.

The men of the church greeted us as long lost children. They met us like family members returning after a long trip. Each man made a formal introduction of himself and then expressed his personal excitement over our decision to follow the Lord Jesus Christ.

They brought us into the building and showed us our respective changing rooms. As we started to change into the baptismal garments we could hear them singing out in the auditorium. They sang just like they did in the first century. No instruments! They just used their voices, exactly as Ephesians 5:19 and Colossians 3:16 described. We had never heard anything like it before. It was loud, primitive, uninhibited, and even off-key at times, but it was also beautiful and soul-stirring.

While changing in the back room, I listened to the men's singing and searched for a word to describe their singing without instruments. My mind chased after the right word, but I could not land on it. "Stick your tongue out, Mike," the thought went through my mind. "The word is on the tip of your tongue!"

We changed into our baptismal garments and the men continued to sing and pray. The songs were rich in melody and meaning. Their prayers between songs were beyond description. They sang with such fervor that, at one point, I thought dozens more had entered the building while we were back in our changing rooms.

"Don't they know what time it is? Don't they know that they'll wake up the entire neighborhood?" My spiritually-immature mind was not grasping the magnitude of the transformation that was about to take place that night.

It was 1:15 a.m. Jonetta and I stepped to the top of the baptistery. We were barefoot; our hands were locked together, and tears were streaming down our faces. The building resonated with songs and hymns being sung by a group of men who had given their lives to the Master.

Jonetta and I stood at the top of the steps. We looked at each other - about to take *that* step. We knew only one thing for sure - our lives would never be the same.

She kissed my cheek, and the word that I had been searching for rushed to the forefront of my mind. It was the one word that so accurately described the men's singing, pure.

How in the world did a young, white, small-town, materialistic, ambitious, partying, not-too-religious, but members-of-a-big-denomination, married couple get the top of *these* steps?

You are about to find out. However, let me give you an honest and fair warning: this is a crazy, raw, crude, true story that will set you on edge and incite your emotions. Just know that in my humble opinion, your willingness and courage to read this story ***isn't*** a coincidence-

> *And we know that all things work together for good to them that love God, to them who are* **the called** *according to his purpose* (Romans 8:28).

Chapter 2
An Unexpected Friendship

August 3, 1987: Seven and a half Months Earlier

The Shell Convenience Mart at the corner of 17th and Broadway was packed that Monday morning, but no other place else would do. The routine stop had become a comfortable start of every work week.

Standing in line, I glanced down at the newspapers neatly positioned in their respective racks and caught the bold headlines predicting Mike Tyson's KO against the Olympic Super Heavy-weight Gold Medalist, Tyrell Biggs, in the upcoming fight.

"Tyson is a machine," thinking to myself as I collected the change from the Shell cashier who clearly needed more coffee herself.

After paying for gas, coffee (no cream, no sugar), and a bear-claw, I strolled to the car to finish the morning commute. It was only seven more blocks north.

The Mid-South's August morning air was already humid and my crisp, heavily starched, long-sleeved, white business shirt was feeling slightly damp with perspiration. Business etiquette in the south called for starched, long-sleeved shirts year-round, and *real* pros wore white undershirts under their dress shirts. I was not quite a real pro yet.

As I pulled out of the Shell parking lot onto 17th, a redneck almost took the front quarter panel off of my car missing me by only a few inches. I slammed my brakes looking up just in time to see him shoot me the bird while whizzing around the front-end of my car. We were known in the south for our hospitality, so I hospitably returned the gentleman a "Hollywood Howdy" of my own. Life in the big city. At least the coffee was still in the cup being held inside with a plastic sipper-lid. The bear-claw was not so lucky being out of arm's reach on the passenger side floorboard, and face-down on fine GM floor-mats. "Don't sweat the small stuff. It's all small stuff," I said out loud to no one, then turned up the radio and made my way up 17th Avenue. Peter Gabriel's song *Big Time*[1] was playing on the radio. It was a song supremely fit to the Eighties mentality.

OSI Data Solutions, Inc. was a company generating about $20m in yearly revenues, and our business was classified in the Graphic Arts industry. OSI did a couple of things very well. They sold printing presses and peripheral camera equipment (cameras that made plates for printing presses), and they sold paper by the train loads. The company also had several internal departments. One department sold smaller printing systems called mimeograph machines and they sold them to schools, offices, and churches. Lots of churches.

Jonetta and I had moved to Nashville with a specific plan. We wanted to build a life together, and I wanted to go to college at the same time. Nashville was a booming city only three hours from our small home town in southern Illinois. It seemed to be the right fit for our future. We could build a life together in the city, I could obtain a formal education, chase the dream, eventually get hired by a big software manufacturer, transfer to the west coast, become the CEO and make truckloads of cash - a perfect plan.

What we did not know about Nashville was that it, like many American cities, held some interesting secrets. One secret of Nashville was that the music industry was its *second* biggest industry. How could *music* in the *Country Music Capital of the World* take a back-seat to something *else,* and the world not know about it?

What was Nashville's secret number one industry? An industry bigger than country music? Printing. Nashville was a printing giant and I had not had a clue. Actually, most people did not know. Now I was involved in Nashville's number one industry, and it did not even require picking a guitar!

OSI Data Solutions also had other internal divisions that sold a variety of niche systems, systems used by hospitals in their patient-admissions departments, machines used by banks to make credit cards, and office equipment like paper cutters, folders, shredders, laminators, and the like. Everything sold from under the OSI roof had to be installed and tested. Customers required training, and all equipment required follow-up service.

This is where I came in. My official title was Technical Service Engineer. I was factory certified on a plethora of OSI's thing-a-ma-bobs! If OSI sold it, I could fix it. I would arrive each day a little before 8:00 a.m. to review the day's agenda and leave the office around 8:30 to go into the field. I would usually be back at the office by about 4:00 p.m. The last hour of the day revolved around paperwork and administrative duties.

My territory map looked like a triangular wedge. Put a pencil on Nashville, draw a line straight to the east, and then end at Cookeville. Then draw a straight line southwest, stop at Pulaski, and then draw a straight line north ending back in Nashville. It was a huge region that had 17 hospital accounts and over 200 church accounts. All required monthly service calls.

A big salary, full accompaniment of corporate benefits, a car allowance, expense account, a liberal commission program, all-expense paid factory certification trips, quarterly reviews, performance bonuses, and a college tuition cooperative reimbursement program for employees. It was a fantastic job for a twenty year old. Wait a minute, it was a fantastic job for a forty year old!

OSI Data's customers parked on the side lot which meant that employees had to park at the rear of the building. The front of the building acted as a buttress against Charlotte Avenue. There was no real *front* parking area. Parking in the back required employees to enter through the office building's back door located by the loading docks at Shipping & Receiving (S&R). All OSI employees used this one particular door to get to their offices.

I entered the back door that Monday morning with my coffee in one hand and my pseudo-lawyer looking briefcase in the other. There was that guy again. He was upbeat, smiling and working at his consistent above and beyond pace. There was something different about him, but I just could not put my finger on it.

As I began to weave my way through the myriad of S&R pallets hustling to get to my department office with only a few minutes to spare someone hollered, "Hey man! What's your name?" I looked back toward the direction of the voice, not really having the time to make friends. It was that guy. I stopped in my tracks as he approached. I responded while sticking out my hand, "Michael Shank. Mike. And you are–"

"Randall Edges. It's a pleasure to meet you, Mr. Mike!" He shook my hand in what I call a hand sandwich. That is when someone shakes your one hand with both of theirs, so that their two hands are the bread and your one hand is the meat.

Randall was different than the others that worked in Shipping & Receiving, and for a host of reasons. This young, African-American man had a natural confidence and an award winning smile that could set an executioner at ease. While the other guys in S&R seemed to shuffle around as though work was the last thing on their minds, Randall seemed to be that guy that loved his job. Eighties yuppies would have called Randall a mover and shaker. While the others looked disheveled, Randall was always intact and immaculate in appearance. It was as if he was covertly wealthy and his job in S&R was just something to do for fun.

I had never met a man that seemed so out of place as Randall. He was in his early thirties, clean cut, slim build, married with children, physically fit, and far too intelligent for his current departmental employment. Additionally, his attitude revealed a bullet-proof exterior.

"Since you are my new friend, I'm going to give you something," Randall exclaimed.

"Uh, that's really nice, but we just met, and you really don't have to–"

Randall quickly turned and walked to his desk, ignoring me. He tore off a paper towel, reached into a green and white box sitting on his desk, and pulled out two hot Krispy Kreme doughnuts[2]. Wearing a broad smile, he brought the doughnuts over to me, and in the most humble way said, "Mr. Mike, I hope you enjoy these. I might even have something *better* for you a little later!"

He then turned and walked away in a flash behind a stack of boxes before I could thank him. What a friendly and… weird guy. For Randall, my name from that day forth would be, Mr. Mike.

Two hot Krispy Kremes trumped a Shell station bear-claw any day of the week, and the sugar rush made me totally forget the redneck salute flung at me earlier that morning. But what did Randall mean, "I might even have something better for you a little later?" We had just met. We did not know each other.

I had not yet developed any latent skepticism of humanity, nor did I possess any suspicions about the possibility of ulterior motives, so I went about the day.

However, Randall had an ulterior motive.

Chapter 3
Are They Nuts or What?

November 20, 1987

It was now November. During the past three and a half months Randall and I had cultivated our friendship, and it had been intellectually stimulating to say the least. He would ask dozens of thought-provoking questions, all geared toward the spiritual side of life.

"Hey Shank! How many times did you eat today?" were the first words out of his mouth as I returned to the office from a client call one November afternoon.

I thought for a quick sec. "Three, so far."

Randall approached, walking rapidly across the dirty loading dock floors. He responded, "Okay, how many times did you eat of *spiritual* food today?" It was questions like this that had gotten me into the habit of reading my Bible.

"Oh, man! I'm starving to death!"

Randall laughed, and we both knew that nothing else needed to be said. Yes, Randall was a very different sort of Christian. The guy *lived* what he believed. But there was something else, he knew the Bible like no one I had ever met before. Lots of so-called Christians knew a few passages that fit their particular beliefs, but Randall had the most solid, over-arching knowledge of the Bible that I had ever seen. In reality, Randall had more Bible knowledge than any *Pastor* I had ever known. Ask him a Bible topic, and he would know where it was. Randall's understanding of biblical divisions, dispensations, compositions, authors, and intended audiences was truly remarkable. And his ability to recall Bible information from a specific book, chapter, and verse was truly impressive. He was a guy who had spent many years in personal Bible study.

November 20th was a clear, cool Friday afternoon. The last Friday before Thanksgiving week. I had just come in through the S&R rear door to finish up the day's paperwork before my commute back to our little apartment in southwest Nashville.

Randall was sitting at his desk as I came in and swiveled around toward me in his pre-1950's desk chair. It was a chair long reduced to the dusty corner among boxes of paper and ink. He had heard the back door open.

"Mr. Mike, did you know that Christ is coming back?" Randall was on top of his game.

"When is He coming?" I asked.

Without hesitation Randall replied, "Matthew 24:36 says, *of that day and hour knoweth no man, no, not the angels of heaven, but my Father only*." Randall handled me with humility and kindness, because he knew that I was an arrogant little punk who needed a dose of humility and kindness. Actually, I needed a *lot* of work. Randall had his hands full.

He continued without opening his Bible, "Mr. Mike, *seeing it is a righteous thing with God to recompense tribulation to them that trouble you, and to you who are troubled rest with us, when the Lord Jesus shall be revealed from heaven with his mighty angels, in flaming fire taking vengeance on them that know not God, and that obey not the gospel of our Lord Jesus Christ: Who shall be punished with everlasting destruction from the presence of the Lord, and from the glory of his power; when he shall come to be glorified in his saints, and to be admired in all them that believe (because our testimony among you was believed) in that day*. That's in 2 Thessalonians, chapter one, verses six through ten."

Wow! His Bible knowledge was truly amazing.

"Mr. Mike, that verse says that Jesus will take vengeance on them that obey not the gospel of our Lord. The question is, 'Have *you* obeyed the gospel of our Lord?'"

There was a pregnant pause as I considered the question. Had I obeyed the gospel? What the heck did he mean by that?

"I've been saved if that's what you're talking about?"

"How were you saved?" Randall asked respectfully. I could tell that he was sincerely interested in what I had to say.

I scratched my head. "Uh, let's see... I went to a revival at the Baptist Church when I was eight years old. At the end of the service the preacher asked who wanted to go to Heaven. I raised my hand. He then said something like, 'If you've got your hand up, are you saved and going to Heaven?' I knew I wasn't saved and it scared me. I didn't want to go to Hell. He then said something to the effect that we had to be saved to go to Heaven, and that anyone wanting to be saved should come forward.

"Even though I was terrified to go forward, I was more terrified of the thought of going to Hell, so I made my way past the people in the pew and out into the aisle, then I walked to the front of the auditorium. My third grade teacher was standing to the side as I reached the front of the church. She came over to me and told me to get down on my knees with her. She began to explain that I had to admit that I was a sinner and needed God's forgiveness. I admitted that I was a sinner and wanted God's forgiveness. She then asked me to repeat a prayer with her. I think it was called The Sinner's Prayer. I repeated what she told me to say, which included asking Jesus to come into my heart and save me from my sins. At the end of the prayer she said that Jesus had come to live in my heart, that I could trust that all of my sins had been forgiven, and that I was saved! When I died I'd go to Heaven!"

Randall listened with rapt attention, never interrupting. "Mr. Mike, were you ever baptized?" he questioned further.

"Uh, yeah. When I was thirteen," I answered.

"So," Randall said, "you were saved when you were eight years old by saying the prayer with her." Then he paused and got up out of the old swivel chair. "And you were baptized five years later?"

"Yeah, exactly!" I confirmed his accurate recital, happy that he had been listening so closely.

"Why'd you get baptized?" Randall asked.

That took a little more thought, but it came to me after a few moments. I remembered what the Pastor had told me from the baptismal ceremony. I answered, "It was an outward show of an inward change."

Randall, being very focused on my words, asked, "So you were saved *before* you got baptized, right?"

"Of course," I said without hesitation.

Randall was leaning back on the edge of his desk, listening closely, rubbing his chin with his right hand while resting his right elbow in his left hand. He was considering everything that I had shared with him to that point.

I stood there waiting for a positive response. Maybe he would give me an encouraging remark generated out of his normal state of exuberance. Maybe he would say, "That's great! Good for you!" I was sure that he would be excited and encouraging.

However, after Randall pondered my responses for several moments, he said, "Mr. Mike, saying the Sinner's Prayer *isn't obeying* the gospel of Christ. Secondly, *no* one in the Bible has ever been saved that way."

The air went out of my sail. He had not given me the reaction that I expected, and he confused me as well.

"What are you talking about?" I asked with a mixture of disappointment and frustration.

Randall smiled softly and said gently, "Mr. Mike, when Christ comes back He's going to take vengeance on those who haven't obeyed the gospel, so don't you need to know what the gospel *is* and how to obey it?"

He asked an honest question that deserved an honest answer. I was intrigued, but his question also revealed his ulterior motive. Randall was engaging me in a Bible study. It did not matter though, because I really wanted to know what the gospel was and how people obeyed it.

"Yeah, I would," I replied in kind with just a hint of reserve.

Randall asked me to commit to a one-on-one Bible study for the Monday following Thanksgiving. I made the commitment, wrote the day and time in my day-planner, and then went to my office. Larry, my best friend and co-worker, was already in from the field and busy at his desk, located just to the right of mine.

"Hi, Larry!"

"Hi, Mike!"

"Hey, me and Randall are going to have a Bible study after Thanksgiving." Before Larry could respond, Kirk (the alpha-male and the most out-spoken guy in our office) said, "Hey, Mike. Better stay away from that dude. His church thinks they're the only ones going to Heaven!" I looked at Kirk as he held his ink-pen in the corner of his mouth while wearing a gratified expression. He was sitting at his desk in a stretched-back position, the king of his domain. Alexander the Great must have had a similar look on his face after conquering the Persian Empire.

"What? They think they're the only ones going to Heaven? Are they nuts or what? Who'd have the audacity to think they had the monopoly on Heaven?" I shot the questions back at Kirk as my anger swelled; the volume of my voice grew with each syllable. Kirk's smile seemed to grow in direct proportion to my anger.

I jumped up out of my desk chair and walked at a brisk pace back toward Shipping & Receiving. "Forget the paperwork," I said to Larry. "I've just made an appointment with some kind of religious nut-job and I've gotta get out of this thing before I have a high-speed come apart!"

I walked through accounting and book-keeping and then through the paper warehouse simultaneously running the mental scenarios through my mind. I had to figure out exactly what to say to get out of the Bible study. S&R was just around the next corner.

"Kirk told me that you think you're the only ones going to Heaven! Is that true?" I said to the back of Randall's head as he sat at his desk. I had just verbally "sucker-punched" Randall. Randall spun around in his chair with an expression of shock.

"Mr. Mike, I don't judge anyone's soul! That's up to Christ alone, but the Bible says that Jesus bought His church with His blood, Acts 20:28. That's just *one* of the things we'll study about when we get together."

"Randall, let's just wait a while. I'll be real busy when we get back from our Thanksgiving trip, but we'll talk about it, okay?"

Randall was visibly disappointed, and he should have been. I had broken my commitment with him based solely on gossip, but I had to get out of that study. I had a lot of respect for Randall, but Kirk's gossip had infected me, and the seed of doubt had taken root.

Doubt causes indecision. Indecision causes inaction. Inaction causes us to put some of the most important things in life into that place where unimportant things reside. Inactions also causes idleness. Idleness increases doubt. Doubt, indecision, inaction, idleness: all work like dominos that, once falling, lead to more doubt. It's a vicious emotional circle.

This kind of emotional spiral creates emotional walls between the things that should be very important and the things that are unimportant. Once these walls grow, it becomes difficult to know how to tear them down.

However, another seed had been planted in my heart. It was the seed of Scriptures that Randall had planted in my heart when he quoted the Bible.

> *The Lord Jesus shall be revealed from heaven with his mighty angels, in flaming fire taking vengeance on them that know not God, and that obey not the gospel of our Lord Jesus Christ* (2 Thes. 1:7-8).

The verse played over and over again in my mind. What *was* the gospel? Wasn't that one of the books in the Bible? How do you obey a *book*? What did Jesus mean by *that*?

Jonetta was busy planning our trip back home during the weekend before Thanksgiving. She worked in Payroll and Accounting for a small retail athletic store located close to Belmont University.

We always enjoyed the short trips back to southern Illinois where we grew up. Thanksgiving dinner with her family in Harrisburg, then Thanksgiving supper with my folks in Eldorado. Eldorado and Harrisburg were two communities that were sports rivals situated a mere seven miles apart.

These little towns were located in the heart of the coal and corn belts, the two local industries that was the lifeblood of the region. Jonetta and I loved these communities because they represented everything in life that was good. They were full of hardworking, honest, independent, proud people who sacrificed for their families and gave to their neighbors.

A few days later we were on I-24 West heading back to southern Illinois. Jonetta always picked up snacks for the trip (I loved all the little things she did for us) and we were sharing a bag of pizza crackers.

"Randall quoted a Bible verse that said Jesus will take vengeance on everyone who did not obey the gospel," I said to my wife. "Honey, what is the gospel?" I asked her.

She took a drink from her water bottle and said, "Michael, the first four books of the New Testament are called the Gospels. Is that what you're thinking of?"

"Uh, maybe… no. I don't know." Randall's words from the Bible were stirring me and making me wonder. "No, that can't be it because you can't obey four books of the Bible. It doesn't make any sense."

When someone asked, "Are you saved," I would say, "Yes." But no one had *ever* asked me if I had *obeyed the gospel*. I had no clue what that meant.

The more I thought about it, the more it bothered me. Was the gospel and the Sinner's Prayer somehow connected? Of course! They had to be. But I needed to make sure, because even though I was young, arrogant, foolish, self-centered, sinful, abrasive, materialistic and shallow, I knew that the concept of eternity was an infinite amount of time. Hell would be a hot place to spend an infinite amount of time.

The conversation with Jonetta moved to the many other topics of life: love, hopes, dreams, past, future, and the bugs that get splattered all over the windshield when you're driving 79 mph on I-24 West (the pizza crackers suddenly lost their appeal).

She finally fell asleep at the Cadiz exit, and I sped along the interstate thinking about money, the in-laws, and a Thanksgiving turkey. Well, maybe not in that order.

Chapter 4
Yellow Scrap of Paper
November 30, 1987

Was I religious? Nah. No more religious than the next guy. Did I believe in God? Sure. Did I believe that Jesus Christ was God's Son? Absolutely. But I was not brought up in what you would call a religious home. My parents simply did not go to church when I was little. I got started in church by a little elderly woman named Eula who lived next door to us. Eula knocked on our door one day when I was about five years old and asked my mother if it would be alright for her to take me to church with her. Mom agreed, and from that point forward, I went with Eula every Sunday, being slowly trained up in Eula's faith. The Baptist faith.

Most of my friends went to the same Baptist Church, as well. Attending church was like going to school, the grocery store with mom, basketball camp in the summer, or our small-town Dairy Queen. The Baptist Church became a part of life.

Church was a weekly event just like our family vacation was a summer event. However, was I religious? No. Ask me if I was a Christian and I would say, "Sure!" However, I believed that, due to my salvation experience at the wise old age of eight, I could live pretty much any way I wanted, because I was saved. I did not really need to worry about it, and that is how most of the people I knew thought about it too.

The reality was that, while I wore the name Christian, Christ could rarely be found in my everyday life. Getting saved was an event that everyone did, but it was not a lifestyle. I compared it to buying a fire insurance policy with a one-time premium. I paid the premium when I was eight, but it did not require me to live in the insurance office so to speak.

My teenage years were wild. It was the Eighties, and I had the hair, the clothes, the music, the selfish drive for money, personal ambition, and a love of partying. I liked to drink beer, experimented with marijuana, cursed like my friends, and lived like the rest of the world. My friends and I all wore the label of Christian, but there was little difference between my lifestyle and the world around me. It all seemed very normal at the time. After all, I had been saved, and once I was saved I would always be saved, so it did not really matter what I did.

Little changed in my personal lifestyle after getting married. I went to church once in a while, did not kill anybody, did not rape anybody, never stole anything, did not do any serious drugs, obeyed the law, worked hard, paid my taxes, took care of my wife, gave a little bit to charity during TV telethons, and even gave a dollar to the homeless guy holding the cardboard sign around Music Row once in a while.

For all intents and purposes, I was a good guy, right? That was enough. Besides, I just did not have much time for religion. Jonetta and I were building a life together, and we wanted the finer things that life had to offer. We wanted a big home with an Olympic-sized pool in a pretentious suburb, a 7-series BMW, a Range Rover, a summer home in Colorado, a winter home in the Keys, residual income from investment accounts, fine clothes, vacations around the world, expensive jewelry, a yacht moored in the Carolinas, a house-keeper, a grounds-keeper, an accountant, a stock-broker, an attorney on retainer, and of course, an aggressive college account for our future brood. All of the things that young and aspiring materialists desire. God's program simply did not fit very well into my program.

OSI Data Solutions was just the first small stepping stone. My ultimate goal was to become a software CEO in the Silicon Valley with a seven-figure salary and stock options.

We arrived in Nashville after a much needed Thanksgiving break. We were back in the city to chase the dream.

A mixture of sleet and snow was falling that Monday morning when I stepped through the back door of OSI Data Solutions. Randall was not around the shipping area. I was relieved that he was not there because I was still a little uncomfortable over backing out of our Bible study the way that I did. Oh well, you cannot unring a bell.

I went back to my office, organized the day's agenda, and then followed the rest of the herd toward the company's outdated conference room on the second floor for a mandatory company meeting.

Jackson "Jack" Stayvick owned OSI Data Solutions, and he had some news to share with the organization. Jack was soft spoken but formidable. When the room quieted Jack announced that his son would be taking over as CEO. It was as if he had announced that the company was shutting the doors.

Ledger, Jack's son, had no experience in the industry, nor had he earned the respect of the employees. Ledger was young, arrogant, and very full of himself. He had a six-thousand square foot home in Brentwood given to him by daddy. He drove a 325i convertible BMW[1] that always had his over-sized touring bag of Ping[2] golf clubs in the back seat. Ledger loved to flaunt what his daddy had earned while giving the pretense of his own importance and self-worth.

The "kid" was a complete contrast to the modest, hard-working, get-your-hands-dirty, kind of guy that Jack was, and the OSI employees resented Ledger deeply.

At any rate, after the news of change filled our ears, everyone filed out of the smoke-filled meeting room. Randall caught me midway down the wooden staircase that exited into the paper warehouse.

"Hey Shank, wait up," he said in his chipper way.

"Hi, Randall, what's going on?" I replied.

"I want to ask you something," Randall said as he sidled alongside. "Do you have to be baptized to be saved?"

"Of course not," I said without any pause.

Then he handed me a small torn piece of notebook paper. It was a corner piece from a yellow legal pad. A Bible verse was scribbled on the scrap:

1 Peter 3:21

He said, "Check this out man. I'll catch up with you later." Off he went.

I was scheduled to go to Lawrenceburg that morning (83 miles from Nashville). Our company had a MetaCard patient-admissions system at Crockett Hospital, and the system was down.

Trouble-shooting the hospital's system had taken all morning, but the final diagnostics test was successful and the admissions staff was back in business. It was the lunch hour, and Lawrenceburg had a McDonald's. I opted for the drive-thru, then escorted my Big Mac[3] and fries over to the David Crockett State Park to eat in solitude. There was no ambient hospital noise or nurses complaining in the background. Just AM talk radio.

There was a new guy on WLAC 1510 out of Nashville. Rush Limbaugh was his name, and from what I could tell it was some kind of political talk show. He was an entertaining guy, no doubt, but WLAC's weak signal carried a lot of static that far out of Nashville.

The yellow scrap of paper laid there in the console. 1 Peter 3:21.

"What does that say?" It would have to wait. I did not have a Bible in the car. Strange, no one had ever handed me a Bible verse. That was an odd thing to do, wasn't it?

As I pulled into OSI's lot at 4:45 p.m. Larry was walking out to his car. He was already heading home for the day. Larry had just started carrying a Bible in his briefcase, but don't ask me why.

"Hey, Larry," I hollered across the lot through my rolled-down window. Larry turned and smiled when he saw that it was me.

"Hi Mike! You go to Pulaski today?" he asked.

"Lawrenceburg," I corrected.

"Oh. Mileage check is going up!" Larry grinned.

I laughed, "So are gas prices!" Gas was running $1.05 per gallon. Ridiculous! How high were they going to get?

"Hey, grab your Bible, would you?" I said to Larry as I got out of my car. He was over at his red Pontiac Sunbird. Did everyone at OSI drive Pontiacs now?

"You doing that Bible study with Randall?" Larry asked remembering our pre-Thanksgiving conversation that Kirk had interrupted.

"No, I got out of that, but he did a hand-off after the meeting this morning, and he gave me this." I showed him the yellow slip of paper with the verse on it. Larry took a look.

"I'm curious to know what it says," I said.

Larry took his Bible out of his briefcase and opened it on the trunk of his car. He thumbed through the gold-edged pages having trouble navigating the conglomerate of names in the Holy Book. After finding the right book, Larry asked for the chapter and verse again. I repeated it, and he found it.

He handed his Bible over, and I read the verse quietly to myself. The verse said,

> *The like figure whereunto even baptism doth also now save us (not the putting away of the filth of the flesh, but the answer of a*

good conscience toward God,) by the resurrection of Jesus Christ (1 Peter 3:21).

"Larry, look at this," I said, handing his Bible back to him while pointing at verse 21 with my index finger. "Have you ever seen this verse?"

He read it quietly to himself. "No, I guess I haven't, but it's faith that saves us, isn't it?"

"Well, yeah, of course. Baptism is some kind of work. Hey, I'm going to ask my Pastor about this verse, and I'll get back to you. Thanks, Larry."

"See ya later, Mike."

I walked toward the office as Larry drove away, wondering about the verse and why Randall had done the *hand-off* thing that morning, but everyone in S&R was already gone for the day.

This verse required a religious expert.

Chapter 5
The First Duel

December 1987

"Don't worry about it," he stated with smug, Pastoral confidence. "It's taken out of context. Ephesians 2:8-9 says that we're saved by grace through faith, not works. Baptism is a work."

I suddenly felt much better about my Baptist faith. Our quick, after-services counseling session with our Baptist Pastor was paying off. My wife, who by the way, had the longest natural eye lashes that God ever gave any woman, sat in a padded chair next to me in the Reverend's upscale office. I glanced at his wall calendar: December 6.

Our Pastor, the religious expert, advised us that Randall had indeed taken 1 Peter 3:21 out of context. Interestingly enough, even though we called ourselves Baptists, we believed that baptism had nothing to do with salvation. I had, as most every Baptist member since the inception of the Baptist Church, had been taught that baptism was not part of being saved; however, baptism *was* necessary to become a member of the Baptist Church.

I was now armed with a new level of religious confidence and loaded for bear. Looking back, I was a fool. I went to church, but didn't read my Bible. Now I was becoming a religious expert by running back to my Pastor so that he could instruct me on how to think and what to say in all things pertaining to religion.

The next day I was ready with a Bible in my briefcase and my Baptist Pastor's words well scripted and ready to be fired as mortar rounds into Randall's camp. I arrived fifteen minutes early for the duel, and I was nervous. Religion was not my forte. Randall, however, was as skilled in the Bible as my Baptist Pastor. Maybe I should have brought the Pastor with me?

I stepped through the back door of the office, and there he was running around the Shipping & Receiving floor at his breakneck pace looking crisp with his million-dollar attitude lighting up the place. Randall saw me come through the door and hollered, "There's the man that can fix anything! How you doing, Mr. Mike?"

I smiled back and waved him over, pulling out my Bible at the same time. Randall beamed with excitement when he saw my Bible. "Alright, Mr. Mike! You must have read the passage I gave you!"

"Yeah, Randall, but it's out of context," I repeated with great confidence, staying on script.

"What do you mean, my friend?" Randall asked sincerely, with no animus.

"Well," I was gearing up, "Ephesians 2:8-9 says that we're saved by faith, not works, and baptism is a work." Pulled it off! I had successfully mimicked my Pastor's level of confidence.

"Mr. Mike, you're absolutely correct about faith, and I'm proud of your willingness to study your Bible. Man, you're doing great! God tells us in 2 Timothy 2:15 that we're to *study to show thyself approved unto God, a workman that needeth not to be ashamed, rightly dividing the word of truth*! You're also correct in saying that we're saved by faith and not by works, but my friend, baptism is not a work. Let me show you with your Bible," and he asked for my Bible.

I thought to myself, "Hang on a second! Where's the fight?" Randall had disarmed me. I went in prepared for a Bible battle, and he was not fighting. In reality, his persona magnified something I'd rarely seen in others who wore the Christian label. Love and humility.

Randall quickly flipped through the pages of my Bible as we stood over his desk. While waiting on him to find his text, the back door swung open. It was Kirk (the Alpha-male of our office and the one who'd told me to stay away from Randall).

I knew as soon as Kirk saw me standing with Randall that I was busted. The look on Kirk's face said it all. His facial expression said, "Mike, you idiot! I told you to stay away from that guy, and there you stand disobeying my supreme inter-office dictate!"

"Mr. Mike," Randall regained my attention as he landed in the book of Ephesians. "Chapter 2 verse 8 says, '*For by grace are ye saved through faith; and that not of yourselves: it is the gift of God.*' Verse 9 says '*not of works, lest any man should boast,*' so you're correct in saying that we're saved by faith and not of works. But it is you, my friend, who is pulling this out of context."

"Me?" I was heating up.

"Yeah," Randall said softly, "but let me show you why." He went on. "Listen man, Paul wrote this letter to the church at Ephesus to a group of Christians who were being heavily influenced by new Jewish converts to Christianity. You see, these Jews, who formerly were under the Law of Moses, were now trying to teach new *Gentile* Christians that they had to go back to the former works of the Law, the Law of Moses. Those Jews were teaching those new Gentile Christians that they had to be circumcised. That was the work Paul was talking about. It was a former work of the flesh. Now Mike, that old Law of Moses was abolished on the cross along with the Jewish works of the flesh."

Randall moved forward. "Look here in this same chapter at verse 15 (Ephesians chapter 2), '*having abolished in his flesh the enmity, even the law of commandments contained in ordinances; for to make in himself of twain one new man, so making peace.*' Paul was correcting the new Christians at Ephesus, telling them here in Ephesians 2:10-22 that Christians were no longer under the former works of Moses.

The new Jewish converts to Christ had been boasting that they were more righteous and more sinless because they had obeyed the previous law of circumcision, which is the work that Paul refers to here. But Paul corrected them, stating in verse 9 that our faith was not of works. Our faith is not of *old Jewish practices.*

"Mr. Mike, the works Paul speaks of here in Ephesians 2:8-9 is clearly the works of the Law of Moses. Paul was correcting their erroneous thinking, lest any *Jewish-Christian* should boast. Do you see that?"

"Yeah," I understood the context. Randall was right, and the scripture made a great deal of sense in context. My Pastor had not explained the context of Ephesians chapter 2, nor had he brought any of this up during our meeting.

"My friend," Randall said, "if we try to go back to the Law of Moses, we actually fall from God's grace, because Galatians 5:4 says, '*Christ is become of no effect unto you, whosoever of you are justified by the law; ye are fallen from grace*.' Those Jews who became Christians at Ephesus were trying to incorporate some of the former laws of Moses like physical circumcision. They were fallen from grace and that's why Paul emphasized not of works. He was talking about the previous works of Jewish Law."

"But Mike," Randall continued at a fast pace, "Paul isn't saying that we do *nothing* to access the grace of God. As a matter of fact, faith only or faith alone is a false doctrine! Do you know that there is only *one* place in the whole Bible where you find the phrase 'faith only?'"

I shook my head in the negative. I didn't know, nor did I know where it was found.

Randall, seeing the nod, moved on, "It's right here in the book of James, chapter 2, verse 24. '*Ye see then how that by works a man is justified, and* ***not by faith only***.' Look here at verse 17 – '*Even so faith, if it hath not works, is dead, being alone*.' And verse 19 – '*thou believest that there is one God; thou doest well: the devils also believe, and tremble*.'"

Randall was schooling me in the lost art of reasoning the Scriptures together. It was an art that I was completely unfamiliar with.

"Mike, James says that faith, being by itself, is dead! It cannot and will not save any man! The devils also believe, but they're not saved, are they?" Randall asked, and waited.

I finally looked up at him, thinking that it was a rhetorical question, but I ultimately blurted out, "Of course not!"

Randall laughed and agreed with me. "Then why, Mr. Mike, do men think that faith *only* saves them today, while the book of James, and many other passages in the other books of the New Testament, clearly teach that faith only does *not* save them?"

There I stood unsure and shaking my head. I was out of my depth having just seen passages that I had never seen before.

Smiling, Randall finished his own question. "Again, it's because *they* pull scriptures like this (Ephesians 2:8-9) out of context trying to make Paul's statement mean something that it does not mean! No disrespect, Mr. Mike, but lots of denominations tear up the Bible by ripping passages completely out of context."

I had heard Ephesians 2:8-9 quoted throughout my life, and we, Baptists, always used it to refute, discredit, and negate any action toward salvation. I had never heard Ephesians 2:8-9 in its proper context, nor had I ever read the entire chapter. I did not realize that the Apostle Paul was speaking of the Jewish Christian converts who were trying to bring in the previous Jewish laws like circumcision. It was the Jewish Christians who were boasting about the Jewish works that they had done, and they were trying to convince the Gentile Christians to follow the former works of the Law of Moses–physical circumcision.

Now, of course, many of my Baptist counterparts would say, "Well, I would have taken him to this scripture or that scripture," but so what! I wanted to deal honestly with the part of the Bible that was put before me. The problem with religious men who are steeped in their existing beliefs is that they will not reason together honestly. They will not sincerely listen and consider the current topic. Instead, they busy their minds by searching for other passages to jump to rather than really listening and considering the arguments before them. Their minds run away in defense of their religious position which prevents any real listening and logical reasoning of the Bible together.

Why don't we Baptists confront the fact that we have used Ephesians 2:8-9 out of its proper context for hundreds of years to defend the faith only platform? How about we confront the fact that this passage, in its context, does *not* teach, instruct, support, or advocate the faith only idea at all? Why won't we deal honestly with the context of Ephesians 2:8-9 and accept the Bible fact that Paul was talking about the works of the former Law of Moses?

How are we Baptists so completely inconsistent with our faith only platform? We are inconsistent when we teach that someone is saved by faith *only*, but in reality we require that faith must be accompanied with repentance, coming forward at an alter call, and asking Jesus into our hearts by praying a prayer such as the Sinner's Prayer? That is hardly *faith only*.

I knew another reason why we were so inconsistent. It was easier to believe something I had heard a thousand times before than to believe something I had never heard in my life!

"Mr. Mike," Randall went on, "I want you to take a simple teaching to bed with you tonight."

I asked, "What's that, Randall?"

Randall turned the pages of the Bible to another book, found his target, and read, "*As also in all his epistles, speaking in them of these things; in which are some things hard to be understood, which they that are unlearned and unstable wrest, as they do also the other scriptures, unto their own destruction.*" Randall put a special emphasis on the latter part of the verse.

"What does that mean?" I asked.

"That means," Randall answered, "that some of the things in the Bible take more study to understand than others, and people who haven't studied their Bibles (the unlearned and the unstable) wrest the Bible. They literally twist the scriptures and the end will be their own eternal destruction.

"Mr. Mike, that's what's happening all over the world right now. Unlearned and unstable men twist the scriptures to support their own beliefs, and they do so to their own spiritual destruction."

"Where is that verse found?" I asked.

He turned the Bible around and pointed to the verse with his index finger. It was 2 Peter 3:16.

I felt something vibrating on my hip. My pager was going off! I looked at my watch. It was 8:07 a.m., and my boss was looking for me. I was inside the building, but not at my desk.

"Randall, I gotta go, but we need to talk about this more, alright?"

"Oh yeah, Mr. Mike. I'll catch you later!" Randall said with a smile and a nod.

Randall Edges was definitely different. He was encouraging, meek, respectful, full of Christian love, and God's grace! It was evident that he truly and sincerely loved God with all of his heart. But the biggest difference? He defended his position with the Bible, and that was something I had never seen anyone do quite like Randall did.

As I walked away from him, he quoted a scripture to my back, "'*If any man speak, let him speak as the oracles of God.*' That's 1 Peter 4:11, Mr. Mike!" I smiled and kept walking.

Could he read minds, too? Weird. Regardless of what Kirk had said about the guy, Randall's nature was different. It was compelling.

No more time to talk. The boss didn't put up with tardiness in his employees, especially future software CEO's.

But I knew one thing for sure… if I was an *honest* man, I could never again use Ephesians 2:8-9 to support the *faith only* doctrine. This was, at least in this one instance, a demonstration of how we Baptists were guilty of wresting the Scriptures of God. I didn't want to be guilty of wresting the scriptures.

Chapter 6
Am *I* Going to Hell?
Later that Morning

Kirk was the office leader, and I wanted his acceptance. But I had infringed on his advice, and he had caught me discussing the Bible with Randall. Kirk said little to me throughout the rest of the morning. He was pouting over my disobedience.

All of us worked at our desks until lunchtime. We smoked, talked, mulled over paperwork, told office war stories, drank automatic-drip coffee, and shared the latest industry gossip.

At lunch a couple of the guys were packing up, and getting ready to leave the office to make service calls. Larry was on the phone. One of the engineers was installing a heat-roller into a GBC Laminator. Kirk was focused on organizing contracts for his biggest account, Vanderbilt Medical Center. I closed up my files and got ready to go into the field.

"Mikey," Kirk said to me, getting my attention. Kirk was about eight years older than I was, and he had called me Mikey ever since we had met. I never knew why.

"Yeah, Kirk," I said, turning to him as I lifted my briefcase from my desk.

"You know that guy Randall believes that Baptists, Methodists, Presbyterians, Catholics – everybody but *his* church are all going to Hell?"

"Kirk, I haven't really found out what the guy believes, because we haven't discussed it that much yet," I replied.

"Just a heads up, buddy," Kirk warned.

"Thanks man." I was leaving the office with the feeling that my infraction had been forgiven.

But was that *really* what Randall believed? How could anybody believe that? Cults believed that kind of thing, didn't they? Weren't we all headed to the same place, but just taking different roads to get there? At least that is what I had heard people say many times before. How about the phrase I had seen printed on the backs of semi-trailers, "Join the church of your choice?" It was a mantra that seemed intelligent, reasonable, and tolerant. Wasn't I an open-minded guy? Why are there so many churches anyway? Why couldn't people agree? Wasn't there just one Bible? Wasn't there just one God? Wasn't there just one Jesus? Was there a correct teaching?

Through the myriad of mental questions sprouting up in my mind, a central premise came to the surface:

> *All denominations teach conflicting doctrines; therefore, it isn't possible that all of them are biblically correct.*

My path to the car took me through Shipping and Receiving right past Randall's desk. I simply could not resist. My need to be liked by Kirk combined with Kirk's gossip about Randall's alleged beliefs was just too strong. I had to bring it up again.

"Randall, I've got to know if it's true," I stopped between his desk and the back door. "Do you think that all denominations except yours are going to Hell?" I had caught him counting boxes of ink on a pallet that had just been forked out of the back of an eighteen-wheeler. Randall would stop everything he was doing to discuss the Bible.

"Mr. Mike, we're not a denomination. It's not that simple." Randall replied as he looked me square in the eye.

I wasn't about to let up. "Randall, you know that I'm a Baptist. Now, if I die, am I going to Heaven or Hell? Just tell me what you think."

"Mr. Mike," Randall hesitated, "I am *not* the judge of your soul. Only God does that, but the Bible says that if you obey the gospel, God adds you to the church of the Lord Jesus Christ, and Christ will save His church."

"It sounds like you're talking in circles or something," I replied with frustration wanting a simple yes or no. Randall knew I was frustrated, but he was not going to discuss religion without an open Bible in a proper setting, and neither of us had the time at that moment.

"How about we get together tonight and study the Bible," Randall countered. I was, however, determined to force an answer from him on the spot.

"Randall, just give me a straight answer. Am I going to Heaven or Hell?" Randall was in a metaphorical corner, and he knew that I was not letting him out without an answer.

He conceded, "Friend, it's not what *I* think that's important. It's what the *Bible says* that's important. The Bible clearly teaches that everyone who's not a part of the church that Jesus purchased with His blood, Acts 20:28, will not be saved."

"Ah, Randall!" I raised my voice and felt as though the top of my head was going to blow off! "Look, if I'm a Baptist, is it Heaven or Hell? Answer me straight!"

"Mr. Mike," he said meekly, "from my understanding of God's Word, if you're a member of a denomination, whether it be Catholic, Baptist, Methodist, Presbyterian, Episcopalian, Mormon – *anything* that Jesus Christ did not establish and buy with *His* blood, there's no question that you're headed toward eternal destruction."

Kirk was right! I couldn't believe it! I was furious! I felt the immediate rush of adrenaline dump into my bloodstream from the bilateral Adrenal glands just above the kidneys. I thought I would punch him in the face! Instead, I turned and stomped out the back door toward my car, but not before I yelled back at Randall, "You're the most narrow-minded person I've ever met! As a matter of fact, you're so narrow minded that you could look through a keyhole with both eyes at the same time!"

Jumping in my car, I threw the briefcase over the headrest into the back seat, started the engine, and squealed the tires, leaving a trail of smoke behind me. So mature.

"To (*expletive*) with him," I thought. "I'm a Christian, and I'm going to Heaven. I don't give a (*expletive*) about what he thinks!"

Oh yes, what a fine Christian I had turned out to be! It was about to get even better.

Chapter 7
Fight or Flight
Christmas Approaching

Most people have been equipped with the fight or flight mechanism. Dr. Walter Cannon, an American Physiologist and Professor in the Department of Physiology at Harvard Medical School, coined the phrase. His hypothesis and the phrase was introduced in his book *Bodily Changes in Pain, Hunger, Fear and Rage: An Account of Recent Researches into the Function of Emotional Excitement* (Appleton, New York, 1915). Cannon's theory states that animals react to threats with a general discharge of the sympathetic nervous system, priming the animal for one of two subsequent responses: fighting or fleeing.

At my current age of 20 years old, my character craved a good fight. I was independent, strong-willed, and rebellious. Why? Who knows? My aggressive nature was probably due to an accumulation of circumstances.

I had been adopted at birth by a loving, blue-collar family. Dad was an over-the-road trucker who was gone six days out of every week. Mom was an LPN, but during my Seventh grade year she developed Septicemia and almost died. She was never the same after that.

From that point forward my life did a complete turn-about. It was not Mom's fault, it is just the way things were. Dad had to work, so he was never at home. Mom struggled with her health, so it was difficult for her to be a mother. I, out of necessity, became a mom and dad unto myself, and I grew increasingly resentful toward the authority that my father tried to assert over me during his one day at home.

The circumstances of our home life, combined with my teenage hormones, created a situation whereby two loving parents could no longer control an independent, strong-willed, rebellious, self-supportive teenager. It began in my pre-teen years. At the age of twelve, I was cooking, cleaning, checking mom's blood pressure four to six times each day, setting up her meds, and taking care of minor stuff around the house.

At the age of sixteen I began taking care of the family cars, did the grocery shopping, picked up mom's meds from the pharmacy, took her to doctors' appointments, made sure the household bills were paid, and was essentially the man of the house.

It was during that period of time that I met Jonetta. She was a cheerleader and a country-girl who loved to draw and paint. She had aqua-blue eyes that melted me like hot butter and eyelashes that could whip a man from across a room! She was prissy one minute and a tomboy the next.

We dated for the next two years and fell in love. We discussed marriage after graduation. Running a household was nothing new to me, and being with Jonetta at a new address was appealing in every way. It meant that I could get away from the home life that had become a burden and be with the love of my life.

Jonetta and I married shortly after our high school graduation and moved directly to Nashville, Tennessee. It would be another five years before we would have our first child.

Randall's opinion that I was headed to Hell was just what I needed to get me going in a spiritual direction. The fight nature was kicking in, and I was resolved to find the spiritual answers that I so deeply craved. No one would ever put me in a spiritually defenseless position again.

However, something very profound was happening to my spirit that would take much longer for me to recognize. Randall created an interest in me to examine my personal beliefs and actually defend them – a biblical principle in and of itself. This new found interest caused me to start picking up tracts. Tracts are those little religious pamphlets that every church seems to offer. They're normally found lying on a table or placed neatly in a decorative rack in many church foyers. And remember, I had about 200 different churches in my OSI territory, so I had the opportunity to pick them up almost every day.

The tracts I collected covered every topic: worshipping on the Sabbath, drinking, smoking, dancing (all the fun things to do, or so I thought), worshipping God, the authority of the Bible, and matters of salvation.

I became a reading machine, which was a big change to our active lifestyle. Jonetta and I played racquetball and tennis regularly. We golfed together and shopped a lot. Going out to eat several nights each week was the norm and entertaining friends was a must.

Our apartment was located in a Nashville suburb called Bellevue (sounds like the psychiatric hospital) about 13 miles southwest of downtown. It was a nice suburb and really starting to grow during that period in the late Eighties. Our apartment complex had swimming pools, tennis courts, an exercise gym, and tanning beds. A full complement of amenities that would attract Eighties yuppies.

Now many evenings were occupied with reading. Jonetta, always supportive, began to ask questions of her own. We started studying together, discussing the issues, and evaluating the many denominational philosophies. We both started to recognize a common denominator in these little religious books, and our studies brought us to a common conclusion:

> *Read every single one of the tracts from every denomination represented within. Conduct an objective comparative analysis. The conclusion was the same: only one denomination seemed to be able to turn to the book, chapter, and verse for everything they believed and practiced with the Bible. It was the one that Randall belonged to, even though their literature stated that they weren't a denomination.*

Jonetta was wearing her pink pajamas and sitting in the middle of our living room floor wrapping Christmas presents. "Michael," she said, "think about it. When you make spiritual decisions, you're limited. You've got the Bible, your opinions, and denominational teachings. That's it!" She was right. She was beautiful *and* smart!

I sat down in the floor next to her and handed her a cup of hot chocolate.

"Actually, Jonetta, you've got a point. What else is there? Look at all these tracts we've been reading. The majority are written opinions with a few scriptures sprinkled throughout. I hate to admit it, but Randall's church seems to back up *everything* they believe and practice with the Bible. The others offer some scripture, but what they offer seems disjointed and out of context."

Jonetta thought about it for a moment.

"Michael, where *did* the Baptist Church come from?"

"That's a good question!" I exclaimed while admiring her willingness to think beyond the usual boundaries.

"Thanks," she said and smiled. "Now get me some marshmallows for this hot chocolate!"

"Hey little woman," I barked back, and we both laughed loudly!

What a great question! Where did the Baptist Church come from?

Chapter 8
Enough to Make a Guy Cuss!

Christmas Closing In

We went to our Baptist Church the following Sunday. It was filled with the E.T.C. (Easter, Thanksgiving and Christmas) Christians. You know the Christians that only go to church three times a year? We could barely find a seat.

We waited after services for what seemed like an hour until everyone filed out, and we could get some alone time with the Pastor.

"Reverend, we've got a quick question," I said respectfully. He took us back to his spacious, finely decorated office and sat down in his large, leather, executive chair.

"Uh, yes, what can I help you with?" I realized that he didn't remember our names.

"Where and when did the Baptist Church begin?" The good Reverend leaned back in his extravagant chair and scratched his balding head.

"Well, it's my opinion that John the Baptist started the Baptist Church," he responded in a condescending tone that conveyed an unspoken message. It told me I was stupid for wasting his precious time with such a rudimentary and trivial question.

Even though I did not appreciate his tone, the premise made sense. We were, of course, "Baptists." Duh! However, I remembered how Randall backed up everything he said with the Bible, so I asked, "Could you help me find that in the Bible?"

"Look at Matthew 3, and I hope y'all will come back tonight." He gave an obligatory smile and then spun around to face the paperwork on his desk, which was evidently much more important than two young parishioners whose names he could not remember.

Jonetta and I looked at each other. Apparently our meeting was over.

"What a pompous (*expletive*)," I quipped as we walked down the wide, newly carpeted halls of the contemporary church building. My attitude did not reflect good morality – I needed a lot of work.

"Honey, he's just busy," she said forgivingly.

"Yeah, and just think," I said, "that guy lives off of our donations while he parks his fat (*expletive*) in that fancy chair that we pay for, mind you, but he doesn't have the time to open his Bible when confronted with an honest Bible question?"

Jonetta frowned while trying to quiet me down. People were still milling around the building. She was not successful.

"What'd you write that offering check for this morning?" I asked as we walked faster through the lavish hallways toward an exit. "Ninety bucks? I bet he'll take the time to count out those ninety bucks. What do you bet?"

"Michael!" Jonetta exclaimed, but it was no use. Thoughts started flashing through my mind. Churches were becoming all about the money with their multi-million dollar worship facilities, family recreation life centers, gymnasiums with in-door walking tracks, high-tech lighting for entertainment, and sound systems more expensive than Michael Jackson's. Those churches seemed to be replacing Bible content for bigger buildings and better entertainment. Why? To draw bigger crowds, of course. Bigger crowds meant bigger donations. Bigger donations meant bigger paychecks and better lifestyles for the leadership of those churches.

It was becoming apparent that churches were not immune to materialism, greed, or covetousness. Wasn't a big, lavish, expensive church building a display of unchristian opulence? Weren't bigger church buildings designed to appeal to the lust of the eye and to impress those with money? Weren't they designed to lure people?

Money. It was becoming all about the money. TV preachers were raking in millions from little old ladies living on fixed, poverty-level incomes while they lived the lifestyles of Sheiks. Living on money given to them under the guise of giving to God.

Don't get me wrong. I loved free enterprise, capitalism, and profit. We lived in the greatest country on the planet on the greatest planet in the universe. However, greed, materialism, and the gospel of money in the church did not jive with me.

To top it off, arrogant Pastors who lived large from the donations of the church disgusted me. Hey, if a guy wants to make the big bucks in the land of the free and the home of the brave, then by all means he should knock himself out trying. The private sector is the place for him, and the free enterprise system is the perfect financial vehicle.

Nevertheless, preachers, pastors, and evangelists who lived upscale, materialistic, six-figure lifestyles (lifestyles created and maintained by donations) were a sickening and vile breed whose end is destruction, whose God is their belly, whose glory is their shame, and whose minds are on earthly things. The Bible says:

> "*Through covetousness* (their great desires) *shall they with feigned words* (slick speech) *make merchandise of you* (make money off of you)*: whose judgment now of a long time lingereth not, and their damnation slumbereth not*" (2 Peter 2:3).

"Hey Mr. Rolex-wearing, Mercedes-driving, slick-talking Pastor. You won't make merchandise of me any longer."

These were the thoughts rambling through my head as we walked toward the exit of the church building. I knew that *most* Pastors were not in the ministry for the money. However, those

Pastors that lived large from donations put a bad taste in my mouth.

When Jonetta and I reached the heavy glass exit-doors, I said, "But hey, there's a lot of other Baptist Churches in Nashville."

I had to fight Randall with Bible knowledge, and maybe Matthew 3 was the place to start.

Chapter 9
Lower Than a Pregnant Ant

Later That Afternoon

Jonetta whipped up a nice Sunday lunch after we arrived back at the apartment, and I searched Matthew 3 for the beginning of the Baptist Church. We were not entertaining friends that day, and it was too cold to do anything outside. I ate lunch through a long face.

"What's wrong?" she asked.

"The chapter that the pompous (*expletive*) recommended says nothing about John starting the Baptist Church," I replied as though someone had shot me in the stomach. His nickname stuck.

She thought while she chewed. "What does it say?"

"The text speaks of John the Baptist, of course, but it's a description of his activities. It's not a proper name. Matthew 3:6 says that people were coming to him from Judaea, and were being baptized by him in the Jordan River. It doesn't say he started the Baptist Church or any church at all!"

"Do you think maybe the Pastor made a mistake on the chapter," she volleyed giving the Reverend the benefit of the doubt.

"Maybe," I tried to be generous, "but I'll read a little more tonight."

Coincidentally (or Providentially), many of my repair calls during the following week came from my Baptist Church accounts, so I took advantage of the situation and asked the various Baptist preachers the same question, "Who started the Baptist Church?" Some said John the Baptist. Some said that the Baptist Church came out of the Catholic Church during the Reformation Movement. Some said that the Baptist Church was part of the church of the Bible. Some were not sure when or where it began. One thing was clear – none of them could provide any scriptural support proving that the Baptist Church was in the Bible or that it was a part of the church of the Bible. Their lack of Biblical support fueled my frustration.

Later that week Randall met me coming through the back door of OSI with his Bible in hand, but I cut him off. "Randall, I don't want to argue," I said before he could say a word.

But Randall replied, "Mr. Mike, it's my Christian duty to come to you and apologize for offending you." I was floored. I had yelled at Randall during the previous week for no reason other than pressing him into verbalizing his personal convictions, and he was the one apologizing?

He went on, "Mr. Mike, Matthew 5:23 and 24 says,

> *Therefore if thou bring thy gift to the altar, and there rememberest that thy brother hath ought against thee; leave there thy gift before the altar, and go thy way; first be reconciled to thy brother, and then come and offer thy gift.*

"I am truly sorry if I have offended you in any way. Will you please forgive me?"

I was ashamed of myself. I felt lower than a pregnant ant. "Randall, you have nothing to be forgiven of. It's me that needs your forgiveness. Would you forgive me for yelling at you the other day?" I asked with great shame looking down at the dirty concrete floor.

"Absolutely my friend," and he put his arm around me. He was smiling so wide he could have eaten a banana sideways! He was a true Christian.

"Hey, while we're talking, I've got a Bible question for you," I said as I stepped away from the uncomfortable man-hug. "*Some* Baptists believe that John the Baptist started the Baptist Church. What do you say?"

"Now you're talking my language," Randall responded. "Let's step over to my office," he said in a loud, flamboyant voice. We both laughed because his *office* was an old desk in the corner. He flipped through his Bible at Mach speed.

"Look at this, Mr. Mike," Randall said as he laid his Bible down on the top of his paper-filled desk. He was in Matthew 16, pointing at verse 13 thru 18,

> *When Jesus came into the coasts of Caesarea Philippi, he asked his disciples, saying, Whom do men say that I the Son of man am? And they said, Some say that thou art John the Baptist: some, Elias; and others, Jeremias, or one of the prophets. He saith unto them, But whom say ye that I am? And Simon Peter answered and said, Thou art the Christ, the Son of the living God. And Jesus answered and said unto him, Blessed art thou, Simon Barjona: for flesh and blood hath not revealed it unto thee, but my Father which is in heaven. And I say also unto thee, That thou art Peter, and upon this rock I will build my church; and the gates of hell shall not prevail against it.*

"Mr. Mike," Randall continued, "Jesus said that He would build *His* church. Jesus would build it, not John. Notice that Jesus prophesied of this event. Future tense. It would be His church, but it did not yet exist. It didn't exist when Jesus made His statement. Jesus declares unity and singularity in His statement: *I* (singular) will build *My* (belonging to Him) church (singular). Jesus told Peter that He would build one church and that it would belong to Him. Jesus will claim only what belongs to Him.

"Now, John the Baptizer never prophesied about building a church, owning a church, or purchasing a church with his blood."

"What do you mean by purchasing? You've said that before," I asked.

"Let me show you," Randall said as he turned more pages. *"'Take heed therefore unto yourselves, and to all the flock, over the which the Holy Ghost hath made you overseers, to feed the church of God, which he hath purchased with his own blood.'* That's Acts 20:28. You see, the Bible teaches us that Jesus purchased the church with His blood."

"I've never seen that verse," I responded.

"It's okay, Mr. Mike. Many people haven't," Randall replied, "but let the Bible interpret itself. Jesus said He would build His church and Acts 20:28 said that He bought it with His own blood. Colossians 1:18 says that He is the head of the body, the church.

"Does the Bible say that John the Baptizer prophesied that he would also build a church, or that he would purchase his church with his blood, or that he would be the head of his own church?"

I had never seen any of these verses. To be honest, I had never really read that much of the Bible. I was one of those people who would read pieces of the Bible during hard times. If I was in trouble I would ask God for help, but my Bible study habits were poor. My study habits consisted of putting a Bible on the table with the spine down and allowing it to fall open. I believed that wherever the Bible opened was what God wanted me to read. I was beginning to see that this approach was a fool's approach.

"Uh, I'm not really sure, Randall," I replied weakly because I was no longer wrestling with Randall. I was wrestling with my existing beliefs and beginning to see that my beliefs were different than the Bible verses that I was now seeing for the first time in my life.

"Mr. Mike, you dig in your Bible, and you'll see that John didn't prophecy that he would start a church, nor did he purchase a church with his own blood, nor is he the head of any church.

"Dig all you want and you won't find it, because it ain't there! I could go out and start a denomination, call it anything I wanted, and claim that some Bible character started it. But that wouldn't make it so, would it?"

Randall asked the question and I did not offer an answer.

He pressed on, "Notice here in Matthew 16:18 that Jesus said, '*And I say also unto thee, that thou art Peter, and upon this rock I will build my church; and the gates of hell shall not prevail against it.*'" Randall followed the verse with his index finger. "This is where our Catholic friends make one of their first mistakes. You see, they use this verse to say that the Catholic Church is founded on Peter, but it isn't. Here's why," Randall went on, "the New Testament was originally written in Greek. In the Greek you'll find that the word for Peter, and the word for the rock on which Christ was to build His church are two separate words with two different meanings."

I nodded, as if to say yes, showing him that I was still following.

"Now, Mr. Mike, stay with me. The name 'Peter' is Petros in the Greek, which is the masculine gender. However, the word for 'rock' in the Greek is Petra, which is the feminine gender. Petros (Peter) is a piece of rolling rock or fragment, while Petra (rock) is a solid, massive, immovable substructure."

"So, Randall," I interrupted, "what's the point?"

"I'm sorry, Mr. Mike. The point is to identify what it was that Jesus would build His church upon. Was the church to be built on Peter or something else? Jesus said, '*And I say also unto thee, That thou art Petros* (Peter), *and upon this Petra* (rock) *I will build my church; and the gates of hell shall not prevail against it* (Matthew 16:18).' You see, Jesus was not saying that He would build His church on Peter like the Catholics would have you believe. Jesus said He'd build His church on *a rock*. Something distinctly different than the man called Peter. We know this because of the two different Greek words in the text. The church would not be built on Peter but would, instead, be built on something that Peter *said*."

I looked at Randall, waiting for him to give me the answer. He took the cue.

"Peter *said* in Matthew 16:16, '*Thou art the Christ, the Son of the living God,*'" showing me with his index finger again. "Mr. Mike, Christ's church was going to be built upon the confession of faith that Peter made regarding Jesus Christ. It is the same public confession that Jesus Christ is the living Son of God, and that was the same confession that would later kill Christ. The *confession* that Jesus Christ is the son - the Petra – the solid, massive, immovable substructure on which Christ's church would be built."

Randall continued, "Now, the question is this, did John the Baptist start the Baptist Church?"

I seriously considered his question in light of the Scriptures, but I did not answer.

"Mr. Mike, John the Baptist could *not* have started the Baptist Church. Do you know why?"

"Why?" I asked.

"Because in Matthew chapter 14:10, two chapters before Jesus prophesied about building His church, John was dead! John was DEAD! He'd been beheaded by Herod!"

"So, John," I interrupted, "was *dead* before Jesus even talked about building a church?" I could not believe it.

Randall said, "That's right. That's right!"

"'Then John could not possibly have started the Baptist Church?"

"That's correct, Mr. Mike," Randall replied.

"Well, when did Jesus build *His* church, or does the Bible say?" I asked.

"Oh yeah. The Bible reveals that the church began after Jesus' ascension to Heaven, after His being seated at the right hand of God, and on the Day of Pentecost. It's found in the second chapter of the book of Acts," Randall answered.

The most basic Bible points were beginning to take shape. "So, Randall, you're saying that Jesus prophesied about building His church, and the church didn't belong to John. No church was started by John because he was dead long before the church ever began. And you're saying that Jesus ascended to Heaven before His church began?"

"Mr. Mike, I'm not saying it. The Bible says it," Randall clarified. "And you've read the scriptures for yourself. You're understanding it just fine."

Randall had made more sense with his worn out Bible than any preacher I had talked to all week. Benjamin Franklin is quoted as saying, "The sting in any rebuke is the truth." I was feeling the sting, but the truth was also liberating. Jesus said in John 8:32, "*And ye shall know the truth, and the truth shall make you free.*"

"Then who started the Baptist Church?" I asked the question, now mentally exhausted.

Randall smiled and said, "Go to the library, Mr. Mike, because there ain't no Baptist Church in the Bible! John was a baptizer, not a member of any Baptist denomination. And he wasn't the father of the Baptists either."

Bellevue had a small public library, and I just happened to be a card-carrying member. The advice paid off. I checked out a book on denominational history, drove back to the apartment, made a pot of coffee, got into my Nike sweats, pulled on a beater-T, and dug in.

The historical denominational research revealed facts that some pastors did not seem to know (or they did not want to share with me). The Baptist Church began with a man named John Smyth, a Fellow of Christ's College in Cambridge, who had broken his ties with the Church of England. He became a Puritan, then a Separatist, and ended his days working with the Mennonites. Persecution led Smyth into exile to Amsterdam where he and fellow worker Thomas Helwys would come to form the first Baptist Church somewhere between 1607 and 1609 depending on which historian is referenced[1].

When I compared everything in the four gospels to the assertions made by my own denomination, as well as the historical information, the conclusion was loud and clear: The Baptist denomination[2] began in Amsterdam, Holland. It was started by John Smyth and Thomas Helwys[3] (circa 1607 to 1609). That was approximately 16 centuries after John the Baptist.

Maybe some of us Baptists were just trying to be optimistic in thinking that John started the Baptist denomination. Some of us simply did not know our own history readily available at the local library. Some Baptists claimed an unbroken succession from John the Baptist[4], yet their premise was clearly false. There is not an ounce of scripture to support a claim of unbroken succession, nor is there any scriptural support that John started anything. John pointed to the Christ. He was the prophesied forerunner of the Messiah. John prepared men's hearts and men's way for the Christ. He was a servant of the Lord, not the builder of the Lord's church.

Yes, maybe we good-hearted Baptists were just being optimistic. But it was not our denominational optimism that bothered me – it was our ignorance of the Word and our lack of biblical support for our various claims.

Through my own personal research, I had found that the "John the Baptist Origin" was, in reality, a lie.

Why did I believe what I believed? It was how I was raised. I had never known anything else and I had never really studied the Bible.

I was angry, but I was not angry at Randall. I was angry at myself. I was angry at my own personal ignorance of God's Word. Jesus said, *"Ye do err, not knowing the scriptures, nor the power of God* (Matthew 22:29)."

Why do we make religious mistakes? Because we do not know the scriptures.

Chapter 10
Just Don't Drink the Kool-Aid

Christmas Almost Here

"My philosophy is this: any denomination that claims exclusivity to Heaven is probably some kind of a cult," he said as he looked at me over the top of his crossed feet, which were propped up on one of the messiest desks I had ever seen. The Lutheran minister was interesting to say the least. He was a guy in his early fifties, and he looked the part of the quintessential professor. He had wire-rimmed glasses, a graying beard, a ratty corduroy jacket with patches on the elbows, and a pipe hanging out of one corner of his mouth.

His office was an eclectic blend of Victorian antiques, tribal art collected from African missionary trips, stacks of old issues of Scientific American, newspapers strewn all over the place, secular paperback novels on the rear bookshelf, hundreds of religious hardbacks on the opposite wall, a large potted Ficus tree (missing half of its leaves) in the far corner. The office was filled with the smell of pipe smoke mixed with something else. Mothballs, maybe?

I had just finished replacing a computer-board in the church's electrostatic stencil imager and had asked to talk with him about the Bible. It was interesting that he gave me more time than my own Pastor, and I had not contributed one dime to his church.

This particular Lutheran church happened to be one of the largest Lutheran churches in the Nashville area. The Reverend (or whatever the Lutheran Pastors liked to be called) had just finished a phone call in his office. I had overheard him on the phone say, "It's BYOB night, right?" Bring Your Own Beer? Lutherans drank? Huh. I liked to drink. I liked Lutherans immediately. Baptists never drank alcohol!

"And that denomination (the Lutheran Reverend was talking about Randall's church) totally dismisses John 3:16," said the minister. This was a point that I had totally forgotten.

"Yeah," I jumped in. "That's right. I'd forgotten about that verse." John 3:16 was a verse that had been branded into my brain at an early age during Sunday School. I wanted to impress him with my Bible knowledge so I quoted, *"For God so loved the world, that he gave his only begotten Son, that whosoever believeth in him should not perish, but have everlasting life*!" It rolled off my tongue. He had to be impressed.

The Lutheran Reverend puffed his pipe. He was not about to be outdone by some young computer technician. He ignored my quote. "You realize, uh, Mike, that Jesus said in John 15:5 that He is the vine and the various denominations are the branches."

"No!" My mouth dropped open. I did not know that verse. I thanked him for his time and left his office thrilled with this new knowledge. I had a visual in my mind of Christ being like the trunk of a tree and the branches coming out from Him being all of the different denominations.

And Randall's church? Maybe it was some type of cult, but knowing Randall the way I did, the cult thing just did not add up. Randall believed in the Bible. He supported every belief with the Bible.

Driving back to the office gave me time to wind down and think. "At least the Lutheran Pastor remembered my name," I mulled. Points for him!

"Alright." I mentally summarized, "(1) John 3:16. The Lutheran minister said that Randall's church disregards that verse. (2) John 15:5 says that Jesus is the vine and denominations are the branches, and (3) the Reverend said that groups who claimed exclusivity to Heaven were probably cults."

I was headed back to OSI determined to find Randall. I was a man on a mission.

Randall was nowhere to be found. I called the office switchboard and had him paged. Nothing. I was sitting at my desk smoking a cigarette when Larry came in. He sat down at his desk and said, "Those things are disgusting," while pointing at the Marlboro[2] in my hand.

"Where's Randall?" I turned a deaf ear on his anti-smoking comment.

Larry responded, "I heard he's out sick today."

Later that evening Jonetta and I had an excellent dinner at the West End Cooker with a new OSI executive and his wife. After the meal, we went to one of Nashville's dance barns. It was a tourist trap that specialized in couples dancing. We did not do the two-step, so we just watched.

The exec was in his late thirties, and he was already feeling his three-beer-buzz from the Cooker. Jonetta and I were only 20 years old, a biographical fact lost on the intelligent, yet on the way to *Margarita Ville,* yuppie and his equally intoxicated wife. They started buying us drinks. Stop. Let me rephrase. They started buying me drinks. Jonetta didn't drink.

Yes, city life and executive friends had its perks.

The electronic rooster crowed at 6:30 a.m. the following morning. A wave rolled through my stomach as soon as I opened my eyes. I was nauseated and about to lose it right there on our gray and mauve comforter.

"I'm calling in sick today," I moaned.

Jonetta was in the bathroom applying her makeup. "Get your butt out of that bed you little illegal-alcohol-drinking-Yankee." Her words giggled out as she ran out of the bathroom into our bedroom, leaping from the bathroom door threshold toward the bed like one of those flying squirrels you see on the animal channel.

"Don't–" I objected, but it was too late. Her small 100 lb. body landed squarely in the middle of our bed, took a good bounce and landed right on top of me. She squealed and laughed the entire time.

"Get off me," I grumbled, feeling the need to throw up.

"I don't like you after you've been drinking," she complained. I did not blame her. She was right.

"Me neither, but you can lecture me in a minute," I said while running into the bathroom to bow at the porcelain throne. Gross.

West End Avenue was backed up with traffic. No Shell Station coffee this morning. I would cut across Centennial Park, pick up Charlotte, head east over to 18th Street, head south one block, a quick left through Chicken-Shack alley, and I would be in the parking lot. E.t.a. 9 minutes. Commuting in city traffic was an exercise in dynamic logistics.

The concrete ramp leading up to the back door at OSI was covered in ice, and I was wearing new Johnson and Murphy wingtips. They were slick as snot! I almost broke my neck twice before reaching the door at the top of the ramp. I was through the door in one piece. Whew!

There was Randall buzzing around S&R, singing, smiling, and doing his thing.

"Good morning, Randall," I greeted him. He returned a hearty, "Good morning to you, Mr. Mike!"

"Hey, Randall," I said, walking toward him as he worked, "You gotta minute?"

"Sure man, whatchu got?" Randall turned and shook my hand.

"I have some Bible questions that I would like to ask you about, and I was thinking that you might let me take you to lunch today. I have several service calls in the L&C Tower, but I could swing by around noon. Do you want to go?"

Randall held up one finger as to silently say "Hang on." He then hustled over to his desk, picked up the phone, punched the line, and said, "Sir, can you hold for another minute please?" He thanked the person, punched the hold button, and put the phone back down.

"I'd love to go to lunch with you," Randall said. "Are you driving or am I?" he asked.

"I'll drive. Pick you up here at noon," I said, and we went our respective directions for the morning.

I could not wait to talk to Randall over lunch, but I reminded myself, "Don't drink the Kool-Aid!"

Chapter 11
Salt n' Pepper
A Week Before Santa

We squeezed into a booth at the Church Street Diner. It was a small, narrow eatery that had been in the city for decades. The food was excellent! I pulled out my Bible after we placed our order.

"Randall, we talked about faith the other day, and you showed me how faith only doesn't save, but you ignored John 3:16 didn't you?" I metaphorically moved out the first pawn in our biblical game of chess.

"My friend, I ignore none of God's word, for all scripture is given by inspiration of God, and is profitable for doctrine, for reproof, for correction, for instruction in righteousness: that the man of God may be perfect, throughly furnished unto all good works, 2 Timothy 3:16-17," Randall quoted without looking at the Bible. He'd pulled out a Knight.

I pushed forward, "But, Randall, John 3:16 says that, 'God so loved the world, that he gave his only begotten Son, that whosoever believeth in him should not perish, but have everlasting life.'" I showed him that I could also quote Scripture without looking. A Knight for a Knight. "That says that whoever believes in him will have everlasting life," I stated with confidence.

"Mr. Mike, would you mind opening your Bible to John 3:16?" he asked pleasantly. I obliged by finding chapter 3 and moved the Bible to an angle where we could both see the book.

Randall, using his index finger, said, "Look at the verse again – *that whosoever believeth in him should not perish, but have everlasting life*. Notice these two words here in verse 16… should not?"

"Yeah."

"These words represent a condition," Randall said. "If you quote John 3:16 by itself, you're taking it away from its context, and you're ignoring the entire remote text distorting the meaning.

Mr. Mike, I'm not ignoring John 3:16. You're lifting it out of context in an effort to make it mean something it doesn't mean."

"No, I'm not," I responded so loudly that people from surrounding tables looked our direction.

"No need to get upset Mr. Mike," Randall said, trying to calm my emotions.

"How am *I* taking it out of context?" I asked in a more hushed voice.

Randall ran his finger up to the beginning of the chapter and said, "Mike, look here at John 3:1 [Vv.1-5]:

> *There was a man of the Pharisees, named Nicodemus, a ruler of the Jews: The same came to Jesus by night, and said unto him, Rabbi, we know that thou art a teacher come from God: for no man can do these miracles that thou doest, except God be with him. Jesus answered and said unto him, Verily, verily, I say unto thee, Except a man be born again, he cannot see the kingdom of God. Nicodemus saith unto him, How can a man be born when he is old? Can he enter the second time into his mother's womb, and be born? Jesus answered, Verily, verily, I say unto thee, Except a man be born of water and of the Spirit, he cannot enter into the kingdom of God."*

I followed him.

"The believers spoken of in John 3:16 were those who were born again in verses 3-5. Nicodemus didn't understand what Jesus meant by being born again, as seen by verse 4, so Jesus explained it in detail in verse 5. Jesus said, '*Except a man be born of water and of the Spirit, he cannot enter into the kingdom of God,*'" Randall explained. He was moving his Rook.

"Water and Spirit, Mr. Mike," Randall explained. "That's what defines the true believers found in John 3:16."

I scratched my chin still listening.

"Now," Randall looked up from his Bible, "Mr. Mike, let me ask you this. Does this term 'born again' mean to be born of water and Spirit, or is it just believing, as you first implied?" He took a drink of water that the waitress had brought to our table.

Yep. I had been the one who had pulled John 3:16 out of context. Jesus said being born again was to be born of water and Spirit – in the *same* chapter.

"You know, Randall, I've always heard that being born again was to ask Jesus into your heart and to have a salvation experience," I responded without answering his question directly.

"Mr. Mike," Randall said softer, "1 Peter 3:15 says, '*But sanctify the Lord God in your hearts and be ready always to give an answer to every man that asketh you a reason of the hope that is in you with meekness and fear,*'" again without looking at the Bible.

"Yeah?" I responded with a one-word question.

"So," Randall went on, "when a man claims to be a Christian, he is supposed to be ready to give an answer - a Bible answer - to anyone who asks for the reason of the hope that's in him. He must be able to defend his position with meekness and fear."

I nodded my head in agreement, and Randall continued, "Now, Mike, you told me you were saved by saying the Sinner's Prayer, and you base your hope in Christ by believing your sins were forgiven in obedience to the Sinner's Prayer, right?"

"Right."

"Then would you do me a favor?" Randall asked.

"I'll try."

"Will you find the Sinner's Prayer in the Bible for me?" Randall's question was very sincere.

"Well, uh…" I was thinking it might be a trick question.

"Mr. Mike," Randall interrupted, "All I'm asking you to do is to find the Sinner's Prayer in the Bible, or show me anyone in the Bible on *this* side of the cross that was saved by saying the Sinner's Prayer?"

"No problem, Randall," I said confidently. "But could you give me a couple of days? We're kind of busy with the Christmas holidays?" Everyone used the holidays as an excuse. It was not the complete truth. We were no busier with the holidays than anyone else, but I needed time to get back to a Baptist Pastor, because I could not handle this one on my own.

"Sure, Mr. Mike. Would a week be enough time for you?"

"Oh yeah. More than enough," I answered with a smile.

Our food arrived, and it smelled great. Apparently studying and talking made Randall hungry too. He was buttering a roll when I noticed somebody walking slowly by our booth. As they passed by our table, they said, "Hey, a salt n' pepper team!"

I looked up in time to see a middle-aged, heavyset guy wearing a baseball cap and a greasy coat pass by our table. He was looking down at Randall. Randall was black; I was white; everyone in the restaurant knew who the guy was talking about.

I tried to jump up, but got caught between the booth bench and the table. Randall quickly reached across the table, grabbed my arm, and said, "Mike, please sit down." It was not a request. Randall's grip and tone conveyed a measure of strength, posture, and control that I had never seen in him before.

As I slowly sat back down, Randall said, "Romans 12:18 says '*if it be possible, as much as lieth in you, live peaceably with all men,*' so just let it go my friend."

"No, Randall. I'm gonna kick his (*expletive*)–"

"Mr. Mike," Randall interrupted me before the curse word came out. "No violent response is ever deserved."

The man continued to walk toward the door. Randall slowly let go of my arm as I relaxed. Then he smiled at me and took a big bite of meatloaf like it never happened!

Randall had probably endured racism and bigotry his entire life. Is *that* what had made him so emotionally tough? Maybe, but Randall projected something beyond emotional toughness. It was a deep patience and love toward his fellow man. Jesus Christ lived in and through Randall. Love, mercy, kindness, and grace exuded from him. *That* was the difference I had seen in Randall Edges.

"You know, Mr. Mike," Randall said as he chewed, "water and Spirit. John 3:5. This verse brings us back to 1 Peter 3:21. You remember that note I gave you?"

"Yeah, I do," I said, "but I don't remember what it said."

Randall flipped to 1 Peter 3, then slid the Bible across the table.

I found verse 21 and read aloud:

> *The like figure whereunto even baptism doth also now save us (not the putting away of the filth of the flesh, but the answer of a good conscience toward God,) by the resurrection of Jesus Christ.*"

Randall said, "John 3:5 says '*Except a man be born of water and of the Spirit, he cannot enter into the kingdom of God.*' 1 Peter 3:21 says, '*Baptism doth also now save us.*' Baptism is the *water part* of being born again."

"Randall, when you say that somebody has got to be baptized to be saved, it just goes against everything I've ever heard and been taught."

"Mr. Mike, I'm not saying it. The *Bible* says it."

I countered, "But, Randall, what about the thief on the cross? He wasn't baptized. What about somebody on their death-bed who can't get baptized? What if I was on my way to get baptized and got killed in a car-wreck?"

"Slow down, Mr. Mike, slow down," he said waving his hands. "You're bringing up excellent questions, and I promise you we'll discuss every single one of them, one at a time. But your first objective is to find me the Sinner's Prayer in the Bible. If you can find me that Sinner's Prayer in the Bible, I'll become a Baptist!"

I laughed and looked at my watch. 12:52 p.m.

"Randall, we've got to go."

Randall reached for his wallet, but I objected, "No, no! This is my treat." I grabbed the check off the table.

"Well, I'm going to get the tip," Randall said as he smiled. I objected again, but he waved me off and threw a five dollar bill on the table.

Randall thanked me for the lunch as we arrived back at the office, and I thanked him for the study time together. Then he got out of my car and headed to OSI's back door.

As I watched him walk toward the building, I realized something, if Randall *had not* been a Christian, I would probably be sitting in jail that very moment for assault and battery against the 'Salt n' Pepper Team' racist. I could see the headlines in the Tennessean now:

MAN ASSAULTED IN
DINER DURING BIBLE STUDY

Chapter 12
The Holy Ghost & The Porch Swing

Christmas: At Home

We rolled into my mom and dad's driveway with a huge box tied to the top of our car. It was Thursday, December twenty-fourth. The big box on the top was dad's Christmas gift, wrapped in a box the size of a dishwasher, and it had made the trip from Nashville successfully.

Inside the box was a simple family tradition that had started many years before. When I was about six, I had asked mom what I could get dad for Christmas, and she recommended a replacement bottle of Old Spice[1] aftershave. Old Spice was the only aftershave that dad would ever wear. Since that time a bottle had always been included as one of his many gifts, and the practice evolved into a family tradition. Dad loved it! So the big box we had brought from Nashville contained one small bottle of Old Spice wrapped in progressively larger boxes. To top it off, I had put twelve bricks in the bottom of the box just to throw him off the scent – no pun intended!

My parent's small house was filled with relatives from all over the country. Mom and dad, now faithful Baptists themselves, entertained the family who, like so many families, was an unusual blend of people.

Everyone talked, laughed, fussed, discussed, argued, gossiped, napped, and ate some more. The kids screamed; the TV blared; religion nagged at me.

During mom's years of sickness, she and dad started attending the Baptist Church with me. Grandma started attending with us, and then two of my aunts as well. My Baptist faith that had begun with Eula had spread throughout much of our family.

However, my distant relatives were much more diverse. I had a Catholic aunt and uncle, a Pentecostal aunt, two Methodist cousins, a Presbyterian uncle, another cousin who had married a Mormon guy (she was his only wife so far), an aunt who was a foot-washing Baptist, an Agnostic cousin, and several believers with no official religious affiliations.

My Pentecostal aunt was, by far, the most knowledgeable of the Bible among all of my family members.

"Aunt Nancy," I said to her as we sat together on the couch visiting while my young cousins wrestled on the floor. "Where is the Sinner's Prayer found in the Bible?"

"Well, Michael honey, I don't know exactly," she replied offering no help. "Why do you ask?"

"Just a research project," I responded.

Aunt Nancy considered my response for a moment. "Michael, have you received the Holy Ghost?"

"Uh, I'm not sure," I stammered.

"Oh honey, you've got to receive the Holy Ghost," she said with concern as though she had just learned that I was terminally ill. At that point she took my hand, stood up from the couch and said, "Come with me!" Aunt Nancy led me out to my parent's front porch where there were no family members or screaming kids. "Michael, I'm going to pray for you, and I'm going to ask the Lord for His Spirit to move over you and give you the gift of speaking in tongues-"

Aunt Nancy, please don't-," but she took me by the arm and pulled me down onto the porch swing, plopping down beside me at the same moment. She then closed her eyes, raised up both arms, and began to pray, "Dear Lord Jesus, sweet Jesus! I come to you Jesus for Brother Michael, that you would reach down your loving hands and touch him with your great power – the power of the Holy Ghost! Oh Sweet Jesus, bless him with a baptism of your Holy Ghost and give him the gift to speak in tongues,"

I bowed my head slightly, but did not dare close my eyes. Her emotionalism, animation, and the sheer volume of her voice was all so distracting that I could not do anything but watch the show.

Then Aunt Nancy did something very bizarre; she began to speak in tongues. With her eyes still closed and her arms still raised upwards, her head began to bob from side to side, and she said what sounded like:

Otro macha ka shoon dala ton da lay ma kee ero sutro por sala ostro…

As Aunt Nancy continued to pray, the foreign sounds came forth with speed and proficiency. She rolled her R's like a Spaniard, and I would have thought (if she had not been sitting right there beside me) that she had been replaced by a totally different person. I had no idea what she was saying or what any of it meant.

At one point mom opened the front door to see what was going on out on the front porch, but when she saw Aunt Nancy doing her thing, mom quickly shut the door, retreating back into the safety of her Baptist home. Evidently mom wanted no part of the tongues experience. She did not know what she was missing!

Aunt Nancy finished, opened her eyes, hugged and kissed me, and asked me if I felt anything. Actually, I had not felt anything other than curiosity. However, I loved her and truly appreciated her concern as well as her heartfelt efforts. Even though I did not agree with her approach, nor did I understand her practices, I believed that she had a sincere and loving heart.

As for me, could I speak in tongues? Nope. Oh well, back in the house.

I spent the rest of the evening discussing religion and polling my relatives about their religious beliefs.

Where was the Sinner's Prayer in the Bible? Why did they believe what they believed? How did they get into their faith? Why do they stay with their particular faith? What did they get out of their particular flavor of faith? Is everyone going to Heaven? Why are there so many churches? Why do denominations teach opposing doctrines if everyone's going to the same place? How can everyone be religiously correct? How was each one saved in their respective faiths?

It was a fascinating experience. It was also a failure. No one knew where to find the Sinner's Prayer in the Bible.

We drove back to Jonetta's parent's home after eating and visiting with my mom and dad. Her parent's home was a quiet place. They used feather-bed mattresses and heated the house with a coal-burning stove in the basement. There was nothing like it. If you ever wanted a good night's sleep, you could get it in that house! Even in the middle of winter when southern Illinois temperatures dipped into single digits, Jonetta's mother would crack the window in the bedroom so that fresh air could ventilate the house throughout the night. We would get into that feather-bed, cover ourselves with three hand-made quilts, and breathe the fresh country air all night long. Staying there was a small slice of paradise.

The following morning we woke to the rooster's crow, the smell of biscuits, gravy, bacon and eggs filled the house, but that featherbed had felt so good.

"Enjoy it while you can," I thought to myself as I lay there under the warm covers, "because the big city is calling." Today was Friday, December twenty-fifth, Christmas Day. I knew that today would be the day that I would find that elusive Sinner's Prayer.

Surely it was in the Bible somewhere. I just had to find it.

Chapter 13
Cutting Off the End of the Ham

Last Week of December, 1987

"They're cutting off the end of the ham," I said in my mind. It was early during the following Monday morning, December 28, 1987. Jonetta was still asleep, and I was making French Toast in our tiny kitchen thinking about the many religious answers I had received from my multi-denominational relatives back home.

There is a story about a young newly-wed couple cooking dinner together. The new husband watched his new wife prepare a ham. She removed the outer wrapper, cut off the end of the ham, and then threw the end into the trash.

"Why'd you do that?" asked the husband.

"It's how my mother has always done it," the new bride replied.

"Why'd your mother do it?" asked the husband.

"I don't know," said the wife.

"Could you ask her?" said the husband.

"Sure," replied his wife, eager to please her new husband.

The bride went to her mother and asked, "Mother, when you cook a ham why do you cut off the end and throw it away?"

"It's the way your grandmother taught me to do it. You'll need to ask her," said the mother, so the bride went to her grandmother with the same question.

"Sweet child," the grandmother laughed! "I cut off the end of the ham because the ham was too big to fit into the pot!"

Sometimes we develop our religious beliefs in much the same way. We mimic what we have heard, and we repeat what we have been taught without question. Why don't we question what we have heard and been taught? Because we have been taught by good, loving, kind, sincere, honest, decent, moral, and upstanding people. They are the people that represent authority in our life. They are the people that we trust.

Those people have, in the very same way, been taught by people that they have trusted and loved, so the beliefs and practices continue unhindered and without question down through many generations.

Here is where we make our mistake. We confuse the people that we love with the belief that they hold. The example in the story is clear: the new bride would have continued the practice of cutting off the end of the ham and throwing it away if her husband had not asked the question, "Why do you do it that way?" The bride could have easily said to her new husband, "Honey, this is the way it's always been done. This is the way my mother taught me, and if it's good enough for her it's good enough for me. Honey, be quiet, accept it, and leave well enough alone!" Now if that would have been the bride's attitude, the practice of cutting off the end of the ham would have continued from her to her children, her grandchildren and so on.

Think about it; after enough time passes and enough people die, no one will know or remember the reason for cutting off the end of the ham!

This is what is happening in religion today!

It was time to wake up Jonetta. The French Toast was ready, and she would want some coffee.

"Honey, time to get up," I said to her sleeping face. She smiled, not opening her eyes. "You look good without makeup," I said and laughed.

"Yeah, right," she said sarcastically, propping herself up on her elbows. "I'm the one normally waking you up. What's wrong?" She was puzzled.

"Didn't sleep good last night," I responded.

"Mom's feather-bed spoiled you, didn't it?" It was rhetorical.

I padded back to the kitchen in a Tennessee T-shirt, flannel pajama pants, no-peek socks, and a robe. I poured a third cup of coffee, went out to the patio, and lit another cigarette while lost in thought. Those Marlboro's were so good!

The fact of the matter – a fact that I was quickly finding out – was that very few people really seemed to study their Bible. For instance, take my family back home. The reality was:

- They were all good, sincere, moral, kind, and honest people.
- They all thought that faith alone was enough to save the soul from eternal destruction.
- No one knew where the Sinner's Prayer was located in the Bible and nobody could find it.
- All of them, for the most part, felt that everyone was headed to the same place and that the road you took to get there didn't really matter.
- None of my family knew who started their respective Denominations.
- They didn't know who, where, or when their denomination began, and it didn't seem to matter to any of them.
- None of them really knew much about what their respective denominations taught.
- None of them really seemed to be too concerned about their particular system of beliefs.
- Religious apathy prevailed.

There was another thorn in the mix. I had been reading Proverbs and found texts like chapter 14, verse 12:

> *There is a way which seemeth right unto a man, but the end thereof are the ways of death.*

God says that we cannot depend on what we think seems right. In other words, our own feelings and our opinions on matters of faith and religion might seem right to us, but in the end, our own ideas (what seems right in our minds and hearts) may lead to eternal destruction.

Over the Christmas holidays many of my relatives had said to me, "Just trust your heart, Mike." Television shows, movies, books, and magazines say it all the time. Just follow your heart! But I was smarter than that. The heart can and *often* does lead a person the wrong way.

It sounds strange to hear somebody say a thing that is so opposite of what is popularly taught, doesn't it? It sounded strange to me, and *I* was the one thinking it. Why was I thinking it? Because I had started reading my Bible and finding passages like Jeremiah 17:9:

> *The heart is deceitful above all things, and desperately wicked: who can know it?*

So, just follow your heart? Yeah, right. Just follow the thing that the Bible says is the most deceitful thing above all things. The human heart? Feelings?

"That makes a lot of sense," I said sarcastically to myself. No wonder Hollywood is so screwed up. One of Hollywood's favorite mantras is "just follow your heart!"

What made matters worse was the fact that I had been so happy in my ignorance. I was happy in my Eighties, chase the dream, do your own thing, party it up, kind of life. But now God's Word was getting in the way.

My quest to find these spiritual answers was also causing me guilt that I had never before experienced. The quest for answers motivated me to study God's Word, but His Word forced me to recognize the deficiencies in my own personal character. The Bible was a light that illuminated my shallow, materialistic goals. The Bible light drove away the darkness that my soul had been hiding in for so long. The illumination of the Word allowed me to see my sins, flaws of character, and moral deficiencies. I did not like what I was seeing.

As I mentally reviewed the summary, I was glad that my cigarette was down to the butt. I squashed it into the ashtray on our patio (Jonetta would never let me smoke inside the apartment) and jumped back inside through the sliding glass door. It was too cold to stand outside smoking, especially in a robe!

Smoking - what a stupid thing to do to my body!

Commuting to the office that Monday morning gave me more time to think.

"Just let it go, Mike!" I chided myself, but it was no use. Why couldn't I just let it go? It was because of the verses that Randall had quoted:

> *And to you who are troubled rest with us, when the Lord Jesus shall be revealed from heaven with his mighty angels, in flaming fire taking vengeance on them that know not God, and that obey not the gospel of our Lord Jesus Christ* (2 Thess. 1:7-8).

What *was* the gospel, and *how* did man obey it? I was tired of feeling frustrated. Wait a minute – feelings! I did have a feeling when I said the Sinner's Prayer at the age of eight. Feelings *had* to play a part. My excitement grew as I reached backward again into the distant memories of my childhood, and I remembered the feelings that I had experienced after saying the Sinner's Prayer.

"That's it!" I said out loud as I drove the last few blocks of my commute to the office. The feeling I had experienced after I said the Sinner's Prayer *must* confirm the fact that I was saved at that moment!

I considered the emotional feelings that my Aunt Nancy displayed during her prayers, and the feelings I experienced when

I attended church. The feeling that I had after my salvation experience *had* to be the Holy Spirit moving upon me, and I was sure that I was right.

At this point I did not need to find the Sinner's Prayer in the Bible, because the feelings that I had experienced was an adequate confirmation of my own salvation.

Poor Randall thinking that all other denominations were headed to Hell. He is a nice guy and all, but he is not the only one going to Heaven. Somebody needed to pray for *him* for having such a narrow mind. Hey, I would pray for him.

I parked the car in the back lot of OSI, bowed my head, and prayed for Randall's narrow way of thinking. Maybe God would open his mind to a broader way of seeing things.

There. Enough said. Now let's get on with life! Silicon Valley is waiting, but it would not wait forever.

Sometimes things have a way of backfiring.

Chapter 14
Feelings… Nothing More Than *Feelings*

Just a Few Moments Later

I stepped through the rear door into the S&R department with supreme confidence having found the holy grail of faith - personal experiential feelings. I strolled through the stack of boxes dressed in an expensive new suit.

"Good morning, Mr. Mike!" Randall hollered.

"Good morning, Randall," I returned the greeting.

"Hey, my friend," Randall was coming fast, "did you find that Sinner's Prayer in your Bible?" Randall smiled and stuck out his hand for a handshake.

I took his hand and returned the smile, "Randall, I didn't find it, but it doesn't matter. I'm confident in my personal salvation," I said without breaking eye contact.

"Mr. Mike, share with me the reason for the hope that is within you!"

"You know," I began, "I told you that I was saved when I was eight years old."

"Yeah, that's right," Randall said as he nodded his head.

"Well, Randall, I had a great feeling of peace after I said that prayer. After asking Jesus to come into my heart and asking Him to forgive me of my sins," I explained as though it had happened yesterday. "And I've realized that the feeling I experienced was the Holy Spirit moving through me and telling me that I was saved."

"Mr. Mike, do you think God wants us to study His Bible together, or do you think discussing the Bible is something that God does not want us to do?" It was a loaded question, but Randall seemed dead serious.

"You know the answer," I said with audible disgust.

Randall responded, "So you would agree that God would have honest men study His Word together, or that it is, at least, a good thing to do?"

"Of course it's a good thing to do," I patronized him.

"Then would you be so kind as to give me a few more minutes of your time being that it is still early?" he asked. I looked at my watch. 7:29 a.m.

I smiled. "Sure, what the heck."

We walked over to his desk, and he pulled up an additional chair. I took a seat and he pulled out a Bible from his top drawer, but he did not open it.

He spun his chair around toward me, fully facing me, arms at his sides, and his hands on his knees. Then he asked, "Have you ever been on a vacation with your wife?"

"Yeah."

"How long was the vacation?" he asked.

"Two weeks," I replied.

"Think about this," he said. "Suppose for a moment, while you and your wife are on vacation together, your hotel phone rings in the middle of the night. You're startled out of sleep and answer the phone. It's one of your family members from back home. You know it *can't* be good. You ask what's wrong. They tell you that your home has just burned to the ground, and you've lost everything you've got. Every possession that you owned was in that home. Every picture, every keepsake, everything important to you is gone. Now, let's rub a little salt into the wound - you don't have any homeowner's insurance. You hang up the phone."

"Go on," I said.

"Mr. Mike, how do you *feel* at that moment?" "Horrible!"

I replied without hesitation. "That's a no-brainer."

"Of course you'd feel horrible," Randall agreed. "Now, suppose that you and your wife hop on the next plane out of there and fly straight home, but when you arrive you find that your home has not burned down. Everything is fine and just as you'd left it. How do you *feel* at *that* moment?"

"Pretty (*expletive*) off at whoever lied to me about my house burning down!" I exclaimed. "Somebody's gonna get an (*expletive*) whoopin'!"

Randall let out an uncontrollable belly-laugh that resounded through the Shipping and Receiving docks. I started laughing at him for laughing at me. What a couple of idiots!

"Yeah, yeah, okay," Randall said, waving his hands as he regained control of himself, "but what *else* do you feel?"

"Relief," I finally responded.

"But, Mr. Mike." Randall was serious again. "How did you feel when they'd told you that your home had burned down?"

"Yeah, okay," I saw where he was going.

"You see, the feeling you had in that hotel room, was it based on a truth or a lie?"

I was processing Randall's logic. He was very wise.

"My feeling was based on a lie," I reluctantly admitted.

"But even though your personal feelings were based on a lie, that lie still generated a very real and very tangible *feeling* in your heart, didn't it?"

I was never easily influenced, but Randall's reasoning was simply incontrovertible.

"Yes it did," I said.

"Mr. Mike," he continued, "there's no doubt in my mind that you had a wonderful feeling at the moment that you thought that all of your sins were removed. Who wouldn't feel fantastic when they were told that they were going to Heaven? Especially a very young child who had just been told that by a respected adult?"

I listened and considered the possibility.

"Now, Mike, you were how old again?" he asked.

"Eight," I answered.

"My friend, if an adult were to lead a child in any kind of prayer and then tell them that they were saved and going to

Heaven when they died, what feeling would any normal child have at that moment?" Randall leaned forward not breaking eye contact.

"Yeah, I'm with you, Randall. Any kid would have the same feeling that I had that night."

"Mr. Mike, in the vacation story did your initial feelings line up with the truth?"

"No."

Randall pressed forward respectfully, "So, would it be correct in concluding that personal feelings are not always based on truth? And that feelings are not always trustworthy guides for determining what is true and what is false?"

"I'd agree with that statement," I said.

"So, how can you put all of your faith and the eternal destiny of your soul squarely upon human feelings? *Especially* when you were a young, impressionable, innocent, eight year old child? Not to mention the possibility that the good people leading you might possibly be biblically incorrect?" Randall asked.

"But I have a personal relationship with Jesus Christ," I responded.

"No you don't," Randall said flatly.

"What?" I shot back.

"Mr. Mike, you don't have a personal relationship with Jesus Christ."

I felt my eyes widen as I stared at Randall. "How can you say that?" I asked with growing anger.

Randall said, "Listen, Mr. Mike, I'm going to use some strong language with you in an effort to open your eyes–"

"Go ahead," I interrupted. Now I was mad.

"Mr. Mike," Randall spoke evenly, "How can you have something with God that doesn't exist in the Bible and wasn't even taught until the 1930's?"

"What are you talking about?" I was surprised again.

"Listen to me carefully. Having a personal relationship with Jesus Christ was a doctrine concocted by a very well-known evangelist back in the 1930's. He said the phrase during a big revival he was holding, and the phrase stuck. People started running around talking about how they had a personal relationship with Jesus. And how did they get their personal relationship with Jesus? By asking Jesus into their heart."

I was thunderstruck. "Randall, I *have* a personal relationship with Jesus," I said with conviction.

Randall asked, "What does that mean?"

I sat there and thought about it. "Well, I know Jesus."

Randall asked a second time, "What does that mean?"

"It means that I *feel* He lives inside me," I said it before thinking.

"Mr. Mike, are you going on feelings again?"

"Well, in a way-" I responded.

But Randall interrupted, "So let me get this straight. You've admitted that feelings are not an accurate guide, but you now say that feelings are an accurate guide? Which is it?"

"Well, I've always thought I had a personal relationship with Jesus."

Randall opened his Bible and found his target. "Mr. Mike, having a personal relationship with Jesus is a hoax. It's one of the greatest false teachings of modern-day religion. You know why? Because it's not taught anywhere in God's Word. No one was ever told to have a personal relationship with Jesus Christ, nor is the principle taught in the Bible.

A personal relationship with Jesus mocks God because it infers that God is a respecter of persons, and He is not. In Acts 10:34, Peter said '*of a truth I perceive that God is no respecter of persons*.' A personal relationship implies that Christ is not in Heaven because He would have to be here, in the flesh, for you to have a personal relationship with Him. The apostles had a personal relationship with Him, but neither Christ, nor the apostles taught the doctrine of having a personal relationship with Him. Jesus never taught the personal relationship concept. The apostles never taught the personal relationship concept."

My anger was throttled, but I continued to listen.

Randall went on, "All of Christ's disciples are taught to love and obey Him. We are to keep His commandments, John 14:15, and we're to live in such a way that He knows *us*, Matthew 7:23. Mr. Mike, if you love the Lord, you'll live in a way that He knows *you*."

I racked my brain as I searched for scriptures to back up the idea of having a personal relationship with Jesus.

"Mr. Mike," Randall interrupted my thoughts. I looked back at him, and he said, "Do an extensive search of the New Testament, and you won't find the words personal or relationship anywhere in the King James Bible.

"Randall, maybe the phrase '*have a personal relationship with Jesus*' isn't in the Bible, but the concept is there."

"No, it's not, Mr. Mike," he answered back, "and the doctrine is a complete fabrication. As a Christian, I've devoted my heart, soul, mind, and life to the Lord Jesus Christ. I do my best to live in accord with His Word. I sacrifice my money, time, and effort for His cause. I demonstrate my devotion to Him as He has instructed, following His teachings and magnifying Him through my life and body; however, with all of this said, I do not have something that is not taught by our Lord."

"But, Randall, a lot of good people teach a relationship with Jesus Christ," I said in a much calmer tone.

"Mr. Mike, you are correct, but Jesus Christ didn't teach that doctrine, and his apostles didn't teach that mess, either. It's just not taught in the Bible.

"Jesus said in Matthew 15:9 that *in vain they do worship me, teaching for doctrines the commandments of men*. The 'personal relationship with Jesus' concept came from a man, and many denominations teach it as a doctrine of God. You are following a teaching of a man, and that teaching is less than 50 years old!

"Mr. Mike, I love the Lord with all of my heart. If having a personal relationship with Jesus was something that I could find in my Bible, I'd be following it right now, and we'd be reading it out of the Bible at this moment."

I could not defend my position because I did not know where it was found in the Bible. I did not know if it was even in the Bible. I also knew Randall well enough to know that he would do *anything* the Bible said to do.

Randall wasn't a fair-weather Christian. His life magnified Christ and his devotion to the Lord was as clear as the nose on his face.

"Randall," I responded, "are you telling me that you don't *feel* anything with your faith?"

"Of course I do. I feel great! I have a joy that surpasses all human understanding. I rejoice daily because of the knowledge that I enjoy all spiritual blessings found only in Christ. But that's the key, Mr. Mike." Randall explained.

"What's the key?" I asked.

"My feelings are based on the truth found in the Word not on false doctrines. My faith isn't directed by my feelings, either. My faith is directed by the Lord's life and teachings found within the Bible. That's the key, and that's the difference," he said as he smiled at me.

"Mr. Mike," he continued, "Look here at Romans 6:17. Would you read this for us?"

"Sure, give it here," I replied, taking the Bible from his hands.

I read the verse aloud:

But God be thanked, that ye were the servants of sin, but ye have obeyed from the heart that form of doctrine which was delivered you.

Randall said, "You must obey from the heart that form of doctrine which was delivered you. Mr. Mike, Paul said that to become true Christians, we must obey from the heart *that* form of doctrine."

"What form?" I asked.

"The form that was delivered. What was the form that was delivered? It was the form given in the first gospel sermon preached to mankind after the ascension of Jesus Christ to Heaven. And when was the doctrine delivered? The Day of Pentecost. You'll find it in the second chapter of Acts. Mr. Mike, that form of doctrine *wasn't* to ask Jesus into your heart and have a personal relationship with Him."

"Then what was it?" I asked.

"You need to read it for yourself, but it's not the Sinner's Prayer. It's not asking Jesus into your heart, and it's not having a personal relationship with Jesus," he said respectfully.

Randall's Bible knowledge was vast. His respect and love of God was evident. He was not disparaging me. He was simply trying to teach the truth from the Word of God.

"Mr. Mike, I suspect you already know that the Sinner's Prayer ain't in the Bible," said Randall. His grammar didn't fool me. He was a very intelligent man.

"Well, Randall, I'm still looking," I replied without any real conviction.

"I tell you what," Randall said as he stood from his chair, and I followed his lead. "While you're searching, do this."

"What's that?" I asked.

He pulled a piece of scratch paper from the many papers on his desk and scribbled while he spoke, "There's a man named

Saul in the New Testament. That man, like you, also had strong *feelings* about his beliefs. He too thought and felt like he was doing the right thing. Saul found that he, despite his feelings, had been completely wrong about his religious beliefs. Jesus dealt directly with Saul on the Damascus road. You find out how Saul became a Christian, and you'll find the answer to the Sinner's Prayer. You'll also find out how to obey the gospel!"

Randall handed me the paper which had written instructions for the assignment he had just given me.

"Mr. Mike, Saul did not become a Christian by saying the Sinner's Prayer, nor by asking Jesus into his heart, nor by claiming to have a personal relationship with Jesus, or any of those false doctrines of vanity and foolishness," Randall said softly. Then he smacked me on the shoulder and said, "Check it out!"

As I walked toward my office I thought, "I was happier when I was religiously stupid!"

Yes, ignorance is bliss, but spiritual ignorance is eternal damnation.

I remembered the statement again:

It is easier to believe a lie that one has heard a thousand times before than to believe a fact that one has never heard before.

Chapter 15
Snake Bite!

Last Few Days of 1987

What I did not know was that my best friend Larry and Randall were studying the Bible together as well.

Larry usually spent a lot of time at our place. We played golf together, went out to eat together, worked together, and spent many hours discussing politics, computers and world affairs.

Larry was a very clean living guy. He stayed away from the poisons of life (tobacco, alcohol, etc.). His family were Presbyterians; therefore, he was a Presbyterian.

Larry was also an excellent trouble-shooter. He held a computer engineering degree, and OSI was lucky to have him. OSI employees would do ride-a-longs together at times when assistance was needed in troubleshooting problem accounts. Larry and I were partnered together as team troubleshooters, and we spent many days in the field running down system bugs.

But Larry hid the fact that he and Randall had been studying the Bible together. That changed during one bitterly cold evening. Jonetta and I heard a knock at our apartment door, and it was Larry.

"Hey, Larry, get in out of the cold," she said inviting him into our apartment.

"Hi, Jonetta!" Larry said in an up-beat way, despite the weather. She took his coat, and we could tell he was excited about something.

"Larry, what are you doing out here this time of night?" I was glad to see him, but I was also interested in knowing what was going on.

"Mike, I've got some news I wanted to share with you, and it can't wait any longer!" Larry spoke as I motioned him to sit on our wicker bungalow type sofa.

"Well, spit it out," I said impatiently.

"I was baptized today!"

"You what?" the words trailed off as I asked. "I didn't even know you've been thinking about religion."

Jonetta got Larry a cup of hot chocolate. He did not drink coffee. We all got settled in as we listened to his story. He trembled with nervousness as he spoke.

"Mom and dad aren't happy with me," Larry said with sadness. It was evident that he was hurting over the fracture that his baptism had created in his relationship with his parents. "But I have to do what the Bible says to do and what the Lord wants me to do."

"But, Larry," I objected, "how can you be so sure that you've done what the Lord wants?"

He grabbed my Bible from the top of our wicker bungalow coffee table. As he flipped through the pages, I looked up at the wall clock. It was 9:12 p.m. From that point we discussed, argued, and reasoned the scriptures together throughout the night. At midnight, I brought up the thief on the cross. He wasn't baptized, but he was saved. What about him?

Larry was educated and accustomed to due diligence. He had also presented these same arguments to Randall during their Bible study. Larry answered my arguments directly from the Bible.

Regarding the thief on the cross, little is known about his previous history leading up to the cross. It is not known if he had been a faithful follower of Christ, then yielded to the temptation of sin and then caught in the act, and subsequently punished for his crime. Larry reminded me that Jesus was a faithful, perfectly devout Jew who had followed the Law of Moses to perfection. The thief on the cross, in Luke 23:42-43, said to Jesus:

> *Lord, remember me when thou comest into thy kingdom. And Jesus said unto him, Verily I say unto thee, To day shalt thou be with me in paradise.*

Jesus, while being alive on this earth, did as He saw fit. On two other occasions He pronounced forgiveness of sins. He healed the lame, the blind, and the sick. He bid Peter to walk to Him on water. Jesus performed miracles and did signs and wonders to confirm to an unbelieving world that He was God's Son.

But Larry pointed out something else. He showed me Hebrews 9:16-17:

> *For where a testament is, there must also of necessity be the death of the testator. For a testament is of force after men are dead: otherwise it is of no strength at all while the testator liveth.*

The Law of Christ (Galatians 6:2) went into effect after Christ's death; therefore, Christ healed, forgave, and saved men while He was alive just like the thief on the cross. However, Christ's law (or testament) did not go into effect until the moment of His death.

Hebrews 9 made this Bible fact clear. The principle of Christ's will continues to this day. While he is alive, a man can do anything he wants with his estate, but his will goes into effect at the point of his death.

When Jesus lived, all men were still under the Law of Moses if they were Jews, or they were under the Patriarchal Law if they were Gentiles. However, at the point of Christ's death those former covenants were nailed to the cross, and both Jews and Gentiles would be reconciled together into one body, the church, by the cross. Larry proved this point by Ephesians 2:14-16:

> *For he is our peace, who hath made both one, and hath broken down the middle wall of partition between us; Having abolished in his flesh the enmity, even the law of commandments contained in ordinances; for to make in himself of twain one new man, so making peace; And that he might reconcile both unto God in one*

body [the body is also the church, Colossians 1:18] *by the cross, having slain the enmity thereby*:

Larry revealed another biblical point that I had never considered. He brought up one of the many reasons for baptism found in Romans 6:3-5:

> *Know ye not, that so many of us as were baptized into Jesus Christ were baptized into his death? Therefore we are buried with him by baptism into death: that like as Christ was raised up from the dead by the glory of the Father, even so we also should walk in newness of life. For if we have been planted together in the likeness of his death, we shall be also in the likeness of his resurrection.*

Men and women are baptized into Jesus Christ by being baptized into His death. The thief on the cross was not baptized into Christ's death because Christ had not yet died, so the thief *could not* have been baptized into Christ's death. The thief was not subject to Paul's command to be baptized into Christ's death (Romans 6) just like Moses and Abraham and David were not subject to it, because all of those people lived before Christ's death on the cross lived under the Mosaical or Patriarchal Law. Therefore, how could they have been baptized into Christ's death when Christ had not yet died?

He also discussed the veil of the temple, and how the veil was not torn until Christ's death (Matt. 27:51), which was God's demonstration of destroying the middle-wall of partition between the Jews and Gentiles (Gentiles represented all of mankind outside of the Jewish race).

His points were consistent with the other teachings of the Bible. When the Bible is considered in context with all of the books, history, and events being considered, it is impossible to refute.

"But what if a man or woman is on their death-bed and cannot be baptized? What about them? Will they go to Hell?" I countered. Larry started laughing.

"What are you laughing at?" I asked.

"I'm laughing because I used the same argument!" he admitted. "But Mike, let me show you something. In your death-bed argument, the man believes that Jesus is God's Son, but dies before getting baptized, right?"

"Right."

"Okay, so your argument is that God would not send the man to Hell simply because he didn't get the chance to be baptized, correct?" Larry re-phrased the point.

"Yeah, you've got it," I responded.

"Well, Mike, your *God wouldn't do that* argument can then be applied to any of God's instructions. Think about it… suppose you are telling an old man on his death bed the story of Jesus Christ. Half way through your story the guy dies. Using your *God wouldn't do that* argument means that God would not send the guy to Hell because the guy didn't get the *chance* to believe."

"No, Larry," I responded, "everyone knows you have to believe in Jesus Christ to be saved. John 8:24 says, '*I said therefore unto you, that ye shall die in your sins: for if ye believe not that I am he, ye shall die in your sins,*' so God would absolutely send the guy to Hell if he didn't believe."

"But," Larry countered, "the guy didn't get the *chance* to believe. Your *God wouldn't do that* argument demands that God allow the man into Heaven because the man didn't get the *chance* to believe, just as your argument demands that God allow the man into Heaven because he didn't get the *chance* to get baptized."

Larry was right.

"Mike, not getting the chance to be baptized is just like not getting the chance to believe. Both hypotheticals describe a man on his death bed. In both cases the man dies before an opportunity.

In one case he dies before the opportunity to be baptized, but in the other case he dies before the opportunity to believe.

"Mike, you're saying the guy would go to Heaven before the *chance* to be baptized based on your opinion '*God wouldn't do that* [send the guy to Hell].' But you turn around and say that he would go to Hell before the *chance* to believe. The guy doesn't have to obey the command of baptism, but he must obey the command to believe?"

"Baptism isn't a command," I interjected.

"Belief and baptism are both commands and equally essential," Larry countered.

"Where are they both commanded?" I asked.

"Mark 16:16," Larry answered quickly, "He that believeth and is baptized shall be saved; but he that believeth not shall be damned."

"Okay, but it doesn't say 'he that believeth not and is not baptized shall be damned!'" I interrupted.

"Mike, you're not stupid. These are two, equal, main clauses connected by the conjunction 'and.' Jesus said *both* are required for salvation."

"But look at the later part of the verse, Larry," I responded.

"Mike, are you saying that Jesus should have phrased it, '*but he that believeth not and is baptized not shall be damned*?" Larry asked.

"Yeah," I answered. "He doesn't say anything about not being baptized."

Larry sat there looking at me in disbelief. My argument was not logical, but I still could not see the flaw in it.

"Mike," Larry said after a few moments, "if I said that you must chew *and* swallow to live, will you live if you only chew, but not swallow?"

"No," I answered.

"So," Larry pushed on, "from the statement that you must chew and swallow to live, you accept that you must do both to live, right?"

I saw the flaw in the argument at that moment.

"Alright, Larry, I see the point," I said with resistance.

"Okay," Larry replied with a smile, "so then I wouldn't need to say 'if you don't chew and if you don't swallow you will die?'"

Yep, if I had not realized the stupidity of my argument previously, I saw it then.

"Mike, Jesus said it takes two things to be saved, belief and baptism. Belief by itself does not equal salvation. Baptism by itself does not equal salvation."

"Larry, I still can't see that baptism is a necessity to be saved." I was desperate to hang on to my lifelong belief.

"So, you're saying," Larry replied, "Chew [believe] and you will live, but swallowing [baptism] has nothing to do with living."

The argument was painful for me to participate in, and the idea of being baptized to be saved just wasn't copasetic with my thinking, but I started to understand Larry's point from the Bible.

Larry continued, "Jesus said in the latter part of the verse, '*but he that believeth not shall be damned*.' In other words-"

I cut him off, "It wouldn't have made sense for Jesus to go further because belief is the first part of the equation. If the first step is not taken, then the second is eliminated by default."

"Exactly!" exclaimed Larry.

"Mike, it's just like the ark. Noah had preached to his generation that a great flood was coming. He preached while building the ark. Noah's generation thought he was a fool and refused to heed his warnings. When the rains began and the floodwaters rose, could all of those outside the ark of God simply have prayed, 'God, I'm sorry? Please forgive me and save me?'

Could they have expected God to have, at the moment of their sorrowful request, placed them inside the ark where they would have been saved? Of course not. That's a deathbed confession, and it's a play on emotionalism."

"But, Larry," I pleaded with him, "I still think that it's faith that saves!"

"Mike," Larry said, "it is faith that saves us. It's an instructive, biblical, obedient faith!" Then Larry showed me something that hit me hard, like a 2x4 to the head! We opened to the book of Numbers, chapter 21, and he read verses 4 thru 9. The King James Version says:

> *And they journeyed from mount Hor by the way of the Red sea, to compass the land of Edom: and the soul of the people was much discouraged because of the way. And the people spake against God, and against Moses, Wherefore have ye brought us up out of Egypt to die in the wilderness? for there is no bread, neither is there any water; and our soul loatheth this light bread. And the LORD sent fiery serpents among the people, and they bit the people; and much people of Israel died. Therefore the people came to Moses, and said, We have sinned, for we have spoken against the LORD, and against thee; pray unto the LORD, that he take away the serpents from us. And Moses prayed for the people. And the LORD said unto Moses, Make thee a fiery serpent, and set it upon a pole: and it shall come to pass, that every one that is bitten, when he looketh upon it, shall live. And Moses made a serpent of brass, and put it upon a pole, and it came to pass, that if a serpent had bitten any man, when he beheld the serpent of brass, he lived.*

Larry said, "Mike, put yourself in this situation. There you are in the camp with the Israelites. You've worked all day, and now you're back to your tent. You pull the tent flap back and see your brother laying there on his cot. He's pale, sweating and shaking. You look down at his ankle and you see it. Snake bite!"

"You tell him to get up and to come outside to look at the serpent of brass on the pole so that he will live, but your brother yells at you to shut up. He says that he wants no part of 'snake salvation'. He says that God will save him by faith alone! Your brother tells you that all he's got to do is pray and ask to be cured right there inside his tent, and God will save him from his snake bite right there in his tent by faith alone.

"But you remind your brother that God told Moses to make the fiery serpent, set it upon a pole, and everyone who is bitten, when he looks at it, shall live (be saved). But your brother tells you that looking at the snake is a work! He says that man is not saved by works, lest any man should boast, but by faith only! He refuses to get up and go outside to look at the serpent on the pole.

"Now, will your brother live, or die?" Larry asked me sincerely.

I gave it serious thought. God commanded the man to look at the serpent on the pole to be healed.

"He'd die," I responded.

"Why?" Larry asked.

"Because he didn't do what God told him to do to be healed," I responded.

"Mike, that's exactly right. Faith – real faith in God – is to follow His instructions. Faith is demonstrating to God that you believe enough to obey His commands. Obeying God is not a work. It is faith. Faith is the exercise of obedience toward the instructions of God."

I had never heard it put that way. Larry had learned a lot. When did that happen?

Larry continued, "Praying for God to save you right on your deathbed and calling it faith is not faith at all. It's selfish, reckless, disobedience to God. That type of faith doesn't save men's souls.

"John 12:42 says, '*Nevertheless among the chief rulers also many believed on him; but because of the Pharisees they did not confess him, lest they should be put out of the synagogue.*'

"Those priests had faith, but that's all they had. They had *faith alone,* but they wouldn't confess Jesus Christ. Jesus said that whosoever shall deny me before men, him will I also deny before my Father which is in heaven. Well, confessing Christ is an act, an action, a behavior, a task, or a 'work.' Confessing is *more* than faith alone, yet you don't hear people say that confessing Christ is a work, do you?"

I was listening.

"However, when someone points out the truth about baptism and that baptism is an essential part of God's plan of redemption, people want to throw it out, calling it a 'work.' Mike, in light of all that is taught about baptism in the New Testament, the argument against baptism is so weak that it cannot stand. Any honest Bible study will prove that men cannot be saved before being baptized into Christ."

"Well, Larry, I *was* baptized," I offered weakly.

"*Why* were you baptized?" he asked.

"An outward sign of an inward change," I responded.

"Mike, that's not Bible baptism," he said.

"Of course it is," I argued.

Larry turned to Acts 2, and began in verse 36:

> *Therefore let all the house of Israel know assuredly, that God hath made that same Jesus, whom ye have crucified, both Lord and Christ. Now when they heard this, they were pricked in their heart, and said unto Peter and to the rest of the apostles, Men and brethren, what shall we do? Then Peter said unto them, Repent, and be baptized every one of you in the name of Jesus*

Christ for the remission of sins, and ye shall receive the gift of the Holy Ghost.

After reading the verses, Larry said, "Look at verse 38. Why were they baptized?"

"For the remission of sins," I responded.

"And what were they told they would receive after they were baptized?" he asked.

I looked back at the verse and said, "The gift of the Holy Ghost," finding the answer in the latter part of verse 38.

"Mike," Larry said as he made eye contact, "Jesus said that a man must be born of water and the Spirit, in John 3:5." I was already familiar with that verse, and I nodded my head yes.

"Peter's words confirm Christ's words and detail how to be born of water and the Spirit: baptism (water) for the remission of sins (reason) and receive the gift of the Holy Spirit."

When Larry left the apartment I looked at the clock on the wall. 5:42 a.m. I was exhausted, but I still had to jump in the shower to get ready for work. Jonetta had gone to bed right after Larry had arrived the night before. She did her visiting and studying during normal hours like normal people!

As for Larry's all-nighter, I had gotten some answers, but hardheads were hard to break. Larry had pushed me hard, and I did not like it. But sometimes stubborn people have to be pushed.

I was stubborn.

Chapter 16
Hot Wings and Aggrivation

New Year: 1988

The blue ball banked off of the left wall, making a high-velocity ricochet at a sharp angle toward my right, flying close to the hardwood, but I closed the gap swinging forcefully at the wrist. The ball made contact with the sweet-spot on my racquet.

Ryan was at my right side, and he could not get to it in time.

"Ah!" Ryan groaned as I took the winning point, but that was fine because he had beaten me relentlessly all morning.

"Every blind squirrel finds a nut once in a while," I said, and we laughed in unison as we climbed through the half-hatch that led out of the racquetball courts into the outer hall.

Ryan was a young lobbyist who worked around the capital building. A single guy who came from a Belle Meade blue-blood family, but he was a guy who was very grounded. The money had not gone to his head.

Ryan was not a nickel millionaire, either. He also did not come from new money. His family was as close to American royalty as you could find. Multiple generations closely tied to Vanderbilt. His family owned commercial properties all over the city. His father was a prominent investment banker in Nashville. Their home was equipped with a staff of nine full-time servants and assistants at all times.

Ambassadors and foreign political figures were common guests at their estate home, and hanging out at Ryan's house required security clearance. Sometimes I wondered if Interpol was on their speed-dial.

I enjoyed Ryan's company because he was level-headed, interesting to talk with, and was without pretension or arrogance. He had earned an MBA from Vanderbilt and possessed superior listening skills.

We played racquetball together three or four times a month. We also met at TGIF's every other Friday after work to drink beer and discuss Nashville politics.

After a quick shower, I was at my locker putting on a new tie. Ryan was sitting on an adjacent locker-room bench a few feet away, lacing up his wingtips. "Hey, Ryan, what do you know about [Randall's church]?"

Ryan finished lacing up his shoe while quickly working the catalog of his mind. His recall was a remarkable thing.

"Michael, I had a great uncle involved with a man by the name of A.M. Burton. Does that ring a bell?"

"Nope," I responded.

"The largest building downtown, the L&C Tower, that's the Life and Casualty Insurance Building," Ryan continued, "It was founded in 1903 by A.M. Burton. Burton was a member of [Randall's church]. He also helped Lipscomb University get where they're at today." Ryan had an eidetic (photographic) memory. I hated the guy.

"What was your uncle's connection to Burton?" I asked, now more interested.

"Not really sure," Ryan scanned his memory. "I was never told, but from what I understand Burton was one of the finest Christian men that Nashville has ever known. His philanthropy toward orphanages and colleges has never been matched by anyone in the Mid-South. At least that's what I've read."

We walked out of the fitness center toward our cars.

"Why do you ask about that church?" Now Ryan was curious.

"I've been in a Bible study with a guy at the office," I replied.

Ryan pulled his keys out of his pocket as he approached a new Volvo. "Michael, if you make a decision to be a part of that church, you won't regret it. They have some of the best reputations around the hill."

Isn't it interesting what you can find out when you simply ask?

Kenny and Regina, our friends from apartment U-7, were having a New Year's Eve party that night, and we were invited. They were a young couple who lived a few doors over, so we did not have to worry about driving back home.

The party started at nine and things really got rolling around eleven. By midnight the party was in full swing. Their small apartment (a mirror image of ours) was wall-to-wall people. I estimated around sixty.

Jonetta gave a slight tug along the side of my pant-leg close to the pocket. That meant she was ready to leave, and her eyes said that it was past her bedtime.

"Let's get out of here," I said and she smiled in return. We made our rounds through the crowd to say our goodbyes. All of the drunks wanted hugs and sloppy kisses. Most of them wanted to kiss her, of course. I couldn't blame them.

We hurried back through the cold night air into the warmth and safety of our own little apartment. I had not had much to drink that night. To tell you the truth, parties were losing their appeal. Come to think of it, a lot of worldly things were losing their appeal.

Reading the Bible on a regular basis was changing me on the inside, and it was a positive change.

Larry called me on New Year's Day to ask what was going on. Jonetta was going shopping with some friends, so I asked Larry to come over to hang out. We'd eat some hot-wings and watch a game.

A few hours later the hot-wings were gone, and the game was boring. I looked over at Larry, and he was half asleep.

"Hey," I jolted him from his semi-conscious state. "I talked to my cousin on the phone the other day. It was about Acts 2:38."

Larry was looking at me a little more awake now.

"And?" he asked, prodding me to finish.

"And she said that the word 'for' in the verse means '*because of.*'" I lobbed the statement over in his direction with no particular objective in mind.

"Yeah, right," Larry said with a smirk and a chuckle. He thought I was joking.

"Oh yeah. That's what she said alright," I goaded him. "The word 'for' in the verse actually means '*because of.*'"

"That's ridiculous," Larry said in a voice of disgust and disbelief.

"Open it up!" I said as I pushed at the Bible on the coffee table with my socked foot. "Go ahead. Check it out!"

Larry took the Bible from the table and then acted like he was going to hit me with it. He then flipped it open to Acts 2:38 and read:

> *Then Peter said unto them, Repent, and be baptized every one of you in the name of Jesus Christ for the remission of sins, and ye shall receive the gift of the Holy Ghost.*

After the first reading he re-read the passage again inserting the words 'because of' in place of 'for':

> *Then Peter said unto them, Repent, and be baptized every one of you in the name of Jesus Christ [because of] the remission of sins, and ye shall receive the gift of the Holy Ghost.*

"Oh, come on Mike! That doesn't even follow Bible logic. So Peter tells them to repent and be baptized because their sins were *already* gone? You can't tell me you really believe that? It's *totally* inconsistent with the rest of the New Testament's teaching on baptism!"

Larry shook his head at me as if he couldn't believe anyone could be so stupid. I just sat there with a grin on my face, not saying a word.

"Mike, I'm going to look at the original Greek. Your cousin's premise makes no sense, but I know you Baptists will try anything to get out of being baptized for the biblical reason."

"She's a Presbyterian," I corrected Larry, smiling bigger while trying to suppress the laughter that was building inside me.

"Whatever man!" Larry was aggravated and it was funny.

"But Larry, think about it. If we're saved at the point of belief, and then we're baptized because our sins are already gone, baptism *would* be an outward sign of an inward change!"

Larry was shaking his head no. "But Mike, one principle teaching must be consistent with the others found throughout the remote text. Your cousin's point isn't consistent. It ignores the rest of the New Testament. It goes against all of the other teachings about baptism, verses we've already been through together. You *know* those verses!" Larry argued back.

I knew that my cousin's logic regarding Acts 2:38 wasn't consistent with the rest of the New Testament, but I was searching for anything that might help me hang on to my existing beliefs.

There was *something* causing me to want to hang on… something that had not yet surfaced, but it was on its way up.

Chapter 17
We Aim to Please

January 1988

Life was busy. Busy for everyone. Time and responsibility slowed for no one. It is funny to hear people say, "When things slow down I'll..." Things never slow down.

The company I worked for was no different. OSI was booming! Our department had eleven Technical Engineers (TE's). Each TE ran an average of five calls per working day. At an average of twenty-two working days per month, each TE ran a monthly average of one hundred and ten calls.

The bulk of my January calls came from my church accounts due to their unusually high December printing volumes. The holidays created heavier duty cycles on their equipment resulting in higher break-down percentages and an increased need for service.

Between marriage, work, entertainment, and life in general, I was reading the Bible continuously. My knowledge of the Bible was growing, and navigating the Bible was becoming easier as time passed.

I was not a fanatic, nor did I want to be. I simply wanted to be able to defend what I believed with the Bible. This principle is found in the later part of 1 Peter 3:15,

> *...and be ready always to give an answer to every man that asketh you a reason of the hope that is in you with meekness and fear.*

Jesus said,

> *He that rejecteth me, and receiveth not my words, hath one that judgeth him: the word that I have spoken, the same shall judge him in the last day.* (John 12:48).

In other words, it seemed to me that the words of Christ might possibly be the measuring rod (or bench-mark) used in determining man's eternal destiny. Jesus said in Matthew 7:21,

> *Not every one that saith unto me, Lord, Lord, shall enter into the kingdom of heaven; but he that doeth the will of my Father which is in heaven.*

How would any of us figure out the will of the Father without reading the Father's will?

Two things are certain, death and taxes. Some people had figured out how to get out of paying their taxes, but I had not met anyone who had figured out a way of getting out of dying. That meant at least one thing is certain.

If you know without a doubt that you are going to die someday, and Christ said that you are going to be judged, doesn't it make sense to find out what you will be judged by? It does not take a PhD to answer the question.

At any rate, there I was standing in Cookeville, Tennessee in one of the Methodist churches and finishing up a service call on a Gestetner mimeograph.

"What's the damage?" asked the jovial Methodist minister.

"No charge," I replied. "It's under contract, and it's in great shape. Just sign here," I said, putting the service ticket down on the unoccupied secretarial desk and pointing to the signature line.

As he signed the ticket, I tried to decide whether or not to ask him. It was early in the afternoon, the church was small, there was no one else in the building, and the minister looked bored.

"Do Methodists baptize?" I remembered that it was amazing what you could find out if you just asked.

"Yes, of course," he responded as he signed the ticket.

I tore off his copy and handed it to him.

"We sprinkle, pour, or immerse, depending on the individual and the situation," the minister replied.

"You do all three?" I was surprised.

"Sure, but a lot depends on the person," he said.

"But isn't baptism immersing someone?" I asked.

"The Bible doesn't specify the mode of baptism," the minister explained. "Sometimes, in administering the sacrament to young children, you can't immerse them, so sprinkling is the best option. However, some people wish to be immersed, and that's fine, too."

"Methodists aim to please, don't they?" I replied with a smile.

He smiled back, "Well, we certainly try to accommodate."

Driving back to Nashville gave me a considerable amount of time to think about the conversation I just had with the pleasant minister at the Methodist Church. "The Bible doesn't specify the mode." His statement looped in my mind. This was a new one on me. I didn't know if the Bible specified the mode or not, but I knew someone who might have the answer. He was back at the office.

"Randall," I got his attention as I came through the back door.

"What's up, Mr. Mike?" he quickly returned my greeting.

"Grab your Bible preacher-man. I've got a gooooooood question for you today!" I exclaimed as we both made a bee-line toward his desk. Studying the Bible with Randall had grown on me.

"Mr. Mike, you ever gonna find that Sinner's Prayer for me?" Randall asked through a big grin and bright eyes.

"Good things come to those who wait," I replied in a slow mock-radio voice.

Randall laughed and said, "Man, you're full of it! What do you have for me today?"

"Just talked to a Methodist minister who said that the Bible doesn't specify the mode of baptism. He said that sprinkling, pouring, or immersion is just fine. Doesn't matter - it only depends on the person and the situation." I recited my previous conversation with the Methodist minister as accurately as possible.

We heard a loud, shrill, beeping signal and looked toward the left. It was Jeremy backing up a fork-lift.

I looked back at Randall, who was shaking his head in the negative. He had leaned back against his desk with legs crossed and arms folded, considering what I had just told him.

"To think that this man leads others," Randall said, looking toward the floor as if he was talking out loud to himself. He continued to talk to the floor, *"But he answered and said, Every plant, which my heavenly Father hath not planted, shall be rooted up. Let them alone: they be blind leaders of the blind. And if the blind lead the blind, both shall fall into the ditch."*

"Where's that verse?" I asked.

"Matthew 15:13-14," replied Randall without hesitation, but still looking at the floor.

Then he looked up at me. "Mr. Mike, there's good people in *every* denomination, just like there's *some* truth in every denomination. Every denomination does some good; every denomination teaches some truth; and, every denomination is made up of a lot of good-hearted, loving, sincere people. When you and I talk about these things I want you to remember that I'm *not* criticizing the people involved in the denomination. I'm only rebuking their false doctrine, and I'll do so till the day I die! I do it because I love the Truth, and I love their souls."

"Uh, yeah, Randall. I realize that," I said.

"But, Mr. Mike, we must refute false doctrine with the Bible. The Bible refutes their beliefs, for the Bible is the living, breathing, Word of the Almighty God."

I had never seen Randall in such an agitated state. He was clearly frustrated and angry by the Methodist's comments.

Randall continued, "Methodism began with a man named John Wesley in the mid to late 1700's. Wesley was marked as a Methodist because of the methodical way in which he opposed the clergy of the Church of England. His method grew into a movement.

"I tell you all of this to make a point. The point is that John Wesley came out of the Church of England which came out of the Roman Catholic Church. Catholics baptized by sprinkling and pouring, and they believe in baptizing babies.

"Even though Methodism is a form of the Protestant Movement (protesting against the many false doctrines of Catholicism, such as; the Pope being God on earth, worshipping and praying to images, praying to Mary, transubstantiation, etc.), many Catholic practices carried over into the Methodist Church."

I followed him.

"Mr. Mike, the baptismal *mode* is certainly specified in the Bible," Randall emphasized by raising his voice, "and that minister is ignorant of the Greek language. He's ignorant of biblical history, and he's ignorant of God's Word."

Randall was being as harsh as I'd ever seen him be. He began turning the pages of his Bible furiously.

I just watched and waited.

"How could any man call himself a minister of God and be so ignorant of the Word?" Randall was rambling to himself as he looked for his target text. "How could an entire group of people follow such ignorance and never check the Record for themselves? Do they not realize that God will hold them accountable for what they believe and do?" He continued to talk to himself, getting angrier with each word that he spoke.

"Alright, Randall, calm down," I tried to insert as he turned the pages of his Bible.

"I'm sorry, Mr. Mike," he apologized, "but a man's soul is serious business – the most serious of any business. It is not to be played with!"

Randall found what he was looking for and slid his Bible over so that I could read it with him.

"MICHAEL SHANK: COME TO THE FRONT DESK. MICHAEL SHANK: COME TO THE FRONT DESK."

The announcement buzzed through the overhead intercom. It was hard to hear with the fork-lift running behind us, but we both caught the name.

"Randall, I've got to go to the front office-"

"It's alright, Mr. Mike. Just come back here when you're done. This is too important to put off!" Randall said as I walked away from his desk and toward the front of the building.

"I'll be right back!" I shouted back to Randall as I made my way through the warehouse.

It took a minute to get from the back of the office to the front of the building. When I reached the front showroom floor, I saw Jonetta standing there with dinner-to-go in her hands. I had forgotten all about tonight. Monday nights were the one night of the week that the Technical Engineers worked an additional three hours (until 8:00 p.m.), when necessary, to catch up on any backlogged, in-shop repairs. Jonetta remembered that I was scheduled to stay late that evening, so here she was bringing me dinner at the office.

"I bet you're getting hungry," she said as she kissed me on the cheek.

"Pardon me." It was a rigid voice from somewhere behind us. We both moved aside. Ledger Stayvick was trying to work his way around us as we stood in the door that separated the showroom from the accounting offices.

"Mr. Stayvick, I'd like you to meet my wife–" I said, but he interrupted with a curt and snotty, "Hello." He never looked at her, didn't turn to shake hands, didn't even turn his head in our direction when he spoke.

"Jack's son, I presume?" Jonetta asked, already knowing that it was Ledger.

"How'd you guess?" I feigned surprise and we started laughing in unison. "He's such an–"

"Hush," she interrupted my foul expletive. "Look in the sack!" Jonetta was excited about what she had brought. "I've got you something special."

She certainly had. Pulled pork BBQ with hot sauce on the side, a large tub of slaw, a container of dill pickles, baked beans, potato salad, cornbread, and cheese cake - an entire cheese cake!

"Thought you'd like it," Jonetta grinned as she said the words.

"No. I don't like it. I love it! But an entire cheesecake?"

"The cheesecake is for the guys in your department, not for *you*! I'm making you a cake at home tonight."

I hugged and kissed her, promised to be home around eight thirty, told her to be careful on the icy roads, and thanked her for bringing me supper. Things like that made for a happy marriage. Don't think that I didn't return the little things to her. She'd skin me alive if I didn't!

Before going back to Randall, I took the cheesecake over to my department and put it out on the conference table. The guys flocked around it like a bunch of buzzards! They loved Jonetta, too.

I then made a quick stop in the parts department to check on an order. No luck. The parts I needed had not arrived.

Standing there in the parts department, I grabbed the Merlin phone receiver next to the system terminal on the parts counter and dialed S&R. Randall picked up.

"Hey, Randall. You like BBQ?"

Chapter 18
How About Some Cake?

January 1988

The smell hit me as soon as I stepped through our apartment door. German chocolate cake! I kicked off my shoes, dropped my briefcase by the door, threw the keys on the counter, and lifted off the large glass lid that covered Jonetta's latest creation. Four layers with that gooey pecan-coconut stuff in between!

Jonetta was soaking in the tub. I un-snapped the Seiko[1] chronograph from my wrist.

"You're late," she hollered from the bathroom.

"Traffic and ice," I responded. There were no cell phones in the Eighties, or at least none that I could afford.

"The roads were bad when I came home too," and I heard her trip the drain-plug. "You gettin' in the shower?" she asked.

"Not just yet. I've got some Bible stuff to show you. How about we talk about it over some cake," I volleyed.

"Sounds like a plan," she hollered back.

We stood at the counter eating cake. I caught her up to speed. The conversation with the Methodist minister, asking Randall about it, Randall getting amped up, finding out that the part I needed for my one backlogged repair was still not in, so rather than coming on home I asked Randall to split the BBQ with me while we reasoned the Bible together.

"So, you've just spent the last three hours at the office talking with Randall about the Bible?" she asked without showing any surprise.

"Yep," I replied, "and I'll give you the highlights." We opened our Bibles, and I reviewed the biblical conversation Randall and I had at the office and what Randall revealed.

Baptize is a word that was *not* translated into the English language. It was transliterated. Transliterating simply means to change a word's letters into the corresponding letters of another alphabet. It's not a translation from one language into another.

The word baptize comes from the Greek word *baptidzo*[2]. Baptidzo means to submerge, to immerse completely, or to fully go under the surface. However, the translators of the King James Bible had been influenced by the Catholic doctrine of sprinkling; therefore, when they came to the Greek word *baptidzo,* their preconceived belief about sprinkling caused them to transliterate the word rather than to actually translate it into the English word immerse as they should have done.

However, immersion opposed their Catholic doctrine of sprinkling and pouring. What were the translators, who were already influenced by Catholicism, going to do with a word that would ultimately destroy their doctrine of sprinkling and pouring? Transliteration. This allowed the translators to leave the Greek word *baptidzo* in its original form (for the most part), and gave them opportunity to mask the word's real meaning. So, they dropped the "d," changed the "o" to an "e" and voilà – the word baptize was born.

Transliteration of the word allowed the Catholic doctrine of sprinkling and pouring to remain intact, because the word "baptize" was so vague. It was a strange, almost esoteric word; therefore, religious people accepted the false idea (promoted by Catholicism) that the word baptize *could* mean to sprinkle, to pour over, or to immerse.

Most importantly, the word baptize would not directly oppose the sprinkling and pouring doctrine advocated by the Catholic Church.

Consider the impact upon the translation if the translators would have rendered baptidzo into the word "immerse," as they should have done.

Mark 16:16 (KJV) reads:

He that believeth and is baptized shall be saved; but he that believeth not shall be damned.

However, the verse should read,

He that believeth and is immersed shall be saved; but he that believeth not shall be damned.

To baptize does *not* mean to sprinkle or to pour over. To baptize means only one thing - to immerse. To teach that baptism means to sprinkle or pour over is to completely misrepresent the original meaning of the command.

Denominations that sprinkle and pour do so by reading Mark 16:16 in the following way,

He that believeth and is sprinkled, or poured on, shall be saved; but he that believeth not shall be damned.

Sprinkling and pouring is not *baptidzo*. One might as well say, "He that believes and dances under a maple tree shall be saved!" It is the same difference. Remember, if you change immersion into sprinkle, you might as well change it to anything else you like.

Again, what if the translators had *not* transliterated the Greek word baptidzo? What if they would have translated the Greek into English without the influence of Catholicism and without any attempt to preserve the doctrine of sprinkling and pouring? The answer is clear. Everywhere the word baptidzo appeared in the Greek the word immerse would have appeared in the English. The doctrine of sprinkling and pouring would have been destroyed. Infant baptism would have been destroyed, as well.

What we do is critical. Randall said that there were specific "life and death points" found in the Bible.

One of them was found in Matthew 7, verses 21-23:

Not every one that saith unto me, Lord, Lord, shall enter into the kingdom of heaven; but he that doeth the will of my Father which is in heaven. Many will say to me in that day, Lord, Lord, have we not prophesied in thy name? and in thy name have cast out devils? and in thy name done many wonderful works? And then will I profess unto them, I never knew you: depart from me, ye that work iniquity.

This is a scene in the future on the Day of Judgment. Jesus said that many will plead with Him, reminding Him that they did things in His name. They prophesied and cast out devils (demons) and did many wonderful things. However, Christ will cast them away, declaring that He simply does not know them. Why? Because they worked iniquity.

In other words, they practiced things that were foreign to the New Testament. They certainly *did* many things in the name of Christ and their particular religion, but they did not do the will of God.

I was familiar with the verse. It was, in my heart and mind, one of the most sobering verses in the entire Bible. The more I read it, the more I understood it. Jesus painted a visual picture of the many who will plead their case.

Randall said that we need to understand exactly *who* these people will be. The world says that these will be the rapists and the murderers and the child molesters and the porn stars, but that is where the world makes their mistake.

The mistake is thinking that Jesus Christ is speaking only of the scoundrels of society. Why is it a mistake to think this? Because Jesus is giving us insight into the fact that the vast majority of those rejected by Him on the Day of Judgment will be those who believed that they were *Christians* while living on this earth. They will be people who prophesied, cast out demons, and did many wonderful works – all in the name of Jesus Christ.

Look at the text again. They said they had *done* these things in His name, but in the end Jesus will not know them.

There are many people living on the earth at this very moment wearing the name Christian and doing many good works in the name of Jesus Christ, but at the end of time Jesus will say to them, *"I never knew you: depart from me, ye that work iniquity."*

How can we figure out if we are working iniquity or doing the will of God? That's the $64,000.00 question, isn't it?

One thing was clear: Bible baptism was *not* getting sprinkled on or poured over.

Chapter 19
What's a Eunuch?

Same Evening

A quarter of the cake was gone. Jonetta was usually in a coma by ten thirty, but she was wide awake and keeping the pace tonight.

I told her how the Bible showed that immersion was the mode of baptism in the story of the Eunuch, but it was time for a quick break.

Jonetta had to pee, and with that she jumped off the couch and pranced down the hallway. I took advantage of the opportunity to slip out onto the patio and have a smoke. I grabbed my Land's End jacket out of the hall closet and yanked open the sliding glass patio door.

"Hey, neighbor!" I heard Norman greet me through the wood slats from above. We lived on a ground-floor apartment, and Norman lived directly above us. His patio balcony was a wood-deck structure, and he was looking down at me through the spaces between the deck-boards.

"Hi, Norman," I replied.

"Skoal[1] might be a better option than this, huh?" Norman joked, referring to the two of us idiots standing outside in the January air sucking on cigarettes.

"Skoal won't stay lit!" I responded. Norman laughed loudly.

"Hey, that's a good point, Mike!"

After a few puffs I said, "Good night, Norman." I couldn't take the cold air any longer. Yeah, I was from Illinois, but it was southern Illinois – not Chicago!

"Good night, neighbor," Norman replied.

As soon as I stepped through the sliding door Jonetta asked, "Michael, what's a Eunuch?"

"Uh… no wrench in the tool box?"

"Shut up!" she yelped, but it got a laugh out of her.

Randall showed me the story of the Eunuch. It was rich with points. I wanted to share it with her as well. The story was found in the eighth chapter of Acts, beginning at verse 26 and ending at verse 40:

> *And the angel of the Lord spake unto Philip, saying, Arise, and go toward the south unto the way that goeth down from Jerusalem unto Gaza, which is desert. And he arose and went: and, behold, a man of Ethiopia, an eunuch of great authority under Candace queen of the Ethiopians, who had the charge of all her treasure, and had come to Jerusalem for to worship, Was returning, and sitting in his chariot read Esaias the prophet. Then the Spirit said unto Philip, Go near, and join thyself to this chariot. And Philip ran thither to him, and heard him read the prophet Esaias, and said, Understandest thou what thou readest? And he said, How can I, except some man should guide me? And he desired Philip that he would come up and sit with him. The place of the scripture which he read was this, He was led as a sheep to the slaughter; and like a lamb dumb before his shearer, so opened he not his mouth: In his humiliation his judgment was taken away: and who shall declare his generation? for his life is taken from the earth. And the eunuch answered Philip, and said, I pray thee, of whom speaketh the prophet this? of himself, or of some other man? Then Philip opened his mouth, and began at the same scripture, and preached unto him Jesus. And as they went on their way, they came unto a certain water: and the eunuch said, See, here is water; what doth hinder me to be baptized? And Philip said, If thou believest with all thine heart, thou mayest. And he answered and said, I believe that Jesus Christ is the Son of God. And he commanded the chariot to stand still: and they went down both into the water, both Philip and the eunuch; and he baptized him. And when they were come up out of the water, the Spirit of the Lord caught away Philip, that the eunuch saw him no more: and he went on his way rejoicing.*

But Philip was found at Azotus: and passing through he preached in all the cities, till he came to Caesarea.

I revisited the points of the story that Randall had shared with me. Jonetta and I discussed them at length. The points were straight forward and self-explanatory, but I had missed them so many times in all of my previous readings of the story. I figured there was a chance that she had missed the same points.

Randall had shared the following with me:

Philip *preached Jesus* to a religious man who was not able to identify the Christ from the prophecy found in the fifty-third chapter of Isaiah, which was the book the Eunuch was reading from. The Bible says that Philip preached Jesus.

Now why is it important to point out that Philip preached Jesus to the Eunuch? It is important because the Eunuch said to Philip, in verse thirty-six, *"See, here is water; what doth hinder me to be baptized*?"

Hold on just a second! How did the Eunuch know about baptism? Didn't Philip preach Jesus to the Eunuch?

Studying the Bible is like everything else. You have got to use the good sense that God gave you. You have got to approach the Bible as you would any other piece of literature. There are laws that govern grammar like the law of inference, but many intelligent people throw away grammatical logic and reasoning when they open their Bibles.

How did the Eunuch know about baptism when Philip simply preached Jesus? Evidently preaching Jesus required preaching baptism. This conversion account verifies this idea. How do we know? Because the Eunuch said, "See, here is *water*; what doth hinder *me* to be *baptized*?"

This conversion account also reveals a clear, easy-to-understand sequence of events. The sequence teaches us God's scheme of redemption (His plan of salvation for man). What's the sequence of the plan of redemption?

The Eunuch heard the Word preached. Romans 10:17 says, *"So then faith cometh by hearing, and hearing by the word of God."* How did this Eunuch obtain a "split-second" faith with a knowledge of his urgent and immediate need to be put into Jesus Christ by baptism in water? He heard the Word preached by Philip! Faith comes by *hearing*. Hearing what? The Word, it is the simple and total Truth of the gospel and how it can change the life of everyone willing to *hear*!

The Eunuch was a religious man. The later part of Acts 8:27 says, "[he] *had come to Jerusalem for to worship*." This indicates piety, a fear of God, a respect for God, and a penitent heart. The Eunuch was, evidently, a man with a repentant heart. Jesus said in Luke 13:3, *"I tell you, Nay: but, except ye repent, ye shall all likewise perish."*

The Eunuch demonstrated his belief that Jesus Christ was the Son of God. Philip told the Eunuch that he could be baptized "If thou believest with all thine heart, thou mayest [be baptized]." (Acts 8:37)

The Eunuch verbalized his belief that Jesus Christ is the Son of God through his public confession of the Christ. In the later part of Acts 8:37, the Eunuch answered and said, *"I believe that Jesus Christ is the Son of God."* This would have been in the presence of Philip and the Eunuch's attendants.

However, his belief and confession were not enough. The salvation process was still not complete. Acts 8:38 states, *"And he commanded the chariot to stand still: and they went down both into the water, both Philip and the eunuch; and he baptized* [immersed] *him."*

What did it take for this high-profile, Egyptian government official to trust in Philip's words? What did it take for him to stop his entire caravan and risk the security of himself and his attendants? What did it take for that Eunuch to place his eternal future into belief, confession, and immersion? It took faith. This is a picture of true faith.

But there was more.

Jesus had already ascended to Heaven, which means that whatever applied to the Eunuch applies to us today. Why? Because you, I, and the Eunuch are on *this* side of the cross. We are all under the same New Covenant of Jesus Christ.

God's will is revealed in His instructions. Philip was led by God's Holy Spirit. The Eunuch's response revealed a response to Philip's teaching. Philip's teaching came by inspiration of the Holy Spirit. This is God's will seen in action.

The Eunuch believed what Philip preached. He wanted to be saved from his sins. Through God's providence they came upon a body of water.

Notice that it was the *Eunuch* – not Philip - who pointed out the water. Philip seemed to want to know that the Eunuch fully believed that Jesus was God's Son before he did anything else with the man.

Consider this, there were two men on the desert road to Gaza. Ethiopia was approximately 1,580 miles from Jerusalem where the Eunuch had just visited. The Eunuch is now making the long journey back to his homeland in Ethiopia. Do you think he might have been carrying drinking water with him? Of course he would have. A 1,580 mile journey on horse-back or on camels, covering a distance of 25 miles per day, would have taken about 63 days. If the Eunuch had brought no drinking water, he, his attendants, his horses or camels, and every other living thing that traveled with him would have died of dehydration during the trip back to Ethiopia.

Do you think that a guy who had managed to become the treasurer of the queen's wealth was so foolish and short-sighted that he would not have brought plenty of drinking water? Water for himself, his attendants, and his animals for the 1,580 mile journey? Of course he would have been carrying water, a lot of water!

This leads to the baptismal mode. If sprinkling was a God-directed, God-approved mode of baptism, Philip and the Eunuch would not have *needed* a body of water for baptism. The Eunuch had water with him and would have simply said, "See, here is some of my drinking water; what doth hinder me to be baptized?"

He would not have needed to stop the chariot and neither man would have gone down into the water as the story states.

Yes, the Bible is an incredible document.

There was another point that I struggled with greatly. The waiting period.

When I was eight years old, I was told that I was saved after saying the Sinner's Prayer, but I was not baptized until I was thirteen years old. Then, the Baptist Church voted on my qualification as a candidate for baptism before they allowed me to be baptized.

Compare my experience with the Eunuch's conversion account. There was no waiting period for the Eunuch. He was baptized immediately upon his confession of faith. No one voted on the Eunuch's candidacy for baptism. The Eunuch did not wait days, weeks, months, or even years to be baptized as I had done.

My salvation experience and the Eunuch's experience were completely different. Jesus said, "*He that believeth and is baptized shall be saved* (Mk. 16:16)." That's exactly what Philip taught the Eunuch, and that's exactly what the Eunuch obeyed.

Philip was led by an angel and the Holy Spirit of God (Acts 8:26, 29). Since Philip was being led by the Holy Spirit, why didn't the Holy Spirit lead Philip to tell the Eunuch to say the Sinner's Prayer? Why didn't the Holy Spirit direct Philip to tell the Eunuch, "Ask Jesus into your heart?" Why didn't the Holy Spirit cause Philip to tell the Eunuch to be baptized with the Holy Ghost and speak in tongues? Why didn't Philip tell the Eunuch to receive Jesus into his heart and then wait to be voted on as a candidate for baptism (as the Baptists did with me)? Why didn't the Holy Spirit direct Philip to do any of these things people are being told to do today?

Here's the hard-core, undeniable, incontrovertible Bible fact that the Baptists, the Methodists, the Presbyterians, the Pentecostals, the Holiness Movement, the charismatic Church of God, the Community Churches, the "faith-only" crowd, and the Televangelists do not understand or refuse to accept – the doctrine of faith only, the Sinner's Prayer, and asking Jesus into your heart to be saved are utterly and thoroughly false to their very core. These teachings are leading people to eternal destruction en masse! This might upset you, but please do not be offended by Truth!

Jesus Christ said,

> *Howbeit when he, the Spirit of truth, is come, he will guide you into* ***all truth****: for he shall not speak of himself; but whatsoever he shall hear, that shall he speak: and he will shew you things to come* (John 16:13).

Honestly, if ***any*** of the previously mentioned doctrines were ***all Truth***, wouldn't the Holy Spirit have directed Philip to teach them to the Eunuch? Wasn't Philip being guided into all truth by the Holy Spirit, just as Jesus said they would be? Wasn't Philip simply conveying the message that he was receiving from the Holy Spirit to the Eunuch? What message did he convey? He *preached Jesus*. What is the result of total Truth hitting an honest heart? The Eunuch's response is the result.

Notice what Philip *did not* teach: faith-only, the Sinner's Prayer, asking Jesus into the heart, baptism as an outward show of an inward change, waiting to be voted on as a candidate for baptism, speaking in unknown tongues. This is clear proof that none of these doctrines and teachings were a part of the Truth that Jesus said the apostles would be guided into. Remember Christ's words:

> *Howbeit when he, the Spirit of truth, is come,* ***he will guide you into all truth****: for he shall not speak of himself; but whatsoever he shall hear, that shall he speak: and he will shew you things to come* (John 16:13).

Jonetta and I finished talking at eleven thirty. We were mentally exhausted.

I had reached a decision and was saddened by it. The Baptist Church was filled with some of the greatest people I had ever known. They were loving, kind, moral, upstanding, sincere, hard-working, God-fearing and zealous people. They did many wonderful works.

My own family had filled the Baptist Church back home, but I had now studied enough of the Bible to realize one thing. No matter how much I loved and respected them, no matter how many wonderful people were in the Baptist Church, and no matter how much good I knew that they had done, they were clearly wrong about God's process of saving man.

It made me sick to my stomach to think about it, but when I compared the Bible's teachings about salvation with the Baptist Church's teachings about salvation, there were simply too many discrepancies.

No Baptist Pastor, from the dozens of whom I had spoken with over the previous weeks and months, had been able to show me the Sinner's Prayer in the Bible. I was starting to realize it was because the Sinner's Prayer was not *in* the Bible.

The Baptist Pastors had not been able to give me a single example of *anyone* in the New Testament that had asked Jesus into their heart to be saved. They could not show me in the Bible where *anyone* was baptized as "an outward sign of an inward change". They could not show me one example of anyone in the Bible who was voted on as a candidate for baptism. Why? Because *none* of these things are in the Bible.

Some of those same Pastors, even though they were very sincere men, alleged that John the Baptist started the Baptist Church. The Bible clearly revealed that he did not. Biblical and secular history revealed that John Smyth started the Baptist Church around 1607 to 1609, a historical fact that some of them didn't seem to know.

And no, this was not bashing my Baptist family and friends – the people I loved very much! Instead, it was admitting that the Baptist *doctrines* were the problem – not the good people in the Baptist Church.

I wanted only *one* thing. I wanted to support what I believed with the *Bible*.

How could I, in good conscience, invite someone to the Baptist Church and risk them asking me to help them become a Christian. What would I tell them? Would I go along with the Baptist teaching, even when I knew it could not be found in God's Word? Should I tell them to do something different than what Philip told the Eunuch to do to be saved?

What was I supposed to think when I read Christ's words in Mark 16:16, *"He that believeth and is baptized shall be saved,"* but my Baptist Pastor preached, "He that believeth and is **not** baptized shall be saved?"

By my Baptist Preacher's own words, it was easier to get into Heaven than it was the Baptist Church. He said all you had to do to get into Heaven was to believe, but to get into the Baptist Church required you to be "voted on," and then be baptized, according to the Hiscox Standard Baptist Manual (Hiscox, 1965). What a contrast to God's instructions.

I simply wanted Bible support for my beliefs. I did not want opinions, arrogant responses, creed-books, misinformation, suppositions, and statements about the Bible that were completely false.

Yes, I had arrived at a decision which saddened me deeply. I would renounce my Baptist faith and withdraw my membership in the Baptist Church immediately. At the age of twenty, I was now going to be a religious generic. A believer with no denominational affiliation.

Slowly, painfully, and gradually answers were coming. It was late, and I was preparing for bed. I brushed my teeth and thought about John 6:45:

> *It is written in the prophets, And they shall be all taught of God. Every man therefore that hath heard, and hath learned of the Father, cometh unto me."*

The faith of Jesus Christ was not based on opinions, emotions, feelings, traditions, creeds, human institutions, man-made churches, or ignorance of Scripture. The faith of Jesus Christ is an instructive faith based on God's will revealed in human language. The book that we call the Bible.

I set the alarm clock and slipped under the covers. Jonetta was already asleep. I closed my eyes. I was leaving the Baptist Church.

What would mom and dad think?

Chapter 20
Kicked Out of Sunday School

January 10th

I just laid there... listening. It was seven thirty in the morning, and Jonetta was already in the kitchen making breakfast. Sounds were coming through the thin walls of our small, two-bedroom apartment at the Knollwood Apartment Complex. It was the couple next door again, going into round two of one of their frequent domestic disturbances.

"Should I call the police?" I wondered as I lay in bed. From what I had been able to gather, the fighting couple next door lived together. They had no kids, were in their mid-30's, and *she* was the abuser of the pair. She (his live-in girlfriend) outweighed him by about a hundred pounds, and he wasn't small, either.

Jonetta and I had witnessed her verbal abuse toward him more times than we could count. We had also seen her hit him on several previous occasions. The Bellevue PD seemed to be on a first name basis with the couple.

I got out of bed, walked down the hall, came up behind Jonetta, and wrapped my arms around her while she worked at the stove.

"You goin' over to help him?" I asked softly into her ear as she flipped pancakes.

"The poor guy probably needs a little help," Jonetta said sympathetically, "but I don't think that the three of us could take her. Michael, she's a big, mean woman."

"Yes, she is!" I said while pouring the first cup of coffee. The noise emanating from their apartment seemed to evaporate during our second cup.

"You think she killed him?" I asked, grinning a little as I grabbed another piece of sausage from the serving platter.

"Don't say something like that!" Jonetta scolded.

"Maybe he killed her," I said, grinning bigger, "and now he's trying to figure out what to do with the body!"

"Oh! I'm gonna smack you now," Jonetta blurted out.

"Hey, hey! She's rubbing off on you!" Jonetta ignored me. "You know the Bible says that bad company corrupts good morals."

"Speaking of that," Jonetta jumped in, "where are we going to church this morning?"

There we were between the proverbial rock and the hard spot.

I had, up until that point, acquired enough Bible knowledge to recognize that many denominations were the manifestation of Christ's statement:

> *But in vain they do worship me, teaching for doctrines the commandments of men* (Matthew 15:9).

I thought about our church situation and I was discouraged with the options: Catholicism or Protestantism.

The hours I had been spending at our local library researching denominationalism and their respective doctrines was paying off. Catholicism was out of the question. There were so many unbiblical doctrines in the Catholic church that I didn't know where to begin: praying to Mary, recognizing the Pope as God on earth, transubstantiation (the bread and wine turning into actual flesh and blood), calling the priests father, the auricular confessional booth, the Vicar of Christ, ad nauseam.

The Apostle Paul wrote,

> *Now the Spirit speaketh expressly, that in the latter times some shall depart from the faith, giving heed to seducing spirits, and doctrines of devils; Speaking lies in hypocrisy; having their conscience seared with a hot iron; Forbidding to marry* [priests were forbidden to marry]*, and commanding to abstain from meats* [Catholics were to abstain from certain meats during

> Lent], *which God hath created to be received with thanksgiving of them which believe and know the truth* (1 Timothy 4:1-3).

Jesus said,

> *And call no man your father upon the earth: for one is your Father, which is in heaven* (Matthew 23:9).

I was trying to get closer to God's Word not farther away from it! Catholicism would never be an option. Anyone who spent any amount of time reading the Bible quickly found that Catholicism's doctrines were erroneous, without Bible authority, without biblical origin, and false.

That left the mainstream Protestants (Baptists, Methodists, Presbyterians, etc.), but this was a huge problem in and of itself. First, these groups taught many things that I now knew were not in the Bible. Second, almost every denomination was influenced by Calvinism. I'd spent a lot of time studying Calvinism at our local library. Dr. Richard Bucher[2] (2010) wrote:

> Along with Martin Luther, John Calvin (1509-1564) is viewed as one of the two great Reformers of the Sixteenth Century, and one of the most influential Christian teachers in the history of the Church. He is regarded as the father of Reformed theology and the founder of Presbyterian Church polity. Today, well over 50 million Christians throughout the world consider themselves Calvinist in some sense. All Presbyterian and Reformed churches, and many Baptist denominations consider themselves Calvinist churches…as well as numerous evangelical and non-denominational churches have been influenced by Calvinism.

Calvinism was based on five doctrines that formed the acrostic TULIP. Almost every denomination grabbed on to some, if not all of Calvin's doctrinal viewpoints. Mr. Calvin might have been an intelligent man, and he might have been influential in his day, but how people could subscribe to his religious ideas was beyond me. To accept the Calvinistic points meant that you had to close your Bible. Calvin's five-doctrines are found to be completely false when compared against the Bible. They are:

1. ***(T)otal Hereditary Depravity.*** Calvin incorrectly taught original sin. That every child is born with sin, already guilty of sin and conceived and born totally corrupt (depraved) spiritually. Furthermore, the teaching maintains that people don't have freedom to seek or choose God. This is completely false because every accountable person of sound mind has the freedom to choose to serve God. Deuteronomy 30:19 says:

> *I call heaven and earth to record this day against you, that I have set before you life and death, blessing and cursing: therefore choose…"*

God wanted them to choose life of course, but the point is that God gave mankind free moral agency - the power to choose. But how about the premise that all babies are born with sin? Do infants carry the sins of their parents before them? Do they carry the sins of Adam and Eve? No, they do not. This is easily seen as a false doctrine from passages like Ezekiel 18:20:

> *The soul that sinneth, it shall die. The son shall not bear the iniquity of the father, neither shall the father bear the iniquity of the son: the righteousness of the righteous shall be upon him, and the wickedness of the wicked shall be upon him* (Ezek. 18:20).

The Bible is rich in analogies and examples teaching us that we are not spiritually responsible for the sins of our fathers and forefathers. Children are, until they come to an age whereby they fully understand right from wrong (and are able to choose between the two), innocent and free from the spiritual consequences of sin. The challenge for many regarding this topic is that they confuse the spiritual responsibility of sin with bearing the consequence of sin. For example, a child born to a crack addicted mother is also addicted to crack; therefore, the child bears the physical consequences of the mother's sin.

However, the child did not choose to smoke crack and is not spiritually responsible to God for having crack in its blood-stream. The child does not inherit the spiritual responsibility of his or her parent's sins, and will not incur a spiritual punishment for those sins.

Now, Calvin wants us to believe that innocent babies and children that die before they come to an age whereby they understand right from wrong are going to be eternally damned. God tells us how burning children in fire was detestable to Him, and did not even cross His mind. He said,

> *You must not worship the LORD your God in their way, because in worshiping their gods, they do all kinds of detestable things the LORD hates.* ***They even burn their sons and daughters in the fire as sacrifices to their gods.*** *(Duet. 12:31).*

> *And they built the high places of Baal, which are in the valley of the son of Hinnom,* ***to cause their sons and their daughters to pass through the fire*** *unto Molech; which* ***I commanded them not, neither came it into my mind, that they should do this abomination,*** *to cause Judah to sin (Jer. 32:35).*

Isn't it remarkable? Calvin taught that babies are born with sin. The wages of sin are death. Children having sin would, therefore, be punished eternally. However, we find that burning children in fire was a detestable thing to God. These scriptures show that God hated this practice, and it was an abomination. God did not command it, nor did it come into His mind!

2. ***(U)nconditional Predestination/Election.*** Because God is sovereign, Calvin taught that the eternal fate of all people depends totally and only on God's unconditional predestination before time began. In other words, it was predetermined before you were born whether you will have eternal life or eternal damnation. This is completely false. It is false because it again denies a great gift from our Creator, free will. God does not predestine anyone to eternal destruction. The Bible refutes Calvin's false doctrine in many areas, such as:

> *Have I any pleasure at all that the wicked should die? saith the Lord GOD: and not that he should return from his ways, and live?* (Ezekiel 18:23)

Peter wrote,

> *The Lord is not slack concerning his promise, as some men count slackness; but is longsuffering to us-ward, not willing that any should perish, but that all should come to repentance* (2 Peter 3:9).

God also does not predestine anyone to be saved. God's children are to work at being faithful and remain faithful. Paul wrote,

> *Wherefore, my beloved, as ye have always obeyed, not as in my presence only, but now much more in my absence, work out*

your own salvation with fear and trembling (Philippians 2:12).

According to the Bible, God's children can fall from grace:

Christ is become of no effect unto you, whosoever of you are justified by the law; ye are fallen from grace (Galatians 5:4).

The Hebrew writer wrote about the idea of falling from the grace of God in Hebrews 12:15:

Looking diligently lest any man fail of the grace of God; lest any root of bitterness springing up trouble you, and thereby many be defiled;

Jesus Christ addressed this idea in Revelation 2:10:

Fear none of those things which thou shalt suffer: behold, the devil shall cast some of you into prison, that ye may be tried; and ye shall have tribulation ten days: be thou faithful unto death, and I will give thee a crown of life.

Notice the contingency (if/then clause) of salvation – "*be thou faithful unto death, and I will give thee a crown of life.*" If a child of God is faithful unto death (until they die), then Christ will give them eternal life. The negative is also true. "Be thou **not** faithful unto death, and I will **not** give thee a crown of life."

John Calvin taught that your salvation or damnation was determined by God before you were ever born. According to Calvin, God allows people to be born with no possible way to escape their pre-determined fate in Hell? If this is true, it means that God determines to put a person into Hell before they are ever conceived? This type of god is not the God of the Bible.

3. ***(L)imited Atonement***. Calvinism teaches that the death of Christ atoned only for the sins of the elect (those whom God had predestined to be saved). This is completely false. John wrote:

> *And he is the propitiation for our sins: and not for ours only, but also for the sins of the whole world* (1 John 2:2).

Limited atonement hinges upon or is married to predestination. Do I really need to say more? It is ridiculous.

4. ***(I)rresistible Grace***. This teaches that we are saved by grace alone. This is also completely false. The Bible says the grace of God that brings salvation has appeared to all men, teaching us (Titus 2:11-12a). One of the primary functions of God's grace (unmerited favor) is to teach man ***to*** respond as well as to teach man ***how to*** respond. Irresistible grace says that nothing is done toward salvation other than grace. Repentance, confession of belief, faithfulness, service, right living – everything else must be thrown out.

5. ***(P)erseverance in Grace***. This is also known as "Perseverance of the Saints" or "Once Saved, Always Saved." Calvinism incorrectly teaches that it is impossible for true Christians to lose their faith, because God empowers them to persevere in grace. This is completely false. Hebrews 6:4-6 states:

> *For it is impossible for those who were once enlightened, and have tasted of the heavenly gift, and were made partakers of the Holy Ghost, And have tasted the good word of God, and the*

> *powers of the world to come, If they shall fall away, to renew them again unto repentance; seeing they crucify to themselves the Son of God afresh, and put him to an open shame.*

Someone who has tasted the heavenly gift, partaken of the Holy Ghost, tasted the good word of God, and the powers of the world to come is certainly a true Christian, yet the inspired Hebrew writer teaches that these can certainly fall away.

The Apostle Paul knew that even ***he*** could fall away. He said in 1 Corinthians 9:27,

> *But I keep under my body, and bring it into subjection: lest that by any means, when I have preached to others, I myself should be a castaway.*

I loved "Once saved, always saved!" Yes! Get saved, then live like Hell! If you are saved, you cannot do anything to undo it. If you are not really saved, then you cannot do anything to undo that either.

But, back to our dilemma. What about the Pentecostals and Charismatics? Their religion is not only heavily dependent upon feelings and great emotionalism, their ideas about the miraculous age of the Holy Spirit are deeply flawed. If the Charismatic (Holiness, Church of God, Pentecostals) can truly heal, why aren't doctors, nurses and medical centers put out of business?

Have you ever noticed that they always seem to heal someone with an invisible ailment (someone in a wheel-chair who comes forward to be healed and then rises up out of their wheel-chair)? Have you ever noticed that those healings can never be medically verified?

If these people can perform miracles as they say they can, why won't they use their gift to heal all of the sick? Those people with medically verifiable cancers, blindness, AIDS, and all of the known diseases of mankind?

Why can't they restore missing limbs? Why won't they use their gift outside of their emotionally charged church services? The answer is clear. They do not have what the apostles and New Testament Christians had in the first century. They do not possess the true, God-given, miraculous, direct operation of the Holy Spirit.

The Charismatics reply, "We don't use the power outside of church services because you've got to have faith to be healed!" My response to that is this, "Hey amigo, you're dead-wrong. Your premise is false because you are ignorant of what the Bible says about the direct operation of the Holy Spirit. Go back and read your Bible again. Miracles were not done for those who already believed. They were done for confirmation of the Word of God and to validate the gospel to those who did **not** believe!

The direct operation and miraculous powers given to the apostles during the first century age were given to them for a sign of confirmation of the Word of God to unbelievers. Mark 16:17-20 states,

> *And these signs shall follow them that believe; In my name shall they cast out devils; they shall speak with new tongues; They shall take up serpents; and if they drink any deadly thing, it shall not hurt them; they shall lay hands on the sick, and they shall recover. So then after the Lord had spoken unto them, he was received up into heaven, and sat on the right hand of God. And they went forth, and preached every where, the Lord working with them, and confirming the word with signs following. Amen.*

Try attending one of those spirit-filled, Holy-Ghost-baptized, charismatic revivals sometime and take a bottle of drain cleaner with you. Walk up to the ones claiming to have the miraculous gift of the Holy Ghost, hand them the drain cleaner, and ask them to drink it. The Bible says that those who have the direct operation of the Holy Spirit can drink *any* deadly thing, and *it shall not hurt them*.

You won't find a one of them that will do it. The Charismatic folks, even though they are very sincere, loving, and good-hearted, are practicing error. It is my opinion that many of these good people know in their hearts that *something* is wrong.

In my studies I have found that when the Word of God (the perfect law of liberty) was completed and confirmed, the miraculous powers via the Holy Spirit and the signs that were necessary to confirm the Word were no longer necessary. James called the Word of God the perfect law of liberty:

> *But whoso looketh into the perfect law of liberty, and continueth therein, he being not a forgetful hearer, but a doer of the work, this man shall be blessed in his deed* (James 1:25).

Paul refers to this perfect law of liberty in 1 Corinthians 13:8-10, telling us when these miraculous powers would cease. He said,

> *Charity never faileth: but whether there be prophecies, they shall fail; whether there be tongues, they shall cease; whether there be knowledge, it shall vanish away. For we know in part, and we prophesy in part. But when that which is perfect* [perfect law of liberty] *is come, then that which is in part* [the miraculous gifts] *shall be done away*.

Miraculous prophecies, the miraculous power to speak in a foreign language without any prior training, and miraculous knowledge revealed through the minds and pens of the inspired apostles would vanish away. When? When that which is perfect comes. What is that which is perfect? The perfect law of liberty. The completed New Testament in written form.

The Charismatics cry, "No! The thing that is perfect refers to Jesus!" However, this is false as well. Christ had already come in the flesh, was crucified, buried, resurrected, and had ascended to the right hand of God when Paul penned his words. Paul verified the subject of his premise in the statement, "*For we know in part, and we prophesy in part*." Their knowledge and preaching, at that time, was in part, or not yet complete (perfect). They relied on the temporary assistance of the Holy Spirit for knowledge regarding the faith, and for the ability to prophesy and preach the will of Jesus Christ. Why do you think Jesus told them:

> *"Howbeit when he, the Spirit of truth, is come, he will guide you into all truth: for he shall not speak of himself; but whatsoever he shall hear, that shall he speak: and he will shew you things to come. He shall glorify me: for he shall receive of mine, and shall shew it unto you"* (John 16:13-14)?

Who would guide the apostles into all truth? The Holy Spirit – the Spirit of Truth. It would be the Holy Spirit that would guide and show the Truth to the apostles.

Then Paul clarified, "*But when that which is perfect is come* [the written New Testament], *then that which is in part* [temporary miraculous powers to confirm the Word] *shall be done away*."

Jesus said in Matthew 24:35,

> *Heaven and earth shall pass away, but my words shall not pass away.*

The miraculous powers of the first century would pass away, but the perfect law of liberty and the written New Testament, would never pass away.

If the miraculous gifts of the Spirit passed away at the end of the first century age, how does the Holy Spirit operate today? Through His Masterpiece, the written New Testament. How were the apostles sanctified then, and how are the children of God sanctified today? Jesus said,

> *Sanctify them through thy truth: thy **word** is truth* (John 17:17).

The written New Testament is the Word of Truth. It is the agent by which men and women come to God and the knowledge of His Will. The apostles needed guidance, direction, and an immediate knowledge to preach Christ's message and to establish the practices of the one faith of Christ Jesus.

However, there was no New Testament at the time of the birth of Christianity (Acts 2, circa 33AD). The New Testament had not yet been written, so the Holy Spirit guided the apostles just as Christ promised (John 16:13). The Holy Spirit guided them to write the accounts of Christ's life and ministry (Matthew-John); their actions and conversion accounts (Acts); their letters of faith, instruction, and encouragement (Romans-Jude); and of the ultimate triumph over Satan and death (Revelation).

The Holy Spirit worked through the apostles using miraculous signs to confirm to an unbelieving world that what the apostles preached was indeed the Truth from the Almighty God (Mark 16:17-20). The apostle's written documents became the Holy Script, the New Testament.

The New Testament was the one thing that all of mankind would be required to learn how eternal life exists through Jesus Christ and how man could be redeemed by Christ. The written New Testament would offer the student a venue to obtain complete and perfect knowledge for becoming a child of God, and living as a child of God.

The New Testament was the perfect masterpiece of the Holy Spirit. It would guide all men and women in all things concerning a new life in Christ that God offers to all. The Holy Spirit, through the pen of the Apostle Paul, wrote:

> *All scripture is given by inspiration of God, and is profitable for doctrine, for reproof, for correction, for instruction in righteousness: That the man of God may be perfect, throughly furnished unto all good works* (2 Timothy 3:16-17).

Back to our dilemma, once again. Where were we to go to worship? What about the Episcopalians and the Church of England? These were heavily influenced by Catholicism, as well. Sorry.

How about the Mormon Church? Absolutely not! Paul wrote,

> *But though we, or an angel from heaven, preach any other gospel unto you than that which we have preached unto you, let him be accursed. As we said before, so say I now again, If any man preach any other gospel unto you than that ye have received, let him be accursed.* (Galatians 1:8-9).

Mormons claim that Joseph Smith received the book of Mormon via an angel. A different gospel than the apostles preached in the first century. Galatians 1:8-9 kills the Mormon religion entirely. Again, Jesus told the apostles,

> *Howbeit when he, the Spirit of truth, is come, he will guide you into all truth: for he shall not speak of himself; but whatsoever he shall hear, that shall he speak: and he will shew you things to come* (John 16:13).

The apostles of the first century were guided by the Holy Spirit of God into all Truth, but Joseph Smith wanted people to believe that the apostles *weren't guided into all truth.* Smith advocated the false doctrine that the apostles had not received all truth. Smith wanted people to buy into the idea that more truth was revealed to him hundreds of years after the first century. Wow, that's creative.

How about the Jehovah's Witnesses? They've re-translated the Bible into a document that denies the Divineness of Christ. They claim that their information comes from their Greek version called the emphatic Diaglott, a two-language translation of the New Testament by Benjamin Wilson first published in 1864. The Jehovah's Witness gospel is clearly a different gospel than the one the apostles preached during the first century. Notice the verse again:

> *But though we, or an angel from heaven, preach any other gospel unto you than that which we have preached unto you, let him be accursed* (Galatians 1:8).

Talk to a few Jehovah's Witnesses, and you will quickly find out that their Watchtower Society is, in their minds, just as holy and inspired as the Bible. Isn't it bizarre that they exalt their publications to the same level as the inspired Bible?

Well, what churches did that leave as an option? It left the vague, nondescript, generic, community churches. Jonetta and I decided to visit a Community Church. Maybe they followed the Bible and just the Bible.

We started visiting community churches. One community church we visited had a rock-type gospel band that stirred the audience into a screaming frenzy. Then the minister took the stage and put on an incredible show. He used props, drama, smoke machines, and a laser-light show. The crowd laughed and cried. He was phenomenal and had the audience eating out of the palm of his hand.

And the most amazing part? He preached thirty eight minutes and mentioned only one Bible verse.

Over those weeks that we visited the community churches, we found that they were religious smorgasbords designed to please everyone and offend no one. They stood for almost nothing. They worked so hard at embracing everyone that they could not stand for the most elementary Bible principles. No brain, no backbone, and all fluff.

Paul wrote to Timothy and said:

> *For the time will come when they will not endure sound doctrine; but after their own lusts shall they heap to themselves teachers, having itching ears; And they shall turn away their ears from the truth, and shall be turned unto fables* (2 Timothy 4:3-4).

It was happening before our very eyes. During one of our visits at a community church we had an eye opening experience. It happened on a Sunday morning in early February. We attended an adult Bible class at one of the smaller community churches. The classes were held before worship service. The class we chose was geared toward young married couples. The group seemed to consist of couples that ranged in age from their 20's to 40's, and there was about 40 people in the class.

Around twenty minutes into the class session, the Bible had not been opened, nor had any of it been referenced. It was a big group discussion on the subject of husbands loving their wives and wives loving their husbands. Almost every response began with someone saying, "Well, I think…," but nothing from the Bible was offered.

The class instructor called on me to give my opinion, but I wasn't there to give my opinion. Nor was I there to hear theirs.

I opened my Bible to the fifth chapter of Ephesians and read:

> *Submitting yourselves one to another in the fear of God. Wives, submit yourselves unto your own husbands, as unto the Lord. For the husband is the head of the wife, even as Christ is the head of the church: and he is the saviour of the body. Therefore as the church is subject unto Christ, so let the wives be to their own husbands in every thing. Husbands, love your wives, even as Christ also loved the church, and gave himself for it; That he might sanctify and cleanse it with the washing of water by the word, That he might present it to himself a glorious church, not having spot, or wrinkle, or any such thing; but that it should be holy and without blemish. So ought men to love their wives as their own bodies. He that loveth his wife loveth himself. For no man ever yet hated his own flesh; but nourisheth and cherisheth it, even as the Lord the church: For we are members of his body, of his flesh, and of his bones. For this cause shall a man leave his father and mother, and shall be joined unto his wife, and they two shall be one flesh. This is a great mystery: but I speak concerning Christ and the church. Nevertheless let every one of you in particular so love his wife even as himself; and the wife see that she reverence her husband* (Ephesians 5:21-33).

The room was deathly quiet. Couples looked uncomfortably at one another. Then a male voice from the other side of the room said, "So I take it that you're a legalist?"

"Excuse me?" I did not understand the question, and I couldn't see who had asked it.

"I said I take it that you're a legalist?" The question was asked by a well-dressed man in his late 30's, sitting with an equally well-dressed woman who appeared close to his age.

"I'm sorry I don't understand," I replied.

"A *legalist*. You think that the Bible is a literal guide, and that you've got to adhere to it." His statement wasn't a question. It was more of an accusation or a challenge before the group. How did I always provoke the alpha male in every group?

"Uh, well, I don't know if I subscribe to your definition, but, yes. The Bible is our guide in spiritual matters, and we should always try to do what it says, as much as possible." I returned the volley to the alpha, making my delivery slow and deliberate.

I was truly confused over such a strange question in a *Bible* class, of all places!

"I don't think that the husband being the head of the wife still applies to us today," came another response from a woman right behind us. She continued, "And putting something like that on people today is legalism. You're no different than a Scribe or a Pharisee when you try to make that apply to people today."

"Well," came a young voice toward the front, "doctrine is divisive and creates conflict."

These people were a bunch of idiots! No, my attitude wasn't Christian at that point, either.

"May I say something along that line," I said, interrupting the young man toward the front. The room became deathly quiet again. All eyes shifted to me. The class instructor nodded his head yes.

I read from the Bible, *"Whosoever transgresseth, and abideth not in the doctrine of Christ, hath not God. He that abideth in the doctrine of Christ, he hath both the Father and the Son. If there come any unto you, and bring not this doctrine, receive him not into your house, neither bid him God speed,* 2 John 1:9-10. If we don't abide in the doctrine of Jesus Christ, we don't have God, but if we do, we have both God and Jesus Christ, God's Son. How can any of you call this legalism?"

No one knew what to say. They could not respond. Arguing the point would have meant arguing with the Word. The instructor's face turned red as he looked around the room. He looked back at me and Jonetta.

"You'll probably find another class better suited toward your personal beliefs," he stated flatly.

I took Jonetta by the hand. We got up from our folding chairs, smiled, thanked the instructor, and walked out of the Bible class completely humiliated and in a state of shock.

Wow! Let me add this to my resume:

February 1988: Got kicked out of Sunday School Class for referencing Bible passages relative to the topic, for reading the Bible in Sunday School Class, and for asking Bible-related questions.

The Community Churches that we visited claimed that they were non-denominational. In reality, they were inter-denominational. They took in everyone from all faiths and creeds. They practiced everything and stood for nothing. Their main objective was to attract the masses with feel-good, positive, success-type messages.

They talked about God, love, faith, hope, and a variety of Christian attributes, but did not open a Bible. Why was that? Probably because when you open your Bible you will quickly find that real New Testament first-century Christians stood firm on doctrines defined by the Master.

The doctrines of the Holy Word of God are much different than the sweaty-palmed, weak-kneed, rosy-cheeked, wishy-washy, feel-good, stand-for-nothing, ineffectual, spineless, let's-all-hold-hands-and-just-get-along garbage being dished out by the Community Church crowd.

One more time-

For the time will come when they will not endure sound doctrine; but after their own lusts shall they heap to themselves teachers, having itching ears; and they shall turn away their ears from the truth, and shall be turned unto fables (2 Timothy 4:3-4).

Chapter 21
Muscle and a Shovel

A February Evening

We were watching the Cosby Show[1] when the phone rang. Jonetta picked it up.

"It's Larry," she said as she handed me the phone.

"Hey man!"

"Hi Mike. You got a few minutes? I've got something to show you," Larry said. He sounded excited.

"Sure," I replied. "You want to talk now, or you coming by?"

"Can I come by?"

"Come on!"

Larry kicked the snow from his shoes and then stepped into our apartment.

"How about some hot apple cider, Larry?" Jonetta asked him, already making her way into the kitchen.

"I'd love some, Jonetta," Larry replied.

"Come on in and show me what you've got," I said, wanting to get right to the point. I didn't know what he had going, but I was eager to find out. Dr. Huxtable[1] and his perfect TV family were no longer the center of my attention.

We sat down at our dining room table, and Larry pulled out a thick manila folder along with his Bible.

"Hang on," I said to Larry. "We're not doing another all-nighter, are we?"

Larry laughed. "No, Mike, not tonight!"

I was relieved.

"Mike, your cousin said that the word 'for' in Acts 2:38 meant 'because of', right?" I'd forgotten about our New Year's Day discussion, and goading Larry into doing the research.

"Yeah, that's what she said," I replied.

"She's wrong," Larry said as he opened the folder of papers. "It doesn't mean that at all."

Jonetta placed a steaming cup of apple cider on the table next to Larry's expanding pile of papers. He thanked her as he pulled papers out of the folder.

What Larry was about to reveal would forever change the way I would look at the Bible. It would also demonstrate the power of diligent study and research. The critical importance of treating the Bible with respect and giving it the time that it truly deserves.

He turned to Acts 2:38 and we read it together again:

> *Then Peter said unto them, Repent, and be baptized every one of you in the name of Jesus Christ for the remission of sins, and ye shall receive the gift of the Holy Ghost.*

"Now," Larry began, "your cousin alleged that the preposition 'for' in the phrase '*for the remission of sins*' means '*because of*'. If that were true, the verse would read:

Then Peter said unto them, Repent, and be baptized every one of you in the name of Jesus Christ [because of] the remission of sins, and ye shall receive the gift of the Holy Ghost.

I nodded, and Larry continued.

"On the surface, it seems to make sense because we use *because of* interchangeably with the word *for* in the English language."

"Right," I agreed.

"But, Mike, the original Greek word in Acts 2:38 '*for*' is the Greek word '*Eis*'," Larry said as he pointed toward his Bible. "It's pronounced ice."

"Wait a minute, Larry," I interrupted. "How do you know this stuff?"

"I went over to Lipscomb University's Greek department and had a long discussion with one of their Greek professors," he replied as if to say touché.

"Well done, grasshopper," I volleyed. Larry laughed.

"Anyway," he was moving on, "*Eis'* is the original Greek word in the text. *Be baptized every one of you in the name of Jesus Christ [Eis'] the remission of sins*. But what does *Eis'* mean?"

"Uh, what does it mean, Larry?"

"I've condensed my research into a two-page summary, and here it is." Larry handed over two pages, neatly stapled together. This is what his research[2] said:

> The preposition ***for*** in Acts 2:38 was translated from the Greek *Eis'*. Thayer's Greek Lexicon definition: "into, unto, towards, entrance into; denotes direction."
>
> *Eis'* occurs 1,493 times within the New Testament. *Eis'* is translated in the King James Version in the following ways and in the number of occurrences:
>
> <u>Translated to word; Number of times the translated word appears in the New Testament</u>
>
> Into; 571 times
> To; 282 times
> Unto; 208 times
> In; 131 times
> For; 91 times
> On; 57 times
> Toward; 32 times
> That; 30 times
> Against; 25 times
> Upon; 25 times
> At; 20 times
> Among; 16 times
> Concerning; 5 times
> **Because Of: <u>0</u> times**

The Greek preposition *Eis'* is **never** translated *"because of"* in the New Testament. Any attempt to make the word *Eis'* mean *because of* is, therefore, false. Such a translation and/or interpretation cannot be supported with an accurate, responsible, truthful study of the Greek language.

The test of this truth can be extrapolated from Matthew 26:28. This verse has the identical Greek words – both structure and tense as Acts 2:38. Matthew 26:28 says:

> *For this is my blood of the new testament, which is shed for many* ***for*** *the remission of sins.*

Translating *Eis'* in Matthew 26:28 to *because of* would force the passage to read:

> *For this is my blood of the new testament, which is shed for many because of the remission of sins"*

Applying the "because of" argument used against Acts 2:38 forces the same argument against Matthew 26:28, because the usage and structure are identical. *But,* when you use the same argument against Matthew 26:28, if makes the Bible say that Christ's blood was shed because sins were already remitted!

However, we know that Christ's blood was not shed because sins were already remitted, so the argument that alleges the word "for" in Acts 2:38 means "because of" is totally false.

CONCLUSION: Matthew 26:28 and Acts 2:38 possess the identical Greek phrase. Applying the *because of* translation in Act 2:38 mandates that the translator also applies it to Matthew 26:28. The absurdity of the argument becomes clear, because the argument makes Christ's death on the cross unnecessary and futile.

Consider the entire phrase "*for remission of sins*" in the original Greek: "*Eis aphesin ton hamartion humon.*" This phrase is also found in Mark 1:4 and Luke 3:3. These describe John the Baptizer preaching the baptism of repentance ***for*** the remission of sins. Did John baptize followers because they *already had* forgiveness of sins? The question is ridiculous. John did not baptize because man's sins were already forgiven, just as Peter did not preach *repent and be baptized* because man's sins were already forgiven.

Peter's command to be baptized for the remission of sins means exactly what it says - baptism is for (*entrance into*, Thayer's Greek definition) remission of sins, just as Christ's blood was shed for (*entrance into*, Thayer's Greek definition) remission of sins.

The argument that men and women can be saved *before* baptism is a lie. It originates from the father of lies who was a murderer from the beginning and in whom there is no truth.

Larry gave me copies of his research and left shortly thereafter. No marathon discussions tonight, thank God!

I sat on the couch. The local Nashville news played on our TV in the background, but I was lost in thought. Questions formed in my mind. Why didn't more people know these things? Why were people so careless with the Bible? Why didn't people study the Bible like their eternal souls depended on it?

Then it hit me! Studying the Bible requires hard work. It takes self-discipline and due diligence. It requires prayerful consideration of the text you are reading, along with the remote text of the other books.

Reading the Bible is not a casual read like reading a paperback novel or the daily newspaper. The Bible is a rich, deep, literary, living gold-mine filled with everything that mankind needs for life – eternal life.

Studying and understanding the Bible is not for the lazy. Studying the Bible requires muscle and a shovel. It requires *mental* muscle and a willingness to use *honest intelligence* (the metaphorical shovel) to dig deep beyond all of our preconceived ideas, our false beliefs, and our comfortable traditions. Studying the Bible takes muscle and a shovel.

Peter said to Jesus, in John 6:68, that Jesus had the words of eternal life. How many people today are really willing to take their time and effort to dig down deep where that vein of Truth can be found?

With my metaphorical shovel in hand and an unrelenting willingness to dig deep, my spiritual muscles were being exercised as never before. They were growing. I was determined to persist and to dig deeper, not knowing what I would find next.

But I knew if I was willing to dig deep enough, I would find the location of the most precious element offered to mankind – that flowing river of blood. Christ's blood.

Chapter 22
Unity: A Joke

February 22nd

Have you ever been fed up? Fed up to the point that you were ready to give up?

I was fed up with churches and so-called Christians in general. Jonetta and I had attended a different church every Sunday morning and every Sunday evening for many weeks in our search for Truth, and we were nearing our breaking point. It was the last week of February, and we had agreed to take a break from church.

The funny thing, everyone *claimed* to follow the one Bible. Everyone claimed to be a Christian, yet the concept of unity was a complete joke. There was no unity in the world of Christendom.

Tolerance was substituted for unity, and it did not require an advanced intellect to understand the difference between the two. One definition of unity is the state or fact of being united or combined into one, as of the parts of a whole; unification[1]. The definition of tolerance, however, is a fair, objective and *permissive attitude* toward those whose opinions, practices, etc. that differ from one's own[2].

With these two definitions in mind, consider what Jesus desired, in John 17:21, when He prayed, "*That they all may be one; as thou, Father, art in me, and I in thee, that they also may be one in us: that the world may believe that thou hast sent me.*" That they all may be one. One mind and one heart. This is a singleness of thinking, of believing, and of practicing spiritual things. New Testament Christians did this very thing. In Acts 2:46, the text says that they, "*did eat their meat with gladness and singleness of heart.*" Paul told the Philippian Christians to be "*likeminded, having the same love, being of one accord, of one mind*" (Phil. 2:2). Peter said, "*Finally, be ye all of one mind*" (1 Peter 3:8).

The principle of Christians being of the same mind (like-minded), having a singleness of heart and mind, and all Christians being of one accord is taught throughout the New Testament. Real unity is a group of people who believe, think, and practice the same things under the banner of Christ using the Bible as their only guide.

But today's denominations (divisions) dotted the landscape, each teaching an opposing set of practices and beliefs. Their idea of unity is to keep their individual beliefs, practices, and doctrines, while accepting all other differing – even conflicting – beliefs, practices and doctrines. That's not unity. That's tolerance. Tolerance is not Christ's teaching of unity. Tolerance requires compromise of one's beliefs.

Why does the world look upon the name of Christ with such disdain? Because the world sees so-called Christians splintered into hundreds of man-made divisions, while, at the same time, claiming to follow the one Book, one faith, and one Lord. It makes no sense to the world, and it made no sense to me. Many non-religious people make this accurate observation: You cannot follow one book, one faith, one Lord, and, at the same time, maintain thousands of opposing practices!

Denominations oppose one another in belief, in practice, in name, and in deed. So-called Christians smile and glad-hand one another with great pretense of love and friendship; however, as soon as those with different denominational affiliations leave one another's presence, they mock the other's respective denomination. It made me sick to my stomach.

I had had my fill of the inter-denominational, fall for everything, stand for nothing, Community Church crowd. Inter-denominationalists, or Community Churches, claimed a non-denominational stance, but in reality they accept everything except true Bible unity. Toleration is the substitute.

If the Community Church crowd thought their message was Bible unity, they needed psychiatric help!

It was early Monday morning. The coffee pots at the Shell station were out of order. No problem. OSI had vending machines in the break room. It was early enough that there would still be plenty of time to get to the office, break a bill for change, and get a few cups from the machine.

"Randall," I got his attention. He was standing in front of the coffee unit buying his own cup out of OSI's machine. I wondered if he shopped at the same Shell station, too?

"Hey, Mr. Mike, how you doing?"

"I'm doing fine, Randall. How about you?"

"Man, if I was doing any better I'd be on prescription medicine!" We laughed together.

"Randall, I've got a spiritual dilemma that I'd like to share with you."

I began to explain, and Randall was, as Ross Perot was, all ears. I outlined our spiritual situation and the things we'd been through during the previous weeks with the community churches.

"Mr. Mike, how about you and I do this," Randall suggested as we finally sat down at the break table. "It's time for you and me to talk about the gospel and the church of the Lord. Did you know that His church still exists today?"

"No, Randall, I didn't."

"My friend," he continued, "as I told you before, you can't be saved outside of His church–"

"But, Randall," I interrupted, "that's just too narrow minded for me–"

> "*Because strait is the gate, and narrow is the way, which leadeth unto life, and few there be that find it*, Mr. Mike."

"Where's that found again?"

"Matthew 7:14."

"But, Randall, that can't be right," I argued.

"Why?" asked Randall.

"Because Jesus is the vine and the denominations are the branches!" I was trying to refute his premise that there was only one church.

Randall started to chuckle. "Mr. Mike, who told you that?" He was surprised. "I bet it was one of the those high-paid denominational preachers, wasn't it?"

"Well, uh," I tried to remember back to the conversation it came from, "I think it was a Lutheran minister that–"

"I figured as much," Randall interrupted again. "Mike, the Word does not say that Jesus is the vine and that the denominations are the branches. In the fifteenth chapter of the book of John, Jesus was speaking to His disciples, and He said in verses 5 through 10:

> *I am the vine, ye are the branches: He that abideth in me, and I in him, the same bringeth forth much fruit: for without me ye can do nothing. If a man abide not in me, he is cast forth as a branch, and is withered; and men gather them, and cast them into the fire, and they are burned. If ye abide in me, and my words abide in you, ye shall ask what ye will, and it shall be done unto you. Herein is my Father glorified, that ye bear much fruit; so shall ye be my disciples. As the Father hath loved me, so have I loved you: continue ye in my love. If ye keep my commandments, ye shall abide in my love; even as I have kept my Father's commandments, and abide in his love.*

We were sitting in the company break room without a Bible in hand, and Randall quoted the text verbatim from memory. His mind was amazing!

"Mr. Mike, Jesus said ye (you) are the branches. He was speaking to His disciples. Men are the branches, not denominations. This is proven in verse 6 where Jesus said, '*If a man abide not in me, he is cast forth as a branch, and is withered.*'"

I was going to confirm what he said with my own Bible, but I already knew that he was speaking the Truth. Yes, I had been misinformed again. Misinformed by a nice Lutheran minister who misquoted John 15:5. How many people had the Lutheran minister misinformed and misled over his years as their pastor?

"Stay right there, Mr. Mike," and Randall took off out the door. I knew he was going to get his Bible. I bought a cup of coffee and considered going back to see the Lutheran Reverend.

Randall came back in with his Bible, put it on the break-table, and pointed to a passage. "Mr. Mike, read this with me." He pointed to 1 Corinthians 1:10-13 and we read:

> *Now I beseech you, brethren, by the name of our Lord Jesus Christ, that ye all speak the same thing, and that there be no divisions among you; but that ye be perfectly joined together in the same mind and in the same judgment. For it hath been declared unto me of you, my brethren, by them which are of the house of Chloe, that there are contentions among you. Now this I say, that every one of you saith, I am of Paul; and I of Apollos; and I of Cephas; and I of Christ. Is Christ divided? was Paul crucified for you? or were ye baptized in the name of Paul*?

"Mr. Mike, look at what was happening there within the church of the Lord in the city of Corinth. Christians were beginning to divide up and following after men rather than staying unified in the teaching of Christ."

"Is this where denominations started?"

"Well, it was the seed of denominationalism. Men have always had a tendency to follow after other men rather than to stay with God's instructions. Those at Corinth were already trying to divide themselves up. Look here at verse 12."

Randall pointed at verse 12 and said, "Some of them liked the teachings of Paul, so they started saying that they were of Paul.

Others liked Apollos, so they started following after Apollos. Some liked Cephas, so they followed Cephas."

He continued, "Man, this is just like the Catholics following after the Pope and calling him God on earth, or the Lutherans following Martin Luther, or the Mennonites following Menno Simmons."

I was listening with rapt attention. It was interesting stuff.

"And look at how Paul straightened them out. He asked them a few simple questions here in 1 Corinthians 1, verse 13, '*Is Christ divided? Was Paul crucified for you, or were you baptized in the name of Paul?*'"

Randall went on, "Now, Mr. Mike, remember that Paul was an Apostle. He was under the guidance of the Holy Spirit. He saw those New Testament Christians going down the path of apostasy."

"What is that?" I interrupted.

"Apostasy means to fall away. Those Christians at Corinth began falling away from God's will. They had to be corrected before it was too late."

I listened.

"Paul told them back in verse 10 what God wanted for them. God, Paul beseeched, wanted them to all speak the same thing (to teach the same doctrine of Christ) and that there be no divisions (denominations) among you; but that ye be perfectly joined together in the same mind and in the same judgment (same beliefs, practices, teachings, and behavior)."

Randall's logic was consistent, solid, relevant, and in harmony with the remote text of the New Testament.

"But, Randall," I said to him as I continued to look for obstacles, "I'm a musician."

He looked up from his Bible, "What does that have to do with what we're talking about?"

"Well, you don't use instruments in your church and I love music." It was weak, but I could not think of anything else. I was running out of excuses.

"Mr. Mike, I tell you what. Give me five mornings of Bible study, one hour each morning. Just five mornings, then you decide for yourself. After five mornings you'll have enough information to decide, and it'll be your decision, not mine. After that, I'll never mention it again. Fair enough?"

"We'll continue to be friends either way?" I asked.

"Absolutely!" Randall smiled and stuck out his hand to shake on it.

"You've got a deal," I said as I shook his hand sealing the deal.

"Mr. Mike, would you like to start next Monday morning, February 29th?"

"What time?"

"How about six forty five here in the office?"

"Why not, but you're getting the doughnuts!"

"Krispy Kremes for my man!" Randall shouted as he strolled back to shipping and receiving. That guy was a treat to be around.

As we walked to our respective offices, I realized that Randall had again shown me several passages that I had never seen before, and I had never heard them preached from any pulpit.

How could I have gone this long without knowing these things?

There was a good answer to this question, and it was coming sooner than I realized.

Chapter 23
When Momma Ain't Happy (you know the rest)

Later That Evening

Jonetta carried the sacks through the front door as I followed close behind with her purse, my briefcase, and a bottle of wine. The Italian takeout we had grabbed on the way home smelled fantastic.

She kicked off her high-heels and opened the sacks while I simultaneously pitched my car-keys on the counter and grabbed the bottle opener.

The phone rang! "I got it," she said, reaching behind her to the receiver on the kitchen wall. There was no "Caller ID" in 1988.

"Hello," she said pleasantly into the phone. "Yeah, he's right here. Just a second please." She pressed the phone to her stomach to keep the caller from hearing what she was about to tell me. "It is Mr. Pompous (*expletive*) asking for you!" She mouthed the words to me very slowly and quietly. I don't think an NSA[1] bug could have picked up what she said. Pompous (*expletive*) was not his name, of course, but the nickname had stuck. It was certainly *not* Christian behavior on our part. We had a lot of growing to do.

I took the phone. "Hello?" Jonetta watched and listened. "No thanks and you won't need to call back. *[pause]* Because we've withdrawn our membership from the Baptist Church. *[another pause]* I'm in a Bible study with a man who's a member of (Randall's church) and I'd– *[another pause]*. Excuse me–"

I hung up the phone.

"Why'd you hang up on him?" Jonetta was bewildered.

"*He* hung up on *me*!"

"You've got to be kidding!" she exclaimed.

"You're not going to believe this," I said to her while twisting the bottle-opener into the cork, "but our old Pastor was calling to say that he hadn't seen us in a while. He [I paused while pulling the levers down and popping the cork from the bottle]… wanted money."

"Money?" she asked. "Money?" She said it even louder the second time. I poured the wine.

"Evidently," I continued, "they're building a new Family Life Center with a big gym, and they're having a fund-raiser." The last part came out in a laugh. The laugh couldn't be helped because neither of us could believe the timing of his call, nor could we believe the irony of the whole thing.

During our last meeting with the Reverend, he could not remember our names and did not seem to want to give us the time of day. He also gave us incorrect information and dismissed us in an arrogant manner. After that meeting I had complained that he wouldn't miss us, but he had certainly missed our money. Now, after we had withdrawn our membership from the denomination and had been absent for four months, he calls.

Why did he call? Was he concerned about our health? Was he worried about our spiritual well-being? Was he troubled by our unfaithfulness? Was he calling to say how much we had been missed? Was he curious to find out if we had moved to Brazil? Did he wonder if we had been injured in a horrible car accident? Maybe he was concerned that we had joined a monastery? Maybe he wanted to find out if we were in some type of need and wanted to know if he could minister to us in some way? Uh… not so much.

Why had he called? Money.

"So, that's when you said 'no thanks?'" Jonetta questioned.

I had just poured the wine into a narrowing goblet tulip glass and smelled the fragrance – just like I saw the rich people do in the movies! "Yep. And I told him he wouldn't need to call back. He asked why not and that's when I told him that we'd withdrawn our membership."

Jonetta was shaking her head in disbelief. "So *that's* when you said you're having a Bible study with Randall?" she asked, re-playing the phone call in her mind.

"Yeah, and I was going to tell him that I'd read Matthew chapter three. You remember, the chapter he recommended?

"Yeah, I know. Go on." she said impatiently.

"Well, as soon as I said I was studying with a member of Randall's church, he said that they're a bunch of water dogs."

"Water dogs?"

"That's exactly what the guy said. Water dogs. Then he hung up on me!"

"Water dogs? What in the world does that mean?" She was getting angry, and that was not good. "So," she continued, "he calls here to beg for money, finds out we're in a Bible study with someone from another church, calls the members of that church a derogatory name, then hangs up on you? And *he's* a *Pastor*?" She was seething with anger.

"Calm down, Honey," I said after taking a sip of wine. "I've scheduled a five-day study with Randall that we're starting a week from today, so I'll ask him. Don't worry about it. Let's eat. The food's getting cold."

"I cannot believe the gall of that man!" she growled through clinched teeth.

When momma ain't happy, well… you know the rest. The Baptist Pastor certainly lived up to his nick-name.

Chapter 24
Why I Didn't Know

February 26th

It was Friday night. Ryan paged me earlier in the day. He wanted to go out to eat, which was a good excuse for us to get together to drink beer and talk politics. Jonetta was working late that evening and would eat dinner with her friends at the office. I didn't want to go back to an empty apartment.

Dinner with Ryan was always entertaining. I was still five weeks away from my 21st birthday, but tagging along with Ryan meant getting served at every bar and meeting well-connected people.

I pulled up next to his Volvo and rolled down my window. "Where we goin'?"

We had previously agreed to meet at Union Station to decide where we would go from there.

"Let's park here and walk over to the Polaris," Ryan responded.

"Let's go!" I replied while jumping out of the car.

The Polaris was one of Nashville's premiere restaurants at the time. It was a large round restaurant atop the Hyatt Hotel. In reality, it looked like a UFO that had parked on the top of an office building. The Polaris had glass windows 360° around the exterior of the structure, and it rotated continuously, very slowly, providing an ever-changing panoramic view of the Nashville skyline. The more you drank, the more confusing the experience became.

Ryan and I sat at the Polaris bar drinking Mexican beer, eating salted peanuts, and discussing Nashville politics. He had just introduced me to a friend of his family who was also the current Ambassador to France. Joe M. Rodgers.

Rodgers was a fascinating guy. He was a friend of a prominent Nashville doctor, Thomas Frist. Frist started HCA (Hospital Corporation of America), and Rodgers was a successful well-known commercial construction contractor. Ryan said that Rodgers had built over 200 hospitals for HCA and he had also been the developer of Vanderbilt Plaza, the Third National Bank building, and the Country Music Hall of Fame.

Then Rodgers got into politics. He had served as the RNC's finance chair, served on Reagan's Foreign Intelligence Advisory Board, and had been a big fund-raiser for Reagan in the '84 election. Now Rodgers was into his third year as the current Ambassador to France – an appointment by President Reagan in 1985.

What struck me about Rodgers was his sense of sincerity. He seemed to have a genuine interest in his fellow-man.

"What did the *Times*[1] write about you?" Ryan asked Rodgers.

"Which time?" Rodgers replied with a light chuckle and a magnetic smile.

"Um, six or seven months ago," Ryan responded, but before Joe could give him an answer Ryan said, "Something about you being the leading pick to head the Department of Commerce?[2] I believe they said, and I quote, 'He's the man!'"

"Ryan, don't believe everything you read in the papers!" Rodgers laughed as he started to leave. "And Mr. Shank, watch this guy," Rodgers said to me while pointing at Ryan. "He'll get you into politics!" He turned around, and three other men were standing behind him waiting to meet him.

"Ryan, regarding human behavior," I changed the topic while lighting a cigarette, "Why, in your opinion, will masses of people hold to a set of beliefs without ever checking the facts behind those beliefs? Without ever asking *why* they believe what they believe?"

"I'll tell you what I think if you'll put that thing out!" The smoke didn't bother Ryan. What bothered him was that *I* smoked. None of Ryan's friends smoked. Why did I smoke?

"Alright, mother," I replied as I squashed the cigarette in one of the many crystal ashtrays along the bar. In the '80s you could smoke almost everywhere.

Ryan thought for a moment. "Michael, have you ever heard of Mein Kampf[3]?"

"Sure. Hitler wrote it."

"Exactly. Mein Kampf is German for *My Struggle*. It was Hitler's exposition of his grand political ideology. His 1925 masterpiece of propaganda. In Mein Kampf Hitler said, that people, by means of shrewd lies unremittingly repeated, can be made to believe that Hell is Heaven. People will believe that Hell is Heaven by hearing lies persistently repeated to them."

Ryan was onto something. The waitress came to the bar to notify us that our food was ready and relocation to a nearby table only took a few seconds. The meal was already on the table: steak with sautéed onions, baked potatoes mounded over with sour cream, extra bread, and Tiramisu for desert. Fortunately, the "beer-appetizers" had not killed our appetite.

As we finished off the orange sherbet, I looked at my watch. 8:00 p.m. I was getting tired and the thought of seeing Jonetta pleased me greatly, but I dreaded the commute back to Bellevue through evening traffic. Nashville freeways were always busy, regardless of the time of day.

Ryan and I shook hands as we departed from the restaurant. We agreed to get together the following week.

The drive home gave me time to think. Why had I never questioned what I had been taught in religion? Simple. It came from someone I trusted. Eula. Eula represented trust, love, and authority; therefore, there was no need to question her or her beliefs.

My faith originated from the trusted people in my life. It originated from the particular church that those trusted people attended and people in positions of authority during my younger years.

The people in that church, people who were good-hearted, sincere, honest, loving, and very moral, had received their faith in much the same way that I had received my faith. They had no need to question what they had been taught. Why would they?

Furthermore, everyone depended on one man - the Pastor. The Pastor told the people in the church what the Bible said and what it meant. Now, if the Pastor was in error on a spiritual matter, the probability was high that the entire church would be in error with him. Why? Simple, because of the trust that the people placed in the Pastor and his position of authority. Isn't it normally assumed that the Pastor was right because he was the man of God? Sure. He was the "paid expert."

Why don't more people question what they have been taught in religion? Maybe because most people, in general, just do not want to take the time and effort to check the facts for themselves. They say, "We have someone to do that for us," or "we pay someone to do that," or "only a Pastor can really understand the Bible," or "I don't have the time to dig through the Bible." The reasons and excuses are endless.

In matters of faith and religion, most people cut off the end of the ham.

For example, the Lutheran minister had told me, "Jesus is the vine, and the many denominations are the branches." That minister was seen by society as an expert in religious matters, so the average guy would not question his authoritative teaching on a religious subject.

Most people did what I had done. They would just assume that the Lutheran minister was right because he was the Bible expert. There was simply no need to verify his religious statements. He is a high-paid, well educated, professional clergyman, right?

Why would I need to read John 15:5-10 for myself? I did not think I needed to read it after a *minister* told me what it said. But think about it for a moment, what if I would have just taken the time to have read it for myself? I would have found that men (mankind) were the branches – not denominations.

I had never read 1 Corinthians 1:10-13. Those passages revealed how denominationalism was rearing its evil head during the first century, and how Paul rebuked them for such a thought.

Throughout my entire life I had heard that faith only saves. I did not have a clue that the *only* place the phrase *faith only* appeared in the Bible was a place that said that man is *not* saved by faith only (James 2:24).

I was beginning to realize that I had spent a lifetime being taught that all denominations were going to Heaven. That is not Bible truth. It is not found in the Bible, but it is easier to believe a lie that one has heard a thousand times rather than believe a truth that one has never heard before.

I had spent an entire lifetime attending church and never once hearing any preacher talk about the church that Jesus built, began, and bought with His own blood. The one church found in the pages of the New Testament.

I had been taught to repeat the Sinner's Prayer and to ask Jesus into my heart. The reality is that the Sinner's Prayer is not in the Bible, nor is the principle found. The Sinner's Prayer is a foreign doctrine to the New Testament.

I had depended on my personal feelings and emotions as a confirmation for my personal salvation; yet, as I read and studied the Bible I found that this, too, was not in the Bible. I found that the *opposite* was true. The Bible warns mankind of the deceitfulness of the heart and feelings. It teaches that human emotions are not reliable guides toward Truth.

Before I started reading my Bible I had no idea that being born again was to be born of water and of the Spirit (John 3:1-5).

As a Baptist, if someone asked me, "How is one born again?" I would reply, "Ask Jesus into your heart, and you'll be born again." Asking Jesus into your heart is false because Jesus said that to be born again one must be born of water and of the Spirit. And the fact that I taught someone something *different* than what the apostles taught was to be accursed (Galatians 1:8-9).

Why didn't I know these simple truths? Because I had spent an entire lifetime cutting off the end of the ham. Why had I been so ignorant of the Truth? Because it takes muscle and a shovel to read the Bible. It takes a heart that is willing to dig. It takes an honest heart (Luke 8:15) that is willing to lay aside preconceived ideas.

The Bible speaks of a noble-minded group of people who were noble minded because they checked out everything they were taught with the Old Testament Scriptures. The verse says,

> *These were more noble than those in Thessalonica, in that they received the word with all readiness of mind, and searched the scriptures daily, whether those things were so* (Acts 17:11).

As I pulled my car into the parking spot out in front of my apartment's patio, I realized something. I had spent an entire lifetime listening to what other people told me the Bible said rather than going directly to the book and reading it for myself. However, over the past few months, and for the first time in my life, I was now seeing what the Bible said for myself. I was studying the Word. I was digging.

Previously, I had never been like the noble-minded Bereans, because I had never searched the Scriptures to find out whether the things I had been told were actually so. Again, I had spent my life cutting off the end of the ham.

Up until that point I had been the blind led by blind guides. Those blind guides were loving, sincere, honest, good, kind, moral, great people. They were simply misguided. They had never checked the facts for themselves either. When they actually checked their Bible, they read through a lens of preconceived ideas, notions, and error. Their trust in the leaders of their respective churches, combined with their confidence in the doctrines previously taught to them, caused them to accept the teachings blindly.

I had reached my boiling point. All of the things I had heard throughout my life were lies. Things like:

- Denominationalism is permitted in God's eyes.
- Jesus is the vine, and denominations are the branches.
- Everyone in all churches will go to Heaven.
- Salvation is by faith alone.
- The Sinner's Prayer is God's method of saving mankind.
- Ask Jesus into your heart, and you will be born Again.
- Pastors are the religious experts and are, therefore, correct.
- Join the church of your choice because they are all approved by God.
- The church you attend does not matter.
- The way you worship doesn't matter.
- What you believe does not matter because we are all going to the same place, we are just on different roads.
- Trust your feelings because they are trustworthy guides.
- Follow your heart because it cannot be wrong.
- Confusion, opposing teachings, and doctrinal conflict was permitted by God.
- You will make it to Heaven as long as you accept

Jesus as your personal Savior.

- A personal relationship with Jesus is taught in the Bible.

They were ***all*** lies. I researched *every* previously mentioned premise. None of them are found in the Bible. None are true. None are biblically accurate. None have any biblical support.

While *none* of these things are found in God's Word, they are currently taught by the vast majority of denominations. While none of these things are true, the vast majority of good people accept them as Truth.

Why? Because there is *some* good in every denomination and there is *some* Truth in every denomination. This is the cunning strategy of Satan. Satan is highly intelligent. Furthermore, he has had thousands of years of experience in deception. He knew that people would never follow him openly. Men and women are simply too smart for that. Instead, Satan found that he could lead people away from Truth by having *some* Truth and *some* good mingled with *some* perversion (twisting) of the Truth.

What would be the best way to pervert God's will and devour men's souls? How could the Adversary lead people into apostasy, heresy, and eternal destruction? What is Satan's strategy? Lead mankind into division. Cause each division to hold to *some* Truth and do *some* good. Let them get *close* to Truth, but keep them just at the cusp of rightly dividing the Word. Get them to think they're saved by perverting the simplest elements of God's plan of salvation. Keep them in this state until they die, and the strategy succeeds. Keep people in just enough biblical ignorance, cause them to rely on their feelings and emotions rather than a "thus saith the Lord," whisper in their ears, "We're all headed to the same place – we're just on different roads to get there."

Does this sound unreasonable? Does it cause you to marvel? Well, consider what the Apostle Paul said,

> *For such are false apostles, deceitful workers, transforming themselves into the apostles of Christ. And no marvel; for Satan himself is transformed into an angel of light. Therefore it is no great thing if his ministers also be transformed as the ministers of righteousness; whose end shall be according to their works.* 2 Corinthians 11:13-15

It was becoming crystal clear. Satan transforms himself into an angel of light. He looks and acts like a godly being with a godly message while leading astray multitudes of men and women who are good, moral, loving, sincere, and zealous.

Ministers would also be led away from the Truth, not realizing their error, or the end of their ways. These well-meaning, moral, zealous ministers would remain in their false practices. How is that possible? How would they not know? Jesus said, *"Ye do err, not knowing the scriptures"* (Matthew 22:29). Ignorance of the Bible causes good, moral, sincere people to error in their religious thinking and practices.

God cannot and will not accept religious error:

> *But in vain they do worship me, teaching for doctrines the commandments of men* (Matthew 15:9).

Vain worship is unacceptable to God. Vain worship is just that – ineffectual, unsuccessful, futile, without effect, to no avail, to no purpose, improper, and irreverent. Satan deceived Eve with one, three-letter-word. It was not a dramatic production. He simply inserted the word "**not**". Genesis 3:2-4 states,

And the woman said unto the serpent, We may eat of the fruit of the trees of the garden: But of the fruit of the tree which is in the midst of the garden, God hath said, Ye shall not eat of it, neither shall ye touch it, lest ye die. And the serpent said unto the woman, Ye shall ***not*** *surely die*:

Satan uses this same strategy today. He says, "You do ***not*** need to be baptized. There is ***not*** one body. Denominationalism is ***not*** wrong. Following your emotions is ***not*** wrong. God cares ***not*** how you worship. Your heart is ***not*** wrong. Religious division is ***not*** wrong. The church you belong to does ***not*** matter. Millions of people are ***not*** wrong.

Jesus said,

Not every one that saith unto me, Lord, Lord, shall enter into the kingdom of heaven; but he that doeth the will of my Father which is in heaven. Many will say to me in that day, Lord, Lord, have we not prophesied in thy name? and in thy name have cast out devils? and in thy name done many wonderful works? And then will I profess unto them, I never knew you: depart from me, ye that work iniquity (Matthew 7:21-23).

Consider these verses again. Who are these that the Lord never knew? They are good people who thought, without a shadow of a doubt, that they were saved. Not only did they *think* they were saved, they lived their lives on this earth doing things for the Lord and in His name. In the end, these good people will be cast away into eternal destruction. Can you imagine the shock? The complete bewilderment?

It played through my mind again. It is easier to believe a lie that one has heard a thousand times before than to believe a fact that one has never heard before.

Studying the Bible was removing my blindness. It was giving me spiritual sight. For the first time in my life, spiritual "20/20 vision" was in reach.

Chapter 25
The Church of the Bible

Study 1 of 5: February 29th

Randall was already at his desk with coffee for the both of us and a box of Krispy Kremes as promised.

"Mr. Mike," he began with his Bible open, "let's start with the church."

I put my Bible up on Randall's desk next to his.

"Sounds good." I tried to match Randall's upbeat attitude.

"What do you know about the church of the Bible?"

I thought about it. "Randall, until I met you I didn't know anything about the church of the Bible."

"Surely you've heard sermons on the church of the Bible?"

"No," I responded honestly. "Church, at least from what I remember, was always something that was secondary to salvation. I was taught that salvation and church membership were totally separate issues."

"Were you taught that you had to be faithful to the church to go to Heaven?"

"No. I was saved when I was eight, but didn't join the Baptist church until I was thirteen. In most Baptist Churches it seems easier to get into Heaven than to get into the church, because joining the Baptist Church requires you to go through a process. You have to relate your salvation experience, and then the church takes a vote on you. If the vote is positive, you're given the opportunity to be baptized to become a member of the Baptist Church." While this exact process is not the single universal practice of all Baptist churches, it was the process that was used in the one I grew up in.

"That's why you believe that people from every denomination will go to Heaven?" Randall asked.

"I did, but after all that I've studied to this point, I'm starting to wonder."

"If you didn't wonder a little at this point Mike, I'd think there'd be something wrong with you!" Randall laughed.

"My wife says there *is* something wrong with me," I said, and we both started laughing.

"Alright. Now, let's go back for a minute. In Matthew 16:18, Jesus told Peter that He would build His church, right?"

"Right," I remembered from our previous study.

"Turn to Acts 2," Randall said and we both turned to it.

"Acts 2:38 says,

> *Then Peter said unto them, Repent, and be baptized every one of you in the name of Jesus Christ for the remission of sins, and ye shall receive the gift of the Holy Ghost.*

"Now, look at verse 41:

> *Then they that gladly received his word were baptized: and the same day there were added unto them about three thousand souls.*

"Mr. Mike, not all received what Peter said, did they?"

"Evidently not," I answered.

"How many received his word?" Randall asked.

"About three thousand," I replied after reading verse 41.

"Mr. Mike, do you realize that there would have been about a million Jews in Jerusalem at that time?" Randall asked.

"You're kidding?" I responded.

"No, man, I'm not kidding. This was one of the primary holy events in the life of a Jew at that time. Almost every Jew would have attended the celebration of Pentecost. Now, look at what Peter said here in Acts 2:36." Randall pointed to the verse.

I followed along at verse 36. Randall read, "*Therefore let all the house of Israel know assuredly, that God hath made that same Jesus, whom ye have crucified, both Lord and Christ*. You see, Mr. Mike, Peter proclaimed Jesus Christ to the entire house of Israel – the entire nation of Jews. But only about three thousand souls gladly received Peter's words. Then those that gladly received his word did what?" he asked.

"They were baptized," I said looking at verse 41.

"Exactly. Now do you see where it says *there were added unto them*?" Randall pointed to the text using his index finger.

"Yeah." I answered.

"Who added them?" Randall asked.

"I don't know," I responded.

Randall smiled. "That's okay, man. Look here at verse 47," and he read the verse aloud,

> *"Praising God, and having favour with all the people. And the Lord added to the church daily such as should be saved."*

"The Lord added to the church," I said.

"That's correct. It is *God* who adds to the church," Randall stated. "*Who* did God add to the church?"

"The people that gladly received Peter's words," I answered.

"And what did those people do to receive his words?" asked Randall.

"They repented and were baptized," I answered while looking at the scripture.

"That's right, Mr. Mike," Randall replied, "and what were they called?" he asked while pointing to verse 47.

"It says '*such as should be saved,*'" I replied. "They were called the saved."

"That's right. So God," Randall went on, "added the saved to the church?"

"Yeah," I responded. It was crystal clear.

"So, Mr. Mike, the church is made up of the saved and the saved make up the church."

"That's what is says," I said. "But, Randall, the Baptist I grew up in voted on who got into the Baptist Church."

Randall did not respond. He did not have to. God's Word was being revealed to me one piece at a time.

"Mike, the church was called many things: the body, the bride, the kingdom, the household of faith, the pillar and ground of truth, and a spiritual house. Let's turn to Colossians 1." Randall turned the pages and pushed on. "Look here at Colossians 1:18:

> *And he is the head of the body, the church: who is the beginning, the firstborn from the dead; that in all things he might have the preeminence.*

"Paul said that Christ is the Head of the body, the church. The body and church are one in the same," said Randall.

"So God added the saved to the church, and the church is the same thing as Christ's body?" I asked.

"Absolutely," Randall said. "Now look at Ephesians 4:4,

> *There is one body, and one Spirit, even as ye are called in one hope of your calling. "*

Randall looked up at me. "Mr. Mike, how many bodies did Paul say there were?"

"One," I replied.

Randall asked, "Now, if the church is the body, and Paul said there's only one body, how many churches are there?"

"One," I answered his question as if I had just opened a treasure chest full of gold. "So, Randall," I said as I looked at the words on the page.

"Yeah, Mr. Mike?"

"Is *this* the reason for the bad rap?"

"What do you mean?" Randall was confused at my question.

"Kirk told me to stay away from you because your church believes that you're the only ones going to Heaven. Is this where it comes from?"

"Unfortunately, yes. Good people like Kirk hear bits and pieces, but they never want to take the time to sit down and find out exactly what the Bible teaches. They go off half-cocked and looking to pick a fight, or they spread rumors and gossip trying to stir as much trouble as possible."

"Why?"

Randall thought about it for a second, then said, "*Be sober, be vigilant; because your adversary the devil, as a roaring lion, walketh about, seeking whom he may devour*, 1 Peter 5:8."

"The Adversary was always present and always there trying to lead men away from the Truth." Peter warned Christians to be vigilant.

"Mr. Mike, people have no problem with the idea that there's one God and one faith and one Holy Spirit and one Jesus Christ and one Heaven and one Hell and one Bible. But when you say there's one church, as Paul said, they freak out!"

"Randall, it's because it sounds so narrow. We've been told throughout our entire lives the exact opposite!" I responded.

"Yeah, Mr. Mike, I know that," replied Randall.

"But, Randall, where does the Bible say that Jesus will save the church? I know you've mentioned it in the past, but I'd like to see it again."

"Ephesians 5:23-25,

> *For the husband is the head of the wife, even as Christ is the head of the church: and he is the* ***saviour of the body***. *Therefore as the church is subject unto Christ, so let the wives be to their own*

husbands in every thing. Husbands, love your wives, even as Christ also loved the church, and gave himself for it.

If Christ is the Savior of the body, the church, then it is impossible to be saved *outside* of the church, because *it's* the very thing that He is going to save," Randall explained.

"So when people say, 'Join the church of your choice'?" I asked.

Randall replied, "It's a nice sounding phrase that seems to come from good intentions, but it's rooted in ignorance of the Word. If those people knew what *you* know now, would they say that?"

"No, they wouldn't," I answered.

"Why?" Randall asked quickly.

"Well, the Bible seems to say that when people obey God's instructions to be saved, they don't choose the church of their choice. *God* adds them to the *church of His Son*."

"You've got it, man!"

"So," I asked, "the name 'church of Christ' is a Bible name?"

"It's one of *many* Bible names used in the New Testament to describe the one body of Christ. Romans 16:16 says:

Salute one another with an holy kiss. The churches of Christ salute you.

"A small 'c' is used in the word church because the church of Christ is not a proper name. It's simply a description of Christ's body, His blood-bought church. It's a descriptive term of Christ's church."

"Randall, I've never seen Romans 16:16," I said, surprised again.

"Mr. Mike, that's alright. You see, you can't find the Catholics, the Baptists, the Methodists, the Presbyterians, or the rest of them in the Bible. I'm not being mean – I'm just saying that they're not in the Bible."

"You can't find any of those groups by name or by practice. That's because they didn't exist in the first century. But, you do find the church of Christ in both name and practice. The church of Christ was born, as we see here in Acts 2, on the Day of Pentecost. . ."

"I've just never equated the church with salvation," I interrupted.

"Most people don't know that the church is essential to their salvation. The saved are members of the church and the church is made up of the saved. The two *can't* be separated."

"I've never thought of it that way," I said as the words trailed off.

"Man," Randall continued, "I'm going to show you how easy this is to understand."

"Go ahead," I said.

"God had Noah build a vessel of salvation, right?" he asked.

"Yeah. The ark."

"Right. Now, Noah said to get into the ark to be saved. Get into the vessel commissioned by God for salvation. But it's *your* choice to get in the ark. Don't get in if you don't want to, but if you don't get into the ark you can't be saved," Randall said.

"I've already been thinking about this!" I replied with excitement.

"Excellent! Mr. Mike, was salvation found outside of that ark?"

"Of course not," I answered.

Randall said, "So, you agree that no one was saved who was outside of the ark, right?"

"Right," I replied.

"Now, Mr. Mike, God commissioned *another* soul-saving vessel. The perfect soul-saving vessel, Jesus Christ. The principle from the Old Testament was brought forth and fulfilled in Jesus Christ. You still have the power of choice – free moral agency. Get into the vessel of Jesus Christ, which is the body of Christ, to be saved. You don't have to get in if you don't want to, but if you don't get in, you won't be saved. Man, it's just like the ark." Randall paralleled the two.

"Mr. Mike, is salvation found outside of the ark of Christ?" asked Randall.

"It can't be," I answered.

"Okay, so you'd agree that no one can be saved outside of the ark of Christ?" he asked.

"I'd agree."

"Mr. Mike, the ark of Christ is the body of Christ. The body of Christ is the church of Christ. That is why you must be in the church of Christ for salvation. It's Christ's body! It's the soul-saving ark of God today, just like the soul-saving ark of God during Noah's day was the boat."

This is called Typology, or "picture language". I had no idea how often Typology is used between the Old and New Testaments. The ark was the "type" and the church is the "antitype". Noah, the builder of the ark, was the "type". Jesus, the builder of the church, was the "antitype".

It made perfect sense. The parallel was in complete biblical harmony, and it was amazing

"So, you couldn't possibly get saved one day, then join a church on another day." I was thinking it through, talking out loud.

"Peter didn't teach you could get saved one day and join a church another day, and *he* was being directed by the Holy Spirit! No one practiced anything like that in the Bible," Randall replied.

"Randall," I interrupted again, "I thought that the church of Christ was just another denomination, but you've always claimed that it's not a denomination."

"That's right. It's not a denomination. Denominations are *divisions* from the original. The church of Christ is the original that began on the Day of Pentecost around 33AD. Secondly, denominations have an earthly head, an association, a committee, a board of directors, conventions, etc. The churches of Christ have no earthly head of any kind!"

"Randall, are you telling me that the church of Christ has no associations or boards? How is it held together? Who makes the rules?" I just couldn't get my mind around it.

Randall smiled at my disbelief. "Mr. Mike, every congregation of the church of Christ is completely autonomous, meaning that each is free from the other and self-governed by its own elders. This is what the Bible teaches in 1 Timothy 3:1-7 and Titus 1:5-9. Deacons assist in the service of the church as instructed in 1 Timothy 3:8-12."

I was listening.

"Christ is the only Head. He is seated at the right hand of God, Acts 2:33, and governs over His kingdom, the church. Jesus governs His kingdom at this very moment. That kingdom is His church, Colossians 1:18, and the idea is explained in Ephesians 1:20-23, which says,

> *Which he wrought in Christ, when he raised him from the dead, and set him at his own right hand in the heavenly places, far above all principality, and power, and might, and dominion, and every name that is named, not only in this world, but also in that which is to come: and hath put all things under his feet,* ***and gave him to be the head over all things to the church, which is his body, the fulness of him that filleth all in all.***

"The church of Christ is the fullness of Christ. The common bond that binds one congregation to another in brotherly love and the Word of God. The Word unites us into one faith, Ephesians 4:3-6. We have no man-made statements of faith, no denominational creed-books, no associations, no conventions, and no board of directors. The Bible is our only rule of faith."

Simple, yet profound. Plain Bible teaching with no human opinions. Allowing the Bible to speak where it speaks. A people who desire book, chapter, and verse for every belief and practice potentially prescribed to. Anything not found in the Word would be thrown aside as insufficient. The mystery of the Bible was unfolding before my eyes.

I was reminded of the Eunuch's reply to Philip after Philip had asked him if he understood what he was reading. The Eunuch responded, *"How can I unless someone guides me*?" Someone was guiding me through the Word.

"But, Randall, how do you identify the church of Christ from every other church on the planet?"

"Excellent question, Mike," he said in his encouraging way, "and that'd be a good place to start tomorrow morning!"

The time during our study flew by! I was eager for tomorrow morning.

Chapter 26
So Many Thoughts

Study 2 of 5: March 1st

Randall leaned back in his old desk chair. I had picked up breakfast for the morning - biscuits and gravy.

"Religions usually identify themselves by their names, but what if you removed all of the names from all of the church buildings? How would you know one from another?" Randall asked as he used a piece of biscuit to sop up the last bit of gravy from the Styrofoam, fast-food container.

"What do you mean?" I questioned.

Randall rephrased, "How can you tell the difference between one church and another?"

"By what they teach and practice?" I questioned.

"Right on," Randall continued. "The way you identify the true church of Christ is by the same method. You find out what it teaches and how it practices."

"Go on," I said.

"Mr. Mike, the church of Christ in the New Testament was commanded to worship God in truth and in Spirit, John 4:24. If you'll read all the way through the New Testament you'll find that Christians gathered together upon the first day of the week to worship God through five avenues of worship:

1. They partook of the Lord's Supper.
2. They prayed together.
3. They sang songs, hymns, and spiritual songs.
4. They gave as they had been prospered.
5. And they were exhorted by preaching.

"That's it?" I asked.

"That's it, my friend," Randall replied "no robed choirs, no formalities, no liturgical prayers, just worship to God as taught by the Apostles and their doctrine. Bible Christians met anywhere they could on the first day of every week to offer their heart-felt scriptural worship to God in truth and Spirit."

"Wait a minute, Randall," I stopped him. He had said something that seemed off. "Did you say partake of the Lord's Supper?"

"Yep."

"Every week?" I asked.

"Every week," he said.

"But my Baptist Church took the Lord's Supper quarterly and during Easter and Christmas," I said.

"Why?"

"Uh, Hiscox Standard Baptist Manual[1] I think." I was thinking back to the church I attended growing up. "Or it could have come from the Southern Baptist Convention. I'm not sure."

"*But in vain they do worship me, teaching for doctrines the commandments of men,* Matthew 15:9," Randall said softly as he looked off into space.

Then he looked back at me. "Mr. Mike, *not every one that saith unto me, Lord, Lord, shall enter into the kingdom of heaven; but he that doeth the will of my Father which is in heaven,* Matthew 7:21. We need to seek to do the will of God. The apostles were Divinely guided. Jesus said that they would be guided into all Truth by the Holy Spirit, John 16:13. When the apostles led the early church in taking the Lord's Supper upon the first day of the week, Acts 20:7, they were being *guided into all Truth.* We are to follow that *same* Truth today."

"What verse?"

Randall repeated it, "Acts 20:7. Let's take a look at it."

We turned to the book, chapter, and verse. Randall asked me to read it out loud. I read,

> *And upon the first day of the week, when the disciples came together to break bread, Paul preached unto them, ready to depart on the morrow; and continued his speech until midnight.*"

"But, Randall," I argued, "it doesn't say we've got to do it *every* week."

"You're right, Mr. Mike. It doesn't," said Randall, "but I want you to consider a powerful parallel that comes from the Old Testament. In Exodus chapter 20, God speaks the Ten Commandments to Moses. In the eighth verse, God said to remember the Sabbath Day and to keep it holy. Mr. Mike, what day was the Sabbath day?"

"Sunday." I answered.

"Sunday?" Randall asked.

"Yeah, Sunday. My Baptist preacher always talked about how we shouldn't work on Sunday, the Sabbath Day," I responded.

"Mmm," Randall was thinking. "Mr. Mike, the Sabbath Day was the holy day reserved under the covenant of God for the Nation of Israel under the Mosaical Law. It was the seventh day of the week, Saturday. That's why the Jewish Synagogues of today continue to meet on Saturday," said Randall. I could see he was embarrassed that he had to break it to me like he did.

"Oh, man… I'm an idiot!" I said to him in disgust. I was embarrassed.

"Don't say that, Mike. A lot of denominational people I meet seem to think that the Sabbath is Sunday, but I brought this up to make another point. Let's turn to Exodus 20:8," Randall suggested. We flipped to the text.

"Would you read the verse for us?" Randall asked.

"Sure," I said. "*Remember the Sabbath and to keep it holy,*" I read aloud.

"Mr. Mike, where does it say in this verse to keep the Sabbath *every* week?" Randall asked.

"It doesn't," I replied.

"You see," Randall explained, "God didn't command the Israelites to remember the Sabbath *every* week, but they kept the Sabbath every week. Why'd they do that?" Randall asked.

I'd never considered this point of reasoning, but it made sense. I answered, "Because a Sabbath occurred every week – every seventh day."

"That's it!" Randall exclaimed. "The Israelites kept the Sabbath every week, even though God didn't specifically *say* to keep it every week because a Sabbath day occurred every week.

Now, the structure and the principle of partaking of the Lord's Supper is identical to the teaching of the Sabbath. *And upon the first day of the week, when the disciples came together to break bread,* Acts 20:7. New Testament Christians took the Lord's Supper on the first day of every week. And the reason? Because there's a first day in every week."

"Yeah, I can see your point," I responded. "I may not buy it, but I understand it."

"Mr. Mike, I'm not asking you to buy *anything*. I'm simply showing you the Word," Randall said in a humble way. "New Testament Christians today, just like 2000 years ago, partake of the Lord's Supper on the first day of the week, and there's a first day in every week."

I wanted to argue the point. "Randall," I jumped in, "it doesn't command us to do it though."

"Mike, there's no command for *you* anywhere in the New Testament!" he laughed.

"What does that mean?" I asked, grinning back at him (but I wasn't happy about the sarcasm in his voice).

"The New Testament is made up of four perspectives of Christ's life, a book that records the birth of the church and the record of conversions, twenty one letters, and one book of apocalyptic prophecy," said Randall. I was listening, and he went on, "Matthew through Revelation. Now, we interpret the Bible through commands, examples, and inferences. When we see New Testament Christians partaking of the Lord's Supper on the first day of the week, this is an example that was instigated and approved by God, and demonstrated by the apostles."

"Yeah. So?" I questioned.

"So, if you want to do God's will, you will follow those approved apostolic examples, not just the commands," said Randall.

I understood his point, but I needed more. "You've got to put more meat on this skeleton," I said.

"Alright," Randall was up for the challenge. "A direct command that seems to apply to *all* Christians is found in Matthew 28:19." We turned to the reference and Randall asked me to read it.

> *"Go ye therefore, and teach all nations, baptizing them in the name of the Father, and of the Son, and of the Holy Ghost."*

"Mr. Mike, that's a direct command that we are to follow," Randall stated. "Now turn to Colossians 3:16. Would you go ahead and read that one out loud?"

After arriving at the verse, I read, *"Let the word of Christ dwell in you richly in all wisdom; teaching and admonishing one another in psalms and hymns and spiritual songs, singing with grace in your hearts to the Lord."*

"Mr. Mike, Colossians 3:16 is a direct command, apostolic example and necessary inference."

"How?" I asked.

"It's a direct command because Paul commanded the Colossians to let the word of Christ dwell in them and teaching and admonishing one another. How? In psalms, hymns, and spiritual songs, singing with grace in their hearts to the Lord," Randall explained.

"I get that," I said.

"It is *also* an apostolic example," Randall continued, "because the apostles showed us the approved example of singing; therefore, we follow their example."

"Alright," I said, "that makes sense. Go on."

"This passage also reveals a strong necessary inference. You see, Paul's command to sing in psalms, hymns, and spiritual songs necessarily *infers* the use of our voice, but *also* infers the exclusion of everything additional.'"

"Additional?" I asked.

"Yeah. What's additional to singing? A piano and an organ. Instruments are accompaniments to singing. Paul's specific command necessarily infers inclusion *and* exclusion," Randall explained.

"But David used instruments in the Old Testament. Kirk said that y'all don't believe in the Old Testament," I blurted, not considering the politics. Even though Kirk had said it long before, it might not have been a good decision to tell Randall *where* the allegation came from.

"That's a ridiculous and false accusation. All Scripture is inspired by God. Mr. Mike, we love, trust, believe in and have great faith in the Old Testament. Galatians 3:24 says that the law [Old Testament] was our schoolmaster to bring us unto Christ. Misinformed people make that accusation, because we have a clear understanding that Christians live under and are bound by the New Testament, not the Old Testament. That's the difference."

"Give me an example."

"Alright. Under the Old Testament, Jews were commanded to observe the ordinances of the Sabbath, or Saturday, which included doing no work on the Sabbath. Where the law existed, a penalty for breaking the law also existed."

Randall turned to a book in his Bible. "Mike, Exodus 31:12-15 reveals the penalty of working on the Sabbath. It says:

> *And the LORD spake unto Moses, saying, Speak thou also unto the children of Israel, saying, Verily my sabbaths ye shall keep: for it is a sign between me and you throughout your generations; that ye may know that I am the LORD that doth sanctify you. Ye shall keep the sabbath therefore; for it is holy unto you: every one that defileth it shall surely be put to death: for whosoever doeth any work therein, that soul shall be cut off from among his people. Six days may work be done; but in the seventh is the sabbath of rest, holy to the LORD: whosoever doeth any work in the sabbath day, he shall surely be put to death.*

"So, if you worked on the Sabbath you would be put to death?" I asked as soon as he finished the verse.

"Yes. Now anyone who says that we're under the Law of the Sabbath today *must also* understand that where a law exists, a penalty for breaking the law must also exist and be enforced. Do you know *anyone* enforcing the penalty of death for working on the Sabbath?"

"Of course not," I answered.

I was developing a new understanding of the inconsistencies that I had been taught over the years. The inconsistencies had not been taught to me intentionally. They had simply been due to a general lack of understanding by my denominational teachers and preachers. They did not understand what applied today and what did not. When a law is given, the penalty for breaking the law must also apply and must be enforced.

"What about tithing?" I asked Randall. "My old Baptist Church put a great deal of pressure on us to tithe (giving 10% of our income to the Baptist Church)." Baptist leaders often quoted Old Testament verses on tithing. They urged church members to complete pledge cards, pledge contracts, and the Baptist Church back home had people make "pledge promises" in front of the church.

I despised the public pledge-promise shows. I remembered one lawyer who announced in front of the entire Baptist Church that he had just written the church a check for ten thousand dollars. It was all about who could outdo their neighbor.

"Mr. Mike, true Christians do not tithe. We're not under the Old Testament law of the tithe."

I could not believe Randall had said the words.

"Randall, we've got to tithe. I've heard it my entire life!"

"I'm sorry, but true Christians do not *tithe* their income," he said. "Tithing was required by the Law of Moses. It stated that all Israelites had to contribute 10% of all that they grew and earned back to the Tabernacle or Temple."

Randall cited Leviticus 27:30, Deuteronomy 14:23, and 2 Chronicles 31:5. "But, Mr. Mike, in reality the tithe was about 23 to 25%."

"How's that?" I was surprised at the percentage.

"Because there were *multiple,* accumulative tithes that the Israelites had to adhere to. When you go through the Old Testament and calculate all of the accumulative tithes, it equates to about twenty-three to twenty-five percent. Not ten percent."

"Twenty-five percent?" I could not believe the Bible facts being uncovered before me.

"Yeah, and remember that where a law exists there would also–"

"Be a penalty for breaking the law," I answered the statement for him.

"Mr. Mike, do you realize that when people try to go back under the Law of Moses by binding the Jewish tithe of ten percent, they have fallen from grace?"

"No. What do you mean?"

Randall replied, "Galatians 5:4 says that *Christ is become of no effect unto you, whosoever of you are justified by the law; ye are fallen from grace.* Mr. Mike, the Israelites were to be assessed their original tithes, plus a penalty of another twenty percent if they failed to tithe. The New Testament nowhere instructs, commands, infers, or gives any examples of Christians ever submitting a tithe to the Lord's church. They gave a voluntary, free-will offering, cheerfully, as they had prospered."

I admitted, "Man, I just assumed the ten percent thing was right."

"Hey, man, don't feel alone," said Randall. "Most people spend their lives assuming that their religious beliefs are right. Then they're shocked when they do a serious study of the Bible. Would you mind reading 1 Corinthians 16:1-2 for us?"

I looked up the verse and read:

> *Now concerning the collection for the saints, as I have given order to the churches of Galatia, even so do ye. Upon the first day of the week let every one of you lay by him in store, as God hath prospered him, that there be no gatherings when I come.*

Randall began, "First, this command has the identical structure of the command to remember the Sabbath. There's a first day of the week in *every* week, so we give every week, right?"

"Yeah, that makes sense," I replied.

"You know something else, Mr. Mike?"

"What's that?"

"The denominational folks are a little inconsistent when it comes to giving. They don't see the need to take the Lord's Supper every week, because they say the Bible doesn't say do it every week. However, they take up a collection every week – even though the Bible doesn't say to take up a collection every week. See the inconsistency?"

"Randall, I've got to be honest. You're right." It was true.

"Think about it, Mr. Mike. The first day of the week, according to Paul, is the only day of the week that we're to lay by in store or to give back to the Lord to help *poor Christians*, according to 1 Corinthians 16:1-2."

"But hang on, Randall," I cut in, "the Baptist Church takes up an offering during every service, including Wednesday nights. Are you saying that's wrong?" I asked.

"Mr. Mike, that's not for me to say. The only thing we've got is the Bible. Members of the first century church of Christ gave on the first day of the week. Today's church of Christ gives on the first day of the week as the Bible instructs."

"So, you don't pass the offering plate *every* time the doors are opened?" I asked.

Randall laughed. "No. Just on the first day of the week."

"You've covered so much ground today."

"Mike, don't get bogged down. It's a lot to take in," Randall encouraged. "New Testament Christians are to worship, to lay by in store, as God hath prospered them, to partake of the Lord's Supper, to pray, to sing, and to be edified by the Scriptures on the first day of the week. These are the things the apostles commanded and exemplified in their practices. We're to continue steadfast in the apostle's doctrine today. Nothing more and nothing less than God's Word instructs."

This was so different than anything I had ever been taught, and it was coming straight out of the Bible and only the Bible. That is what was so powerful and compelling about Randall's teaching. Unlike every denominational person I had ever talked to, Randall's primary concern was to speak only where the Bible speaks, and he supported every practice and every belief with the Word of God.

Yes, as narrow-minded as it seems, it is what the Bible says. The Bible says there is one body. The body is the church, one church. Jesus is the Head of one church. Entrance into the one church was given by Peter - repent and be baptized for the remission of sins. Those who gladly received his words were baptized, about 3000 souls. Those 3000 were saved and God added them to the church.

New Testament Christians continued in the apostle's teachings meeting on the first day of the week to pray, sing, give, take the Lord's Supper, and to hear preaching. Regarding their giving they were no longer under the Jewish tithe of ten percent, but they gave as they were prospered exceeding the righteousness of the Scribes and Pharisees.

Each congregation of the church of the Lord was independent of the rest. Each was self-governed by elders and deacons, instead of one Pastor making all the decisions.

The Lord's church was not a denomination, but a blood-bought institution that the saved were added to by God. Jesus Christ is the Head of His church – the *only* head!

Simple, but profound. If the Bible did not say it, Randall didn't teach it. If the Bible said it, he believed and taught it. He proved every point of belief and practice with the Word.

Chapter 27
What About Music?

Study 3 of 5: March 2nd

"Randall, why doesn't the church of Christ use a piano or organ in worship?" It was my first question of the morning. "I know you mentioned inclusion and exclusion, but I'd like to know more about this."

I knew as soon as Randall set his briefcase on top of his desk that it was going to get interesting. Randall did not carry a briefcase.

"You said you were a musician, didn't you?" Randall asked.

"Yeah."

"What instrument do you play?"

I played several. "Alto sax, drums, keyboards. I am trying to learn guitar right now–"

"Whoa," Randall interrupted. "You're a one-man band," he said, laughing and shaking his head in approval. "I love a good sax. You know any Coltrane[1]?"

Trane was the way he was known by serious saxophonists. John William Coltrane, the jazz saxophonist that pioneered the legendary free-jazz mode. Trane died in 1967 at the age of 40. I was only 3 months old when he died, but he became one of my musical idols.

A smile grew across my face. Randall had hit one of my hot-buttons. "You kidding? I can do *Blue Train* in my sleep!"

"Ah!" Randall laughed and smacked his leg. "You've got to play it for me sometime soon."

"I'd love to," I said.

"Mr. Mike, we get this instrumental music question all the time," Randall said as he got back on topic. "There's a short answer and there's a long answer. If you're going to learn the Bible you need both answers."

"Give 'em to me," I said, eager to hear what he had to say. I might not agree, but I was willing to listen.

"The short answer is this. God never authorized instruments in New Testament worship," Randall said flatly.

"What about David? He used instruments and there's going to be instruments in Heaven, right? I'm a musician and that's a talent from God, isn't it?" I fired questions in a machine-gun approach.

"Hold on, hold on. Slow down a second! Yes, yes. I agree with all of those things you just said, but you're confusing the point."

"How?"

Randall opened his Bible, "Mr. Mike, we either do what God says, or we don't do what He says, right?"

"Right."

"Alright. Let's turn to Ephesians 5?"

I turned to the book.

"Let's look at verses 18 and 19," Randall said as he found the verse with his index finger. "Mike, would you read it out loud for us?"

> *And be not drunk with wine, wherein is excess; but be filled with the Spirit; Speaking to yourselves in psalms and hymns and spiritual songs, singing and making melody in your heart to the Lord;*

"What kind of music does Paul instruct the church to use in this verse?" asked Randall.

"Singing," I replied.

"That's right. Now turn to Colossians chapter 3." We turned two books over and got to the chapter. "Mr. Mike, read verse 16 for us please."

Let the word of Christ dwell in you richly in all wisdom; teaching and admonishing one another in psalms and hymns and spiritual songs, singing with grace in your hearts to the Lord.

Randall again asked, "What kind of music does Paul instruct the church to use in this verse?"

"Same thing, singing."

"Right. These verses came from God through the inspired apostles. Peter wrote in 2 Peter 1:20-21:

Knowing this first, that no prophecy of the scripture is of any private interpretation. For the prophecy came not in old time by the will of man: but holy men of God spake as they were moved by the Holy Ghost."

"Sure," I responded.

"This is the way that God has revealed His will to mankind. Remember that the Holy Spirit guided them into all Truth, John 16:13. It was through this guidance into all Truth that God specified what kind of music He wanted the church to use to worship Him. It's a music that pleases God rather than man."

"But, Randall, wait a second. It doesn't say that we can't use instruments," I hammered back.

"You're correct, but if you practice faith based on what is not said or what is not restricted, you tread on very dangerous ground. That'll lead you to presumptuous sin."

"I don't understand." He was losing me.

"Mike, what did the Lord use in the communion meal?"

I thought about it for a second and said, "Unleavened bread and wine from the fruit of the vine."

"That's right Mr. Mike! But why not use meatloaf and ice-tea? Jesus didn't say we couldn't use them, did He?"

"No, but Christ gave us the example of what He wanted us to use."

"Ah, exactly. And this is just what God has done with music. He's given us the specific example of the type of music He desires. That is singing using the instrument made by the hand of God, the human vocal cords."

I still was not getting it, and Randall could see that I was not getting it.

"Let's turn to Genesis chapter six, and let's look at verse fourteen." Randall led us to the book, chapter, and verse.

He read, *"Make thee an ark of gopher wood; rooms shalt thou make in the ark, and shalt pitch it within and without with pitch*. Mike, God gave Noah a specific. He told him to make an ark out of what kind of wood?"

"Gopher," I answered.

"Right. Now what if Noah would have used oak or pine instead of gopher?"

"That's not what God said to use," I replied.

"So when God specified gopher wood, did that exclude every other kind of wood?" Randall asked.

I got it at that moment. Randall asked a question and by asking the question he answered my question. I shook my head in the affirmative.

"You see, if I tell my kids to do a specific thing, I don't need to give them a list of all the other thousands of things that I don't want them to do at that moment. Why? Because my specific instruction excludes everything else."

His illustration was excellent. I had never considered this rule of grammar when reading my Bible, but it was true.

"Mr. Mike, let me show you one even better. Let's look at Leviticus chapter 10." I turned to the book that he requested and he asked, "Would you read verses one and two out loud for us please?"

I read:

> *And Nadab and Abihu, the sons of Aaron, took either of them his censer, and put fire therein, and put incense thereon, and offered strange fire before the LORD, which he commanded them not. And there went out fire from the LORD, and devoured them, and they died before the LORD.*

"Mr. Mike, check this out. These two sons of Aaron, Levitical priests consecrated for the Tabernacle and from the royal priesthood, used an alternative source of fire that the Lord had not authorized. Evidently, Nadab and Abihu had your attitude."

"My attitude?" I asked defensively.

"Yeah. The attitude of God didn't say we can't use another kind of fire," Randall answered.

Ouch. My legs were cut out from under me.

"Mike," Randall continued, "Nadab and Abihu assumed it would be perfectly fine to do something that God had not authorized and that's what millions of people are doing with instruments in worship today.

"God didn't say to use instruments. God said to sing using our voices. Now, if people want to bring in a piano or an organ or drums or all kinds of other instruments, they've got the same attitude that Nadab and Abihu had. And what happened to them?"

"God destroyed them on the spot," I replied.

"Yes, and God did that as a demonstration to make a point. God's point is this - we are to do what He has commanded and authorized. We've got no right to do what we want just because God hasn't said not to do it. That's a foolish attitude. We don't let our own kids get away with that kind of thinking!"

I had learned a powerful lesson from Randall. Throughout my life I had witnessed a plethora of things done in church services all in the name of God. I had seen things that seemed harmless, and I had seen things that were ridiculous and extreme. I had seen things that I knew would never please God, but people said, "God didn't say we couldn't do it!"

Churches were doing anything and everything to attract crowds. Big bands, power-plays, dramas, Broadway-type musicals, even boxing matches for Christ! Churches were imitating the world to attract the world, and they were making fools of themselves in the process.

"Mr. Mike, did you know that there were no instruments of music in the Lord's church for several hundred years after the birth of the church?"

"No, I didn't."

"Instruments weren't used in any church service until somewhere around 657-672AD when Pope Vitalian[1] brought the pipe organ into the Catholic Church." Randall spoke while retrieving papers from his briefcase.

He continued, "The history of music in the church is amazing. God didn't authorize instrumental music in the church of Christ. Secular history reveals that instruments weren't used until almost 650 years after the church of Christ began on the Day of Pentecost.

Hundreds of years after the Lord's church began a large portion of the church fell away from the Truth into apostasy. Corrupt leaders formed the Catholic Church, which was modeled after the existing governmental structure of Rome. They introduced instrumental music into church services along with many other unscriptural practices."

He had my undivided attention.

"But, Mike, this is going to shock you!"

"What?" I asked.

"Early in the Reformation Movement all of the denominations that came out of Catholicism (Ana-Baptists, Baptist movement, Lutherans, Calvinism, Presbyterians, Methodism, Mennonites, etc.) sang *a capella,* without instrumental music. None of them used instruments!"

"What?" I could not believe it.

"Mike, ***none*** of the denominations used instruments! All of them were in unanimous agreement. They believed that instruments of music were idolatry and were not to be allowed into worship." Randall handed me copies of some papers that he had pulled from his briefcase. "I wanted you to see this."

The paper[2] contained the following research:

NO INSTRUMENTS IN ANY CHURCH FROM THE REFORMATION MOVEMENT!

JOHN CALVIN. French Theologian, Bible Scholar, Reformation Movement influence. "Musical instruments in celebrating the praises of God would be no more suitable than the burning of incense, the lighting of lamps, and the restoration of the other shadows of the law. The Papists therefore, have foolishly borrowed this, as well as many other things, from the Jews. Men who are fond of outward pomp may delight in that noise; but the simplicity which God recommends to us by the apostles is far more pleasing to him. Paul allows us to bless God in the public assembly of the saints, only in a known tongue (1 Corinthians 14:16) What shall we then say of chanting, which fills the ears with nothing but an empty sound?"

ADAM CLARKE. British Methodist Theologian, Bible Scholar. "I am an old man, and I here declare that I never knew them to be productive of any good in the worship of God, and have reason to believe that they are productive of much evil. Music as a science I esteem and admire, but instrumental music in the house of God I abominate and abhor. This is the abuse of music, and I here register my protest against all such corruption of the worship of the author of Christianity. The late and venerable and most eminent divine, the Rev. John Wesley, who was a lover of music, and an elegant poet, when asked his opinion of instruments of music being introduced into the chapels of the Methodists, said in his terse and powerful manner, 'I have no objections to instruments of music in our chapels, provided they are neither heard nor seen.' I say the same."

JOHN KNOX. Scottish Clergyman, Notary Priest, Founder of the Presbyterian denomination, Scottish Reformation Leader. Knox considered the organ "the devil's kist o' whistles," and had the one [organ] in the High Kirk of Edinburgh removed (McClintock & Strong's Encyclopedia, Music, Vol. VI., p.762).

MARTIN LUTHER. German Monk, Professor, Theologian, considered to be the Father of the Protestant Reformation Movement. "The organ in the worship Is the insignia of Baal; a sign of the devil…the Roman Catholics borrowed it from the Jews."

CHARLES SPURGEON. Famous Baptist Minister of British decent. "We do not need them [instruments in worship]. They would hinder rather than help our praise. Sing unto him. This is the sweetest and best music. No instrument like the human voice. What a degradation to supplant the intelligent song of the whole congregation by the theatrical prettiness of a quartet, bellows, and pipes! We might as well pray by machinery as praise by it." When asked why, he quoted 1st Corinthians 14:15. "I will pray with the spirit, and I will pray with the understanding also: I will sing with the spirit, and I will sing with the understanding also." (Charles Spurgeon, Commentary on Psalms 42.) Spurgeon preached to 20,000 people every Sunday for 20 years in the Metropolitan Baptist Tabernacle and never were mechanical instruments of music used, or allowed, in his services.

JOHN WESLEY. Anglican Cleric, Theologian, founder of Arminian Methodism. 'I have no objection to instruments of music in our worship, provided they are neither seen nor heard."

As I read through the document, my amazement grew in direct proportion to the comments of the Reformation leaders regarding their thoughts on mechanical instruments in worship. They were unequivocally *opposed* to instruments in worship.

"Randall, when did the denominations bring instruments into their services?"

"The past 150 years or so," he replied.

My mind reeled.

The church of Christ began in the first century. A part of the church would fall away from the simplicity of the gospel. A large and powerful group of the church fell away some time later. That apostate group finally evolved into a corrupt organization that would later identify themselves as the Universal Church, otherwise known as the Roman Catholic Church.

According to Platina[3] (De vitis Pontificum, 1593), Pope Vitalian (657-72) introduced the organ into the Catholic Church services, but the exact year is unknown. Some denominational historians theorize that it was three years after Vitalian's rise to the papacy (circa 657AD).

When the Reformation Movement started, Reformation leaders were in unanimous agreement. They rejected the use of all musical instruments in their worship services, and they eliminated them from their buildings. The musical instrument, in the Reformation leader's minds, was a thing of idolatry and a device of demons. Calvin, Clarke, Knox, Luther and Wesley agreed in unison. Mechanical musical instruments were not to be seen nor heard in worship!

However, musical instruments would later make their way into almost every one of those Reformed denominations. All of these denominations were groups that began as protest movements against Catholicism and all that Catholicism stood for.

Today, instruments in churches are loved, praised, lauded, adored, applauded, and embraced as vital necessities for stimulating worship. However, when the Truth refutes the use of instruments in true New Testament worship, contemporaries cry foul! They resort to emotionalism, alleging that God loves musical instruments in worship. Interestingly enough, they can't find any biblical command or example for the musical instrument in New Testament Christian worship.

In most men's minds, you could not possibly have a worship service without an instrument. As a matter of fact, most people today believe that not having an instrument in worship is some kind of blasphemy!

Our ignorance of religious history, combined with our ignorance of the Bible, and the origins of our beliefs make for a deadly combination. What is that deadly combination? *There is a way which seemeth right unto a man, but the end thereof are the ways of death*[4]. It was a sickening condition. Ignorance of the Bible was a plague that infected good men and women who continued to cling to the lies that they had been told repeatedly throughout their lives.

What had Ryan told me that Hitler had written in Mein Kampf? People, by means of shrewd lies unremittingly repeated, can be made to believe that Hell is Heaven? They, like me, had been led to believe that using a piano, organ, guitar or a drum-set in worship did not really matter. God did not say we could not do it, so it must be okay. That scripture came again to the forefront of my mind:

> *Jesus answered and said unto them, Ye do err, not knowing the scriptures, nor the power of God* (Matthew 22:29).

The instrumental music issue may or may not be a big deal in a person's mind and heart. Ultimately, it boils down to a simple question. Am I willing to do what God said to do?

The Word of God says, "*Speaking to yourselves in psalms and hymns and spiritual songs, **singing** and making melody in your heart to the Lord*" (Ephesians 5:19). Colossians 3:16 says, "*Let the word of Christ dwell in you richly in all wisdom; teaching and admonishing one another in psalms and hymns and spiritual songs, **singing** with grace in your hearts to the Lord.*" There were only a couple of simple verses to show us the way. How many did I need?

Would I be like the faithful New Testament Christians who worshipped God without mechanical instruments (worshipping in truth, John 4:24) or would I be like Nadab and Abihu?

Chapter 28
Don't Ever Call a Man "Reverend"

March 2nd: Afternoon

After spending the day at Vanderbilt Medical Center doing systems troubleshooting and completing a mountain of related paperwork, I looked at my watch. 5:00 p.m. My brisk pace and direction toward the back door said, "Get out of the way!"

"See you in the morning, Reverend," I said to Randall as I passed by him on the way out.

"Wait up, Mr. Mike," said Randall.

"Yeah?" I turned to look at Randall.

"My friend, don't ever call a man Reverend," Randall said. He was not criticizing, nor was his tone harsh. He was simply instructing.

"What's wrong with that?" I laughed.

"The only place you'll find the word "reverend" in the Bible is in Psalms 111:9:

> *He sent redemption unto his people: he hath commanded his covenant for ever: holy and reverend is his name.*

Reverend is an adjective describing the name of God. It's a word intended and used for God alone."

"Randall, every time I'm around you I learn something new. And everything you teach me is backed up with the Bible!"

"Mr. Mike, I appreciate your encouraging words. Do Baptist preachers want you to call them Reverend?"

"Yeah of course. They put their titles on church marquees, in their bulletins, on their business cards," I replied.

"Why?"

"Well… it's their title, I guess."

Randall was thinking again, and then he spoke up, "Isn't that something? Men who require other men to call them by a spiritual title with a word that's used in the Bible exclusively for God's name?"

Even though I had been in a hurry to leave, he now had my interest.

"Mr. Mike, Jesus covered this issue two thousand years ago, but today's denominational preachers no longer endure sound doctrine. They reject Christ's simplest teachings."

"Like what? What are you talking about?"

"Like John 12:42-43:

> *Nevertheless among the chief rulers also many believed on him; but because of the Pharisees they did not confess him, lest they should be put out of the synagogue: For they loved the praise of men more than the praise of God.*

"Denominational preachers seem to love and crave the glory that is of men more than the glory that is of God. They prove this by their actions and attitudes."

"The glory of men?" I asked.

"Yeah, Mr. Mike. The glory that they receive, in part, by the prestige that comes with their title of Reverend," Randall explained. "And denominational preachers today can be likened to the Pharisees in the first century who loved the praise of men and loved their titles. I understand that some of today's preachers will even get angry if you won't address them by their religious title!"

"Now that you mention it," I said, "I had a minister get a little irritated with me during one of my repair calls when I didn't call him Reverend."

"Mike, Jesus said, in Matthew 23:9, '*Call no man your father upon the earth: for one is your Father, which is in heaven.*' Jesus was talking about using the term as a spiritual title. He wasn't talking about calling your biological dad 'father.' To use the word Reverend as a title is very similar to men who wear the title of Father in the Catholic Church."

"I can see that," I agreed.

Randall said, "Even the Apostle Peter, when Cornelius fell at his feet to offer his worship, told Cornelius to stand up for he was also a man" (Acts 10:26).

"Randall, I've learned more from you in the last three days than I have in a lifetime of Sunday School classes!"

"Mr. Mike, you just keep studying your Bible. The power is in the Word. I'm just a servant, but I'm very grateful to God for your wonderful encouragement."

"Well," I said, "I appreciate your time Randall."

"You've got it, my friend!" said Randall. "Hey, think about this on your way home. The Bible refers to preachers as evangelists, but it never refers to any preacher as a Reverend, Father, or Pastor!"

"Pastor? The church of Christ doesn't call the preacher, Pastor?"

"No way, man, but we'll talk about that tomorrow."

As I walked out to my car, a thought came to mind. I wondered if Mr. Pompous (*expletive*) would get his feathers ruffled if I refused to call him Reverend-Pastor.

Sorry, but *that's* funny.

Chapter 29
Killing the "One-Man" Pastoral System

March 3rd

"Good morning, Randall!" I had brought the coffee and doughnuts for the morning.

"Hey, Mr. Mike!" Randall replied. Then he hollered when he saw the doughnuts. "You know the way to my heart, and it is definitely through my stomach!" Randall laughed large at his own jokes.

"Listen, Randall, I know you probably wanted to talk about some specific subject this morning, but could we push that subject to tomorrow?"

"How come?"

"I've got something else I'd like to ask you about," I confessed.

"No problem. What would you like to talk about?"

"What you said as I was leaving the office yesterday. The church of Christ doesn't call their preachers Pastors. What's with that?"

Randall opened his bible. "The term pastor comes from the Greek word *poimen*[1], or *poimaino,* and it means shepherd. The New Testament also calls them bishops and overseers. Pastor, shepherd, bishop, overseer, and elder all refer to the same office and the same person.

Our English word for pastor, which comes from those Greek words, *poimen* or *poimaino,* is found only one time in the New Testament. Let's turn to Ephesians 4:11."

Randall and I opened our Bibles to the chapter and verse.

"Mr. Mike, would you read it for us?" he asked.

I read:

And he gave some, apostles; and some, prophets; and some, evangelists; and some, pastors and teachers.

"First," Randall began, "An evangelist is a herald. A proclaimer of the gospel to the lost. Notice that evangelists and pastors are two separate offices. They're not one in the same as people are led to believe in denominational churches.

Second, a one-man pastoral [shepherd] system is completely unscriptural, and sets the framework for the abuse of power, corruption, and leading away entire groups of believers."

I cut in, "You mentioned during our study Tuesday that each congregation of the church of Christ was independent of the rest, and self-governed by pastors or elders. So the preacher doesn't make the decisions? Is that what you said?" I asked, trying to remember our previous conversation.

"Yeah, that's right," replied Randall.

"So, the preacher is not the pastor?" I asked.

"No, Mr. Mike. The New Testament reveals that the evangelist and the pastor are not the same man."

"And there was always more than one pastor at each congregation in the Bible?" I questioned.

"Absolutely, just as Paul and the apostles commanded," he answered.

"Could you show me where this is found in the Bible?" I wanted to see it for myself.

"Certainly, Mr. Mike!" Randall began searching for his first verse. "But you may want to write the references down because we're going to look at several on this topic."

I grabbed an ink-pen and took notes. He took me to the following verses:

> Acts 11:30; 14:23; 15:2,4,6,22,23; 16:4; 20:17-18; Titus 1:5; James 5:14; 1 Peter 5:1,5.

In these passages, the Bible reveals that elders (pastors) governed each congregation. There were always a plural number of elders, never just one. A pastor was the same thing as an elder, and a pastor was not the evangelist.

"Randall, why do the majority of denominations use the one-man pastor system today? Why do they reject the commands and examples in the New Testament that clearly show how churches are to be governed by a group of qualified pastors (elders) instead of the preacher?"

"Mike, it seems to be another hold-over from Catholicism. The philosophy of one man ruling the church originated in the office of the Catholic Priest and ultimately the Pope," Randall explained. "And there's another big problem with the system."

"What's that?" I asked.

"The one-man pastor system puts a separation between the preacher and the members, and that's a dangerous partition."

"How's that?" I asked.

"It creates a separate class of people within a church: clergy and laity. It exalts the preacher and puts him up on a pedestal. You won't find clergy and laity in the Bible. The apostles didn't do that with each other, and they didn't tolerate others exalting them either. A good example of this is found in Acts 10:25-26:

> *And as Peter was coming in, Cornelius met him, and fell down at his feet, and worshipped him. But Peter took him up, saying, Stand up; I myself also am a man.*

"When Cornelius fell at Peter's feet to worship him, Peter told him to get up because he was just a man. Mr. Mike, be honest. Didn't you see your Baptist pastor as being up on a pedestal? Maybe a little higher than everyone else?"

"Sure I did," I answered truthfully. The pastor was held up as the man who was closer to God than everyone else. He was separate from the rest. He was somebody who had a greater spiritual connection to God. He seemed to have a better understanding of the Bible than anyone else in the church.

"Alright," Randall responded, "If Peter was an apostle, and he didn't allow people to put him on a pedestal, why in the world would today's preachers *want* to be up on a pedestal?"

It was a good question. "They shouldn't let that happen, Randall," I answered.

"That's the point my friend. In truth, preachers are only a speaking member of a congregation. Preachers have absolutely no authority to govern a local congregation. Authority to govern the church is given only to the elders, and only when there's more than one qualified elder at a congregation of the Lord's people."

"Furthermore, every true Christian is a member of the royal priesthood, 1 Peter 2:9. Every Christian is a minister, or a servant of Christ. We're all required to take the gospel to every creature."

"Third, many denominational pastors are not qualified to hold the office of a true Bible pastor [elder]."

"Qualifications? How are they supposed to be qualified?" I asked.

Randall turned to 1 Timothy 3:1-7 and said, "We've talked about this a little in some of our previous talks, but remember that pastor, shepherd, bishop, overseer, and elder all refer to the same office? Paul told Timothy, in 1 Timothy 3:1-7:

> *If a man desire the office of a bishop* [elder, pastor, shepherd, overseer], *he desireth a good work. A bishop* [elder, pastor, shepherd, overseer] *then must be blameless, the husband of one wife, vigilant, sober, of good behaviour, given to hospitality, apt to teach; Not given to wine, no striker, not greedy of filthy lucre; but patient, not a brawler, not covetous; One that ruleth well his own house, having his children in subjection with all gravity; (For if a man know not how to rule his own house, how shall he take care of the church of God?) Not a novice, lest being lifted up with pride he fall into the condemnation of the devil. Moreover*

he must have a good report of them which are without; lest he fall into reproach and the snare of the devil.

Mr. Mike, how many denominational preachers today are divorced and remarried? How many actually have a plurality of believing children who are in subjection with all gravity?"

I just shook my head. I knew a few denominational pastors who did not meet the qualifications found in these passages of text.

"You know what amazes me, Mr. Mike?" asked Randall.

"What's that?" I responded.

"That so many good, highly intelligent people with good sense, entrust their spiritual future into the hands of a single man. That amazes me! And to think that *one* man has *that* kind of power over a group. He can make decisions that might plunge entire groups of people into deeper spiritual blindness!"

Yes, the one-man pastoral system was a model foreign to the Word of God. It was a system open to corruption, abuse of power, and human exaltation. I had seen it first-hand.

Randall and I shook hands and departed one another's company to go about our day's duties.

It was official. I had information constipation!

Chapter 30
The Gospel of Christ

Study 4 of 5: March 4th

It was Friday morning, and my mood was elevated. "The first week of March," I thought to myself as I pushed the Pontiac Grand Am northeast toward the city. I-40 moved unusually fast that morning.

I hit the scan button on the stereo, and it found a station. *Seasons Change* by Exposé[1] was playing. I was thinking about winter turning to spring, and this song was on? How weird was that? Spring, in my mind, had arrived even though it would not technically be Spring for a couple more weeks. I was already thinking about watching our local minor-league baseball team, the Nashville Sounds, spending days off out at the pool, golfing all summer and fall, grilling out, and cool evenings with Jonetta riding around town in our Triumph Spitfire convertible.

I could smell something wonderful when I stepped through OSI's back door. Cinnamon rolls! Randall had brought cinnamon rolls.

We were both glad to see each other. Our friendship had grown over the months we had worked and studied together, and we shared a great deal of mutual respect. Randall was intelligent, articulate, and, like Ryan, he was an exceptional listener.

"Mr. Mike," he opened the dialogue as we finished off our rolls. "I'm very excited about our study this morning, *for I am not ashamed of the gospel of Christ, for it is the power of God unto salvation to every one that believeth; to the Jew first, and also to the Greek,* Romans 1:16."

"I know that Scripture," I said, jumping in the conversation.

"Mike, do you remember when you and I first met? Back in August?"

I laughed a little and responded, "Oh yeah! How could I forget? You gave me a couple of Krispy Kreme doughnuts! You'd think that we would both weigh about five hundred pounds by the way we're always eating!" Randall laughed along with me.

"And do you remember" Randall picked his thought back up, "that I said to you that Jesus Christ is coming back? Do you remember that?"

"Sure I do, because I asked you when He was coming."

"Yeah, that's right," Randall said, "And do you remember the scripture I referenced that tells us what it will be like when Christ returns?"

Even searching strenuously through my memory, I could not remember. We had discussed too many Bible passages. "Man, there's no way I can remember that verse. I've slept since then."

Randall laughed again. "It's alright, Mr. Mike. I just wondered if you were able to recall it. It was 2 Thessalonians 1:6-10. How about we begin there?"

"Let's do it," I replied.

Randall started reading:

> *Seeing it is a righteous thing with God to recompense tribulation to them that trouble you; and to you who are troubled rest with us, when the Lord Jesus shall be revealed from heaven with his mighty angels, in flaming fire taking vengeance on them that know not God, and that obey not the gospel of our Lord Jesus Christ: Who shall be punished with everlasting destruction from the presence of the Lord, and from the glory of his power; when he shall come to be glorified in his saints, and to be admired in all them that believe (because our testimony among you was believed) in that day.*

I knew where Randall was going, but still did not have a clear answer for him.

"Mike, Jesus is going to take vengeance on them that know not God, and that obey not the gospel of our Lord Jesus Christ. In other words, there are only two kinds of people, those who've obeyed the gospel and those who haven't. Have you obeyed the gospel?"

There it was again. After many months I still was not sure what the gospel was, and I did not know if I had obeyed it.

"I'm not sure."

"Fair enough. I appreciate your honesty. Would you like to know what the gospel is, and how it is obeyed?" asked Randall.

"Absolutely," I answered. I was not saying it to be nice, and I was not trying to prop-up the conversation. I really wanted to know.

"Turn to 1 Corinthians chapter 15," Randall said. "Mr. Mike, would you read verses 1-4 for us?"

I read aloud:

> *Moreover, brethren, I declare unto you the gospel which I preached unto you, which also ye have received, and wherein ye stand; By which also ye are saved, if ye keep in memory what I preached unto you, unless ye have believed in vain. For I delivered unto you first of all that which I also received, how that Christ died for our sins according to the scriptures; And that he was buried, and that he rose again the third day according to the scriptures:*

Randall began, "In these verses, Paul explains the gospel in the simplest terms. In verse one, he states that he's getting ready to declare the gospel, verifying that it's the message that the Christians at Corinth had already received. It's the message on which they stood. It's the message by which they were saved if they kept it in memory.

"Then Paul details the gospel. He says that the gospel is this: Christ died for our sins, was buried, and rose again the third day. Paul said that all of this happened to Jesus according to the

Scriptures referring to the hundreds of Old Testament prophecies about Jesus Christ as the Messiah."

"So, the gospel is," I interrupted him, "the death, burial, and resurrection of Jesus Christ? That's it?"

"That's the gospel!" Randall stated.

"Randall, that's an *event* in history."

"Yeah?" Randall asked.

"Well, it makes no sense," I responded.

"What do you mean?" Randall questioned.

"Jesus said He's going to take vengeance on everyone who hasn't *obeyed* the gospel, but the gospel is His death, burial and resurrection – an event in history! How in the world do you *obey a historical event*? It makes no sense!"

"Mr. Mike, that's a brilliant question," he said through a big grin, "And *that's* the question that everyone needs to be asking! Paul gives the answer to that question in the book of Romans chapter 6."

I was on it. We arrived at the verse at almost the same time.

"Which verse?" I asked, wanting to read it.

"Verses three through five. Go ahead and read it aloud for us," Randall encouraged. I needed no encouragement. It said:

> *Know ye not, that so many of us as were baptized into Jesus Christ were baptized into his death? Therefore we are buried with him by baptism into death: that like as Christ was raised up from the dead by the glory of the Father, even so we also should walk in newness of life. For if we have been planted together in the likeness of his death, we shall be also in the likeness of his resurrection*:

My body went numb, and my mouth went dry. I had read it before, but I had never made the connection. Baptism was a burial. It was burying the old man of sin. Being raised up out of the water was being raised up to newness of life. Raised up out of the water was coming out of the grave which was the likeness and representation of *Christ's* resurrection.

All of those years that I had been told that baptism was not necessary and that it had nothing to do with being saved. Now I find in my own Bible that we are buried with Christ by baptism and planted together by baptism in the likeness of his death. I was angry. I read it again. Randall was speaking, but I was not hearing his words. It was just background noise.

I read the passages a third time. After reading through it the third time, I was staring off into space numbed by the realization–

"Mr. Mike?" His voice broke through.

"Yeah," I blurted.

"You alright?" he asked.

"Yeah. Fine." I answered. I lied. I was not fine.

"Mr. Mike, you want me to go on?" he questioned.

"Yeah, go on," I replied. The shock of the realization continued to surge through my mind and body.

"Okay, Mr. Mike, to obey the gospel is to *reenact* the gospel. The gospel consists of Christ's crucifixion, His burial, and His resurrection.

"First, we must die to a life of sin. This reenacts the crucifixion. Our willingness to die to sin is repentance. It's turning away from the regular practice of sin. Repentance is making a conscious decision to turn your back on your sins and on the world. It is to turn toward the cross of Christ. We die to sin as Christ died on the cross; therefore, we're reenacting His death on the cross. We crucify our old man of sin on the cross through our willingness to repent.

"Second, in baptism we reenact Christ's burial. Paul says in verse three that when we're baptized, we are baptized *into* Christ's death. So, we're reenacting Christ's burial in the tomb, but our burial is in a watery grave instead of a tomb. Paul says that we're baptized into Christ, verse three, and we're buried with Him by baptism into death, verse four. Baptism into Jesus Christ is where we're *planted together* with Him in the likeness of His death, verse five.

"Finally, we reenact the resurrection. Paul says that like Christ was raised up from the dead by the glory of the Father, even *we* also should walk in newness of life, verse four. When we're raised up out of that grave of baptism, we're reenacting the likeness of Christ's resurrection.

"The great hope of every faithful Christian is to be resurrected unto eternal life. Paul makes a special mention of this fact, in verse five, by saying that we shall be in the likeness of His resurrection ***if*** we've been planted together in the likeness of His death.

Mr. Mike, here are life and death points. If we are not baptized, we are ***not***:

- ✓ Put into Jesus Christ (Gal. 3:26-27)
- ✓ Added to His body, the church (Acts 2:47; Col. 1:18)
- ✓ Baptized into His death (Rom. 6:3)
- ✓ Buried with him (Rom. 6:4)
- ✓ Planted together in the likeness of His death (Rom. 6:5)
- ✓ Raised up in the likeness of His resurrection (Rom. 6:5)
- ✓ Raised to walk in newness of life (Rom. 6:4)
- ✓ Obedient to the gospel of Jesus Christ (2 Thes. 1:6-10)
- ✓ Forgiven of past sins (Acts 22:16)
- ✓ Safe in the saving ark which is Jesus Christ (Eph. 5:23-25; Acts 2:47)"

Randall was showing me the comparisons made by the Apostle Paul, and they were indisputable.

"Now, Mr. Mike, consider all of the remote text of the New Testament. Jesus said that a man must be born again in John 3:3. Born again is to be born of water and spirit, John 3:5. Peter confirmed Christ's teachings by telling the Jewish audience on the Day of Pentecost to *repent and be baptized for the remission of sins,* and they would receive the gift of the Holy Ghost, Acts 2:38.

"Jesus said, in Mark 16:16, *He that believes and is baptized shall be saved*. Philip preached Jesus to the Eunuch, and *that* teaching contained teaching about the absolute necessity of baptism, which led to the *immediate* baptism of the Eunuch.

"Paul said that there's only *one* baptism in Ephesians 4:5. 1 Peter 3:21 says that *baptism doth also now save us*."

As I considered his words, I was astounded over the consistency of the teaching and how remarkably it all tied together in perfect harmony.

"There's nothing holy about the water, Mr. Mike. The idea is obedience to God and what He's commanded."

"So, this is why he called you water-dogs," I said, thinking out loud.

"What's that?" asked Randall.

I explained what happened with our former Reverend, and how he had called members of the church of Christ a bunch of water-dogs before hanging up on me.

"Water-dogs," Randall repeated the phrase. Then he started laughing. "What a thing to say about New Testament Christians! Hey man, I wouldn't lose any sleep over it. If doing God's will makes people call us a few names, so what. If God commanded us to be immersed in sheep's wool, I guess that'd make us sheep-dogs!" Randall exclaimed! I was laughing along with him.

"Mr. Mike, false teachers will always speak evil of the way of Truth," Randall added.

"Yeah?"

"Check out 2 Peter two." Randall was already turning to the text.

"What verse?" I asked.

"Verses one and two. Here, man, listen to this,

> *But there were false prophets also among the people, even as there shall be false teachers among you, who privily shall bring in damnable heresies, even denying the Lord that bought them, and bring upon themselves swift destruction. And many shall follow their pernicious ways; by reason of whom the way of truth shall be evil spoken of.*

"This may sound harsh, but that man is, according to the Bible, a false teacher. Many are following his doctrines that deny the Truth of Christ's Word. Then, just like Peter says here in verse two, that false teacher speaks evil of the way of Truth."

I read, listened, and worked through his words in my mind. To be honest, the contrast between my former Baptist preacher and Randall (the contrast in their attitudes and the huge chasm between their level of Bible knowledge) was completely remarkable. Randall knew the Bible front to back. He bent his own will and thinking to what the Bible said.

Randall also had real Christian love. Randall lived in the grace of God. God's Spirit was evident in his life. His Christian love, his excitement for Jesus Christ, his passion for the gospel and the lost, and his sincere humility were all traits of a true Christian. His devotion to Jesus was unparalleled by any man or woman I had ever met. This was a man who knew the Lord, and the Lord knew him! Randall was a man who demonstrated God's love, God's grace, and God's mercy like no other man.

"Mr. Mike, Acts 5:41 says that Peter rejoiced that they were counted worthy to suffer for Christ's name."

"I've heard Kirk call you a Campbellite. What's he mean by that?" I asked without meaning to change the topic.

"He's speaking out of ignorance. Kirk is a good man, and he means well, but he doesn't have the information that you now have. This lack of information is the real problem. He hears people say negative things about us and simply repeats it to others thinking that he's helping them."

"What's it mean? Campbellite?" I asked again.

"They call members of the church of Christ Campbellites because Alexander Campbell[2] was one of *several* pioneer preachers who helped bring about the Restoration Movement[3]. Campbell's family were Scotch-Irish Presbyterians, but Campbell became a well-known Baptist preacher. He published a widely circulated paper called *The Christian Baptist*[4].

Campbell began to recognize the church that Jesus founded within the pages of the New Testament. He began to point out his findings and encouraged others to look at it for themselves. Through his continued studies, he found that his own Baptist doctrines were not supported by the Bible.

"Over time Campbell rejected his own Baptist creeds, desiring instead to be a Christian only. He was one of many men during the nineteenth century who began to urge all believers to throw away denominational creeds and names and restore the church of the Bible.

"In reality, Campbell started nothing. He started no church or religion. He simply pointed people back to the Bible. His plea was the restoration of the first century church and practices that were supported by the Bible. He encouraged people to leave denominationalism and be unified under the banner of Jesus Christ and the Lord's church, as found in the New Testament.

"The Baptists grew to hate Campbell. Denominational preachers from *many* different brands began to hate him, because in order to unify under Jesus Christ and Christ's church meant they had to denounce the false doctrines of their respective denominations. The denominations started losing people by the thousands to the church of the Lord."

"Randall," I broke in, "How do you know all this stuff?"

"Ah, Mike, I've studied religious history for years. All you got to do is read!" Randall replied.

"No wonder the Baptists and Methodists and Presbyterian preachers disliked the church of Christ," I said.

"Well," Randall responded, "Campbell really fired them up when he made a public declaration calling for a rejection of the Baptist Confession of Faith."

"A public rejection?"

Randall responded, "Campbell said that all authority for religion came from the Bible. With that, he began a type of campaign slogan, 'Where the Bible speaks, we speak. Where the Bible is silent, we are silent.' Campbell rejected man-made creeds. And the one he railed against the loudest? It was the Philadelphia Confession of Faith[5]. This was a Baptist creed printed in 1742 by Benjamin Franklin. About ninety years later the Philadelphia Confession had a powerful influence among southern and northern Baptists.

"Mr. Mike, at the first Southern Baptist Convention, around 1844 to 1845, there were about 300 Baptist delegates in attendance, and they *all* subscribed to the Philadelphia Confession of Faith."

I continued to listen as Randall continued to teach.

"Mr. Mike, let's get back to the gospel for a moment. The gospel is so simple that every person of sound mind and of accountable age can understand and obey it if they choose to. When men and women read their Bible and obey the gospel, God adds them to the church of His Son, the church of Christ. Jesus said in Matthew 18:20,

For where two or three are gathered together in my name, there am I in the midst of them.

"When honest-hearted people follow the Bible's plan of salvation and obey the gospel, *they* are *the* church of Christ. When they follow the New Testament pattern and worship through the commands and examples found in the New Testament pattern, they *restore* the first century church of Christ."

Randall was reasoning the Scriptures with me. Following the Bible in salvation and worship made a great deal of sense. If you plant a corn seed, you get a stalk of corn. If you plant a watermelon seed, you get a watermelon. If you plant the gospel seed, you get a New Testament Christian. You get a Christian *only*, with no denominational ties or labels.

"But, Mr. Mike, let's get back to our topic of baptism. Is saying the Sinner's Prayer obeying the gospel?" Randall asked.

"Randall," I said, "For the first time in my life it's clear. The Sinner's Prayer *isn't* obeying the gospel of Jesus Christ."

Randall went on, "Saying the Sinner's Prayers doesn't allow men and women to reenact the gospel, as Paul instructs in Romans 6, does it?"

"No."

"Saying the Sinner's Prayer doesn't put us into Christ's death; it doesn't bury us with Him; it doesn't plant us together in the likeness of His death; and it doesn't allow us to be raised up as in the likeness of His resurrection, so that we may come forth in newness of life, does it?"

"No, Randall. Repeating the Sinner's Prayer doesn't do *any* of the things that Paul describes. And you know something? I've spent my entire life believing, and telling others that baptism isn't necessary to be saved." I was so ashamed.

"Mike, you don't know what you don't know. Satan is shrewd. He's more intelligent than you and I–"

"Listen, Randall," I interrupted. "I see what Satan has done."

"Oh yeah?" Randall asked.

"Yeah. Look at Genesis 3:2-4," and we turned to the text. I read:

> *And the woman said unto the serpent, We may eat of the fruit of the trees of the garden: But of the fruit of the tree which is in the midst of the garden, God hath said, Ye shall not eat of it, neither shall ye touch it, lest ye die. And the serpent said unto the woman, Ye shall not surely die."*

I pushed on, "Satan inserted one three-letter word, twisting God's commandment into a lie. Satan inserted the word ***not***. He said to the woman, '*Ye shall not surely die.*' Satan has done the same thing with the way *we're* saved. Jesus said, in Mark 16:16, '*He that believeth and is baptized shall be saved.*' Satan is using the same tactic today that he used on Eve. He's inserted the same three-letter word into the text, deceiving millions upon millions by leading people to believe the phrase, 'He that believeth and is ***not*** baptized shall be saved.'"

"Mr. Mike, that is correct!" Randall exclaimed.

"Randall! That's exactly what's happened to me, my family, my friends–"

"Mr. Mike, won't you repent and be baptized in the name of Jesus Christ for the remission of sins, and you'll receive the gift of the Holy Ghost?" He wanted me to obey the gospel. He wanted me to have forgiveness of my sins and become a new creation in Christ Jesus. Randall wanted me to become a true, New Testament Christian.

I sat there in silence. I was filled with anger, but not toward Randall. The emotion was indirect and lacked a target. Something was holding me back.

"We've got one more study, don't we?" I answered his plea to obey the gospel with a question.

"Yeah. There's one more study that we didn't get to do because we had to push everything back a day. However, I'll be out of town with my family all next week. Could we do the last study a week from this coming Monday?"

"Do you have a calendar we could look at?" I asked him. He pushed papers around on his desk and found a spiral bound calendar.

"March fourteenth. How's that sound?"

I thought about the date. "That'll work. Same time?"

"Same time is excellent, Mr. Mike!"

As always, we shook hands and went our separate ways for the day.

The gospel of Christ was Christ's death, burial, and resurrection. Obeying the gospel was to repent and be baptized for the remission of sins, reenacting the gospel.

Something was holding me back. I had to figure out what it was.

Chapter 31
A Little Comedic Relief

March 4th: That Evening

Friday evening's I-40W rush hour was especially slow. Go a few yards; abrupt stop; sit a few minutes; and repeat the process.

"Rats in a maze," I said to the steering wheel. It didn't matter. The weekend had arrived, and Jonetta had a plan. She paged me earlier and suggested Kobe Steak House[1] for dinner, then a comedy club on 8th Avenue South.

A little comedic relief sounded like a great plan!

By the time I made it home to Knollwood Apartments, Jonetta was changed, made up, and ready to go.

"You look fantastic!" I said as I threw my briefcase on the couch.

"Thank you," she smiled and kissed me warmly on the cheek. "Now jump in the shower. Robert and Julia are meeting us at Kobe at seven, so we don't have much time."

"Wanna take the convertible?" I asked optimistically.

"We'll freeze to death you knuckle-head!" she said as she laughed.

"You're a Yankee. You can handle it," I hollered back to her as I walked down the hall into our "master" bath (the *only* bathroom).

Five minutes later I was standing in the shower shampooing my hair when I felt an instant shock come over my head, arms, and shoulders. I yelled out thinking that battery acid had just found its way through our shower-head. That's when I heard her laughing.

"Oh! I'm going to get you!" I growled at her.

"What? You can't take a little ice-water in the shower, but you want to take your little red convertible out in *March*?" She laughed harder. That woman had thrown a glass of ice-water over the top of the shower curtain right on top of me!

"Alright, alright. Just remember," I said.

"Remember what?" she asked through laughing.

"Paybacks!"

The valet took our car, and we walked up the restaurant's steps. Robert and Julia waited for us at the entrance doors.

"Hello, my young prodigy," Robert shook my hand, and the girls greeted one another as old friends. Robert was an up-and-coming computer sales executive. From my vantage point, he was doing exceptionally well.

He and Julia had just bought property in Franklin, and they were getting ready to build a new home on the property. They were in their mid-30's and loved life.

And they also bought adult beverages for us, but Jonetta refrained from alcohol as usual. We were seated around a large "U-shaped" hibachi grill. The Japanese chef appeared through a curtain after the waitress took our orders, and the performance began - ninety minutes of Japanese cooking showmanship right at our table. Several courses were served to each person seated around the table. Each course uniquely excellent. It was a treat that everyone should try at least once in their life.

We made it to the comedy club by nine-thirty. Robert was a personal friend of the comedy club's managing partner, so he was able to get us a stage-side table. The table *literally* butted-up against the stage. It was so close that you could reach out and grab the ankle of the comedian, if you so pleased (which would have caused several big bouncers to have been pleased to grab you by your neck and throw you into the street).

The show was incredible. Two opening acts and then the headliner was introduced. It was a guy we had never heard of. He did an act about power-tools and grunted like a cave-man. We laughed until tears streamed down our faces!

I experienced "boomerang" thoughts. Thoughts that would fly in from out of nowhere during the times when my mind had an idle moment. I was fighting and resisting my need to obey the gospel of Christ. Why? I did not know yet. I told myself, "God doesn't want me. I can't live the Christian life. I can't give up drinking beer. I can't give up my materialism. I can't stop smoking. Surely God didn't really want me?"

I know. I would *prove* it to Him. I would prove to God that I was no good. I would prove that He was wasting His time on me. I would run from God. I was prepared to run and resist.

Our bottles were getting low. "Robert, we need more beer," I said. "I've got the next two rounds," I told him over the laughter in the room, and I pulled out my credit card.

Yes. I would *run* from God. Tonight I would drink… a lot. *That* would prove to God that I could not be a *real* Christian.

The headliner's bit about power-tools was a hit! The crowd loved him. At one point the comedian started talking about "passing gas," and Robert and I could not stop laughing. The power-tool guy stopped his act, pointed at me and Robert sitting at the stage-side table, and said to the audience, "These two guys know exactly what I'm talking about. I feel sorry for their wives!" It was hilarious.

The girls did the driving home. We talked about the comedian for months to come, using his one-liners and jokes while bantering back and forth. We did not have a clue that the comedian we saw that night would become very famous. His name was Tim Allen.

Jonetta was driving, and she was mad. I had drank too much.

"If you can't shut it off at three, you need to stop it all together!" She was letting me have it! "And the next time you plan on drinking that much, tell me in advance. I'll just stay home!"

"Honey–" I said, trying to get her attention.

"Don't 'honey' me!" she cut me off.

"But, honey–" I tried again.

"Michael, I said don't 'honey' me–" Jonetta continued in a fury.

"Sweetheart!" I raised my voice.

"What?" she raised her voice in return?

"You'd better pull over," I warned.

"Why?" she asked, still angry.

"The beer. It's coming back up–"

Chapter 32
That *Something*

March 10th

The week was uneventful. Randall was out of town with his family and gone from the office, so there had been no early morning Bible studies, no positive greetings, and no Krispy Kreme doughnuts.

I had been thinking a lot about my life and especially the sins in my life. I drank socially, got drunk periodically, smoked, and cursed a little like everyone else, I was driven by materialism, had thoughts of sexual immorality, looked at a porn magazine once in a while, and coveted all of the nice things the world had to offer.

A diligent effort to live a truly pure life seemed impossible. My family back home smoked. Many of my Christian friends drank, and almost everyone I knew cursed a little. Guys always talked about sex and women, so that seemed normal. Materialism, financial goal setting, and objects of desire were the common motivators of successful business people in the Eighties. Therefore, materialism was the accepted norm. And most of these friends of mine called themselves Christians.

Had I not met Randall, my life would have remained the same. I would have continued down the original path of my own selfish desires in complete spiritual ignorance.

Before meeting Randall I lived in religious error, assumptions, misinformation, false quotes, false doctrines, and the teachings of men (denominationalism). My beliefs were based on traditions, feelings, emotions, and denominational practices that I had held for many years.

I had been cutting off the end of the ham.

I was young, immature, abrasive, self-centered, arrogant, hot-tempered, and impatient. This personal realization was very painful. The more I read the Bible and spent time around Randall, the more ashamed I became of myself and my actions.

"Ignorance is bliss," went through my mind. It would have been so much easier if I had never met Randall. I would not know any of these things about the Bible. But it was not Randall's fault. He put no personal bias on the Bible. He had simply shown me book, chapter, and verse.

Randall read the Bible and allowed Christ's words and commands to shape him into a fine Christian man. He allowed the Bible to determine his future.

I read and reread the things we studied together. I read from my own Bible. The Word of God did not support the denomination I had followed my entire life. No matter how hard I tried to make the Bible fit my old Baptist faith, it simply did not fit.

There was the dilemma. The Bible can be likened to a suit coat. A man will either cut the coat to fit himself, or he will cut himself to fit the coat. Every accountable, responsible man and woman seeking God has a choice set before them:

- They will cut the Bible into a book that fits *their* own kind of faith/denomination.

- They will cut *themselves* (change their minds, their hearts, their actions, and their behaviors) into the type of person that God calls them to be.

- They will accept His Word in full and obey what it says without modification, or they will choose their man-made religion.

That *something* that had been holding me back came to me on Thursday, March 10th, 1988. I was eating breakfast in a downtown Nashville café. A glance at my watch. 7:19a.m. Plenty of time to finish breakfast and make it into the office before eight.

I sat at a window-side table reading a copy of USA TODAY while thinking about the appointments for the day. A sip of coffee and a turn to the next page. Headline:

RELIGION IN AMERICA:
MOST BELIEVE THEY WILL GO TO HEAVEN

The article did not matter. It was the headline! My thoughts went back to Kirk's remarks about Randall and the church of Christ.

"His church believes they're the only ones going to Heaven!" I could still hear Kirk's words in my mind. "You know that guy, Randall, believes that Baptists, Methodists, Presbyterians, Catholics – everybody but *his* church - are all going to Hell."

What did the Bible say?

Jesus said, "*Narrow is the way, which leadeth unto life, and few there be that find it* (Matthew 7:14)."

No, Randall didn't say that! It was not Randall at all. It was the Bible!

It's the *Bible* that reveals the one body (Ephesians 4:4), and that the one body is the church (Colossians 1:18). The church began on the Day of Pentecost (Acts 2:36-47). Jesus is the one Head of the one body (Colossians 1:18). Jesus is the Savior of the one body (Ephesians 5:23-25), the church that He bought with His blood (Acts 20:28).

The *Bible* reveals the gospel (Romans 1:16); the death, burial, and resurrection of Jesus Christ (1 Corinthians 15:1-4), and commands all men everywhere to obey that gospel (2 Thessalonians 1:8).

It is the *Bible* that reveals how to obey the gospel of Christ (Romans 6:3-5), and reenacting the gospel through repentance, baptism, being buried with Christ, and raised with Him in the likeness of His resurrection.

It is the *Bible* that warns us that Jesus Christ will return to this earth to take vengeance on them that know not God, and that obey not the gospel of our Lord Jesus Christ (2 Thessalonians 1:6-10).

It is the *Bible* that reveals that there are only two types of people on the earth: those who obey the gospel and those who do not.

It is the *Bible* that reveals that Peter and Paul preached an identical message (Galatians 1:8-9). A message that man must repent and be baptized for the remission of sins (Acts 2:38; Acts 22:16), and following this God-given instruction is how mankind accesses God's marvelous grace (Colossians 2:11-13).

Grace is God's unmerited favor which instructs us. God's grace *teaches* us! Paul told Titus, *"For the grace of God that bringeth salvation hath appeared to all men, teaching us…* (Titus 2:11-12). Grace brings salvation. How? By instructing and teaching us. Grace teaches, and men must obey. Faith is our exercise of obedience to His instructions (Hebrews 11).

It is the *Bible* that reveals that upon our obedience to God's instructive faith (Acts 2:41), He adds the saved (Acts 2:47) to the one body of Christ (Ephesians 4:4), the church of Christ (Romans 16:16).

It is the *Bible* that tells us there were about three thousand people who heard these words first preached by Peter and gladly receiving it were baptized (Acts 2:41). Those New Testament Christians continued in the apostle's teachings (Acts 2:42-46). They met on the first day of the week to pray (Acts 2:42; 20:7), sing (Ephesians 5:19; Colossians 3:16), give of their means (1

Corinthians 16:1-2), to partake the Lord's Supper, and to be exhorted by preaching (Acts 20:7).

It is the *Bible* that reveals how true Bible Christians sang using their voices without instruments (Eph. 5:19; Col. 3:16).

It is the *Bible* that reveals the *only* instruments authorized, sanctioned, and endorsed for New Testament worship to God are human vocal cords – those beautiful, biological instruments!

It is the *Bible* that reveals how true Bible Christians gave as they had been prospered (1 Corinthians 16:2), as they purposed in their heart, not grudgingly or of necessity, but cheerfully (2 Corinthians 9:7), upon the first day of the week (1 Corinthians 16:2), no longer bound under the Jewish Law of Tithing (Galatians 5:1-4; Ephesians 2:13-16; Colossians 2:14-15). However, New Testament Christians were to *exceed* the righteousness of the Scribes and Pharisees (Matthew 5:20).

It is the *Bible* that teaches each congregation of the church of the Lord to be self-governed by qualified elders (1 Timothy 3:1-7) and not a single "pastor" (Acts 14:23). There was never *one* man to make all of the decisions for the church of the Lord (1 Timothy 5:17; Titus 1:5).

The Lord's church was not then and will never be a denomination (Ephesians 1:22-23). The Lord's church is a heavenly, blood-bought, spiritual institution that the saved are added to by God (Acts 2:32-36; 20:28; 1 Timothy 3:15; Acts 2:47). Men have never "voted" other men into the blood-bought church of Christ or His body (Acts 8:36-38). Voting on candidates for baptism is foreign to the Bible and a man-made invention.

It is the *Bible* that rebukes human doctrines, human creeds, and human opinions (Matthew 15:9; Proverbs 14:12). New Testament Christians used nothing but the Bible as their guide (James 1:25; 2:12). They had no earthly associations, conferences, councils, committees, presidents, or popes (Ephesians 1:22-23). *None* of these can be found in the New Testament church. Jesus

Christ was, is, and will *forever* be the church's *only* Head (Ephesians 1:22-23).

It is the *Bible* that reveals how the New Testament church used many names for the one body of Christ, the church of Christ, Romans 16:16. A Bible name suited for a Bible thing.

So, what was that *something* that was holding me back? It had nagged me relentlessly. It had caused me to cling to my denominational faith. It had been the thing that prevented me from happily receiving and obeying the Word. It was surfacing again, but this time I could not hold it back.

It was pride.

That thing that had been holding me back was pride. Is that why God lovingly warned that pride goes before destruction?

You see obeying the gospel meant that I had to admit to myself that I had been wrong. I did not want to do that. It also meant that I had to accept the possibility that millions of other *good* people were also wrong. I did not want to do that, either.

Reading the Bible had opened my eyes. It caused me anger and resentment because it opposed so many of the beliefs that I had previously held so close to my heart. They were beliefs that I ***thought*** came from the Bible.

I found out that my beliefs had not originated in the Bible, but they had originated from the denomination I had been a part of throughout most of my life.

Larry was already at his desk when I arrived at the office. I shared my concerns with him, and he said that he had shared some of the same concerns before he obeyed the gospel.

However, we did not have time to talk. Customers were waiting, and we both had a big day scheduled.

Life does not always work out the way we plan, does it?

Chapter 33
Conditioning an Elephant

March 11th

A story was told during an OSI Data Solutions sales conference about elephant poachers in the Republic of Chad in central Africa. It was said that the poachers would capture baby elephants, haul them into camp, and lock iron collars around one of their rear ankles.

The collar was the critical component and a brutally cruel device. The inside of the collar was lined with iron teeth that were approximately three quarters of an inch long and sharpened at the ends (like a spiked dog collar turned inside-out).

With one end of the collar fastened to the elephant's ankle, the other end was secured to a heavy chain about three feet in length. That *loose* end was secured to a heavy iron post fastened in the ground with cement.

After the baby elephant was secured, it would pull against the chain, trying to escape. The teeth inside the collar would pierce through the elephant's thick hide, causing immediate pain to the animal. Within a few short weeks the elephant would begin to realize that it could only move within a six foot radius without pain.

The captors would keep the elephant in the collar, secured to the base for about eighteen months or until it became completely mentally conditioned. After eighteen months, the poachers would remove the ankle collar from the fully-grown elephant, and replace it with a small rope secured to *nothing*!

As long as the elephant feels the rope around its ankle, it will not move from that six foot radius. Mental conditioning.

A full-grown, fourteen thousand pound, male elephant, with the power to squash a small car and kill dozens of men, could be easily managed to a small area with a thin piece of rope tied to nothing!

We know that the elephant has the power and opportunity to escape, but the *elephant* does not know. Mental conditioning.

Men and women spend lifetimes becoming mentally conditioned. We become shackled with routines, bad habits, negative thoughts, and poor behaviors.

We become shackled with religious beliefs that are false. Regardless of how false these beliefs might be, they can be extremely difficult to break free from.

Our lives are shaped by our beliefs that have taught to us to be good, moral, loving, sincere, zealous, honest, reputable, kind-hearted, well-meaning, trusting and trusted family, friends, advisors, and religious leaders. These beliefs are taught to us over long periods of time. Mental conditioning.

Without knowledge of our situation, we become trapped. We are spiritually trapped within that small metaphorical radius of false teachings; tethered at the ankle by that slim metaphorical rope. And look closely at the metaphorical rope. There are words written on it. The handwriting is Satan's, and it says:

"A lie I've heard a thousand times"

That metaphorical rope is tied to something that is, in our mind, very unbreakable. But, just like the Elephant's tether, our tether is tied to *something* that has no power to hold us. That something is *pride.*

I will be open with you. *This* is where I found myself. I finally found the Truth and should have been the happiest man on the planet, not letting anyone or anything stand between me and the water of baptism! Instead, I felt that rope around my ankle.

I wonder if *this* where you find *yourself* right now? It is an awful place; I know. I do not know you, but my heart truly goes out to you.

Chapter 34
Just in the Neighborhood

March 12th

Saturday arrived, and the weather was still cold. I really wanted to get the top off of my convertible, but all of the positive thinking in the world would not get the warm weather into middle Tennessee any faster.

Jonetta wanted to go to the Hickory Hollow Mall in Antioch. After several hours at the mall, she had a craving for Chinese food, and it sounded good to me too.

We finished our Crab Rangoon while discussing the possibility of a movie. A new Cineplex had just opened adjacent to the mall. I looked at my watch. 4:30 p.m. We could catch an early show.

The lines at the Cineplex were crazy long, but they were moving fast.

"Let's jump in line. It's moving pretty quick."

"Which one do you want to see?" she asked.

"I don't care." I really didn't. What sounded good to me was a nap!

"She's Having a Baby," said Jonetta.

"Who?" I asked, and Jonetta exploded in laughter.

"No, Michael! That's the name of the movie I've been wanting to see. *She's Having a Baby*[1], with Kevin Bacon and Elizabeth McGovern."

Great, another chic-flick! I would get a nap after all.

We got back to the apartment around 7:15 p.m., changed into sweats, and Jonetta started a batch of chocolate chip cookies. I had just stepped into the kitchen when our door-bell rang. Jonetta squealed like somebody had poked her in the rear-end with a steak-knife! The door-bell always startled her, which made me start laughing.

"Shut up!" She said as I walked to the front door.

I opened the door.

"Randall? What in the world are you doing here?" I was pretty surprised to say the least. Randall and I grabbed each other's extended hands.

"Hello, Mr. Mike! I'm so sorry to bother you at your home like this–"

"No, no, Randall, not at all," I responded while pulling him inside the warmth of our apartment. "It's a pleasant surprise. Get in here!"

Jonetta came out from the kitchen, and I introduced them to each other. I encouraged Randall to pull off his coat while Jonetta went to get him a cup of coffee.

We went to the living room and sat down.

"Mike, it's wonderful to see you outside of work," Randall said as he reclined on the sofa across from me. "I won't stay too long. I don't want to wear out my welcome."

"Please don't worry about doing that, Randall," I minimized his apprehension. "You're more than welcome here anytime."

"Thank you, my friend, but I have a reason for stopping by," he said.

"Oh yeah? What's that?"

"I talked to Larry on the phone today, and he mentioned that you had a concern after our last Bible study," Randall explained.

I looked at the floor, reaching up to rub the back of my neck at the same time.

"Well, yeah, Randall. I just... I'm having a tough time coming to a decision."

"Why is that, Mr. Mike?" he asked sincerely.

"Because for me to do what the Bible says, I'll have to accept the fact that my grandfather might possibly be in Hell–"

"Wait a minute, Mike," Randall interrupted, holding up his hands as he spoke. "It's not your place or mine to judge your grandfather's eternal destiny, but let me ask you something." Randall scooted up on the edge of the sofa cushion.

"What?" I asked.

Jonetta handed Randall a cup of hot coffee. "Would you like cream or sugar?" she asked.

"Neither, dear lady, but thank you for your kindness," Randall said to her as he took the cup from her hands. He looked back to me.

"What would your grandfather want you to do?"

Several seconds passed as I looked at the beige carpet under the glass-top coffee table. "I'm not sure how to answer that Randall."

"Fair enough, Mike," Randall admitted, "but could I show you something in your Bible?"

"Sure," I responded, grabbing my Bible from the end table.

"Let's take a look at Luke 16, starting with verse 19. Would you mind reading it for us?"

I read:

> *There was a certain rich man, which was clothed in purple and fine linen, and fared sumptuously every day: And there was a certain beggar named Lazarus, which was laid at his gate, full of sores, And desiring to be fed with the crumbs which fell from the rich man's table: moreover the dogs came and licked his sores. And it came to pass, that the beggar died, and was carried by the angels into Abraham's bosom: the rich man also died, and was buried; And in hell he lift up his eyes, being in torments, and seeth Abraham afar off, and Lazarus in his bosom. And he cried and said, Father Abraham, have mercy on me, and send Lazarus, that he may dip the tip of his finger in water, and cool my tongue; for I am tormented in this flame. But Abraham said, Son, remember that thou in thy lifetime receivedst thy good things, and likewise Lazarus evil things: but now he is comforted, and*

thou art tormented. And beside all this, between us and you there is a great gulf fixed: so that they which would pass from hence to you cannot; neither can they pass to us, that would come from thence. Then he said, I pray thee therefore, father, that thou wouldest send him to my father's house: For I have five brethren; that he may testify unto them, lest they also come into this place of torment. Abraham saith unto him, They have Moses and the prophets; let them hear them. And he said, Nay, father Abraham: but if one went unto them from the dead, they will repent. And he said unto him, If they hear not Moses and the prophets, neither will they be persuaded, though one rose from the dead (vv.19-31)."

"Mr. Mike, both men died and both went to the Hadean world. The King James Version translates the Greek word *hades*[2] into the word Hell, but the text reveals that the place was two separate places divided by a great gulf. One man in Torments and the other man in Paradise.

"They could see one another. They could communicate with one another, and they clearly remembered their previous lives on the earth.

"Notice that the rich man had five brothers, and he didn't want them to end up on the side of Torments when they died. So, the rich man asked Abraham to send Lazarus back to his home – back from the dead – to warn his brothers.

"Abraham told the rich man that his brothers had 'Moses and the prophets', which was the way that the Jews referred to the Old Testament. The rich man countered by saying that his brothers would be more apt to listen to someone that had risen from the dead. However, Abraham responded by telling the rich man that if his five brothers wouldn't listen to the words of the Old Testament, neither would they listen to someone that rose from the dead."

"It's a good story, Randall, but what's the point?" I asked.

"Mr. Mike, the point is this. The dead want the living to read their Bible and do what it says. The dead have no second chance. They realize that no second chance will be given to them, but they also have a hope that their families, who are still alive on the earth, will have the good sense to repent and obey the gospel. Isn't *that* what your grandfather would want you to do?"

My grandfather had been a good man. He'd been a widower left to raise 13 children on his own. My grandfather's wife died when my dad was 13 years old, and Granddad Shank had done an excellent job raising all those kids all alone.

What would he want for me? He would want me to follow the Bible. He would want me to repent and obey.

"He would want me to do what the Bible says."

"I'm sure that's exactly what he'd want, Mr. Mike." Randall got up from the couch, hugged Jonetta, thanked her for the coffee, shook my hand, put on his coat, and walked toward the door.

"Michael and Jonetta," Randall said as he smiled gently, "Thank you, again, for the coffee and for your kind hospitality."

"Hey, Randall," I got his attention as he stepped through our door into the cool night air. I was following him out the door.

"Yeah," he replied as he swung around to look at me.

"Why'd you take your time to come all the way out here tonight? Aren't we getting together Monday morning? For our last Bible study?"

Randall smiled and said, "Mr. Mike, the answer to your question is found in 1 John 4:7."

He turned and walked to his car.

I waved goodbye, ran back inside, and grabbed my Bible. 1 John 4:7 said:

Beloved, let us love one another: for love is of God; and every one that loveth is born of God, and knoweth God.

Chapter 35
The Last Study

Study 5 of 5: March 14th

"But it doesn't say anywhere to ask Jesus into your heart to be saved," I repeated with finality.

Yes, we were already into the last study. Randall and I were the only two at the office. It was early Monday morning. Most of the doughnuts were gone, and I was working on my third cup of coffee.

"Nowhere. That's one of the biggest misconceptions in religion today. Mike, Jesus doesn't get *into* us. We get *into* Him."

"Show me again." Even though I knew Randall was speaking the Truth, I had to see it again.

"Yeah, but why do I keep thinking that the principle is there, somehow?" I persisted.

"The principle of Christ living within us is taught, but not in the way *you* mean," Randall replied.

"What do you mean, 'The way *I* mean?'"

"1 John 4:4 says:

> *Ye are of God, little children, and have overcome them: because greater is* ***he that is in you****, than he that is in the world.*

"So, the Scriptures teach that the Lord lives in and through us, but at what point does that take place?" asked Randall.

"As a Baptist, I was always taught that Christ comes into you when you ask Him to forgive you of your sins, and ask Him into your heart," I responded.

"But, Mr. Mike, you *now* know that the Bible doesn't teach that. Heaven and eternal life were promised only to those who repented and were baptized. It wasn't promised to those who repented and asked Jesus into their hearts," Randall repeated tirelessly.

"Look one more time at Acts 2:38."

I scanned back to the verse:

Then Peter said unto them, Repent, and be baptized every one of you in the name of Jesus Christ for the remission of sins, and ye shall receive the gift of the Holy Ghost.

Randall and I spent the next few minutes reviewing this verse, along with Romans 6:22-23.

"And those people didn't step into the water *thinking* that they were already saved either. If you get into the water of baptism *thinking* that your sins are forgiven before you get into the water, you're not being baptized for the Bible's reason. That's not Bible baptism."

Randall reviewed Acts 2:39 through verse 47. He answered questions about the miraculous gift of the Spirit, as well as speaking in tongues, the promise to all who the Lord shall call, how God was not the author of confusion (1 Cor. 14:33), and the miracles performed by the apostles.

Randall then asked me to turn to Ephesians 1:3.

"Mr. Mike, would you read this for us?"

I read:

Blessed be the God and Father of our Lord Jesus Christ, who hath blessed us with all spiritual blessings in heavenly places in Christ.

"Mr. Mike, this says that all spiritual blessings are ***in*** Christ, right?"

"Right."

"Grace, the love of God, the answer to prayer, forgiveness of sin," Randall listed them.

"Yeah," I said.

"Then *what* spiritual blessing is found outside of Christ?" he asked.

Was it a trick question? "There aren't *any* spiritual blessings outside of Jesus Christ," I answered.

"Right! There aren't any. All spiritual blessing are in Christ. Now, if all spiritual blessings are in Christ, we've got to get *into* Christ to have access to all spiritual blessing found in Him. Make sense so far?"

"Yeah." I was following him.

"The question is this. How do we get *into* Christ?" Randall asked.

I just looked at him waiting on him to answer his own question. I already knew the answer.

"Mr. Mike, Galatians 3:26-27 tells us how to get into Christ. Let's turn there." I was already headed that direction.

I started reading it out loud before Randall got to the text:

> *For ye are all the children of God by faith in Christ Jesus. For as many of you as have been baptized into Christ have put on Christ.*

There it was again. For as many of you as have been baptized into Christ have put on Christ - baptized into Christ.

"Mr. Mike, let me say again that there's nothing holy about the water. It's the obedient act of following God's instructions and having enough faith in His divine commands to follow His commands.

"When we follow the instructive faith of baptism for the remission of sins, we're literally translated into Jesus Christ, and into the kingdom [the church] of His dear Son, Colossians 1:13, 18. That's what the Apostle Paul said."

"Randall, this continues to blow me away. As I read the Bible, I realize how much I *haven't* read."

"That's okay, man. Let me show you another one that'll blow your mind. Turn to Colossians 2:11-13." I found the text quickly and read:

> *In whom also ye are circumcised with the circumcision made without hands, in putting off the body of the sins of the flesh by the circumcision of Christ: Buried with him in baptism, wherein also ye are risen with him through the faith of the operation of God, who hath raised him from the dead. And you, being dead in your sins and the uncircumcision of your flesh, hath he quickened together with him, having forgiven you all trespasses*."

"Mr. Mike, when a man or woman hears the gospel, they must obey it if they want to be saved from eternal destruction. That means that they must repent of a life of sin. They must then make a public confession of their belief that Jesus is the Son of God just as the Eunuch did in Acts 8. Then they must submit themselves to be immersed in the watery grave of baptism.

"Paul said, here in Colossians, that we're buried with Him in baptism. It's a circumcision made without hands – literally, an operation performed by God!

"Men want to discredit the need for baptism by calling it a work. Well, it's a work alright, but it's not a work of man. It's a work of God! That's what the Bible says.

"We undergo an operation by the hand of God within the passive event of baptism; whereby, God symbolically circumcises the individual. Then, we're risen up out of the water in the likeness of Christ's resurrection. We rise with Him through faith. Paul says that we're 'quickened' together with Jesus Christ through this process. It's here, in the grave of baptism, that we're forgiven of all trespasses.

"The Apostle Peter made it as clear as it can be. He said, in 1 Peter 3:21:

The like figure whereunto even baptism doth also now save us (not the putting away of the filth of the flesh, but the answer of a good conscience toward God,) by the resurrection of Jesus Christ.

"Peter likened baptism to the flood. He said that the flood was the type (foreshadow) of baptism.

"Paul wrote in Ephesians 2:8:

For by grace are ye saved through faith; and that not of yourselves: it is the gift of God."

I had heard this verse quoted a thousand times in the Baptist Church, but they did not know what it meant. *I* had not really understood what it meant either.

By grace are ye saved through faith. Not *faith alone,* but Bible faith, faith defined by the Bible.

What was the Bible's definition of faith? Take the New Testament as a whole, and it becomes clear. The Bible definition of faith: Belief, repentance, public confession of belief that Christ is God's Son, baptism for remission of sins into Jesus Christ. That is Bible faith.

For by grace (God's offer of unmerited salvation) through faith (our exercise of obedience to God's instructions to believing, repenting, confessing Jesus Christ and being baptized for remission of sins), and that not of yourselves (not by maintaining the former law of Moses) you are saved. It is the gift of God (the gift of God is Jesus Christ and access to His blood through Bible faith).

I compared Ephesians 2:8 with Colossians 2:12. It says through the faith of the operation of God. What is the faith of the operation of God? The answer is in Colossians 2:12:

> *Buried with him in baptism, wherein also ye are risen with him through the faith of the operation of God.*

That's saving faith. Bible faith. New Testament faith. It is the faith that harmonizes with everything in the New Testament.

"Mr. Mike, there is no rational, spiritually-honest person in the world who can refute God's plan of salvation," Randall said.

He was right.

"Listen, man," Randall continued, "We've gotta wrap it up right here, but there's something that you need to do for yourself. We won't be finished until you do this, okay?" He was writing something on a piece of scratch-paper.

"Yeah, Randall. What do you want me to do?"

He handed me the paper.

"I want you to find out on your own how Saul of Tarsus became a Christian. How did Saul of Tarsus become the Apostle Paul? Promise me you'll do this," Randall pled.

"Sure, Randall. I promise."

"There's a reason you need to do this, Mr. Mike," he explained. "It's because you are a lot like Saul before his conversion."

"You've said that before," I remembered.

"You're hot-headed, strong-willed, and you've depended on your past feelings and emotions to guide you in religion. Like you, Saul sincerely thought that he was doing the right thing. He thought he was saved and he thought he was living in God's good grace. But Saul found out something that changed his life. I believe you'll find the same thing."

I looked at the scratch-paper that Randall had handed me. It said,

John 9:31 / Acts 22:16

"Start with these verses," Randall said as he pointed to the note.

I stood up from the old chair situated next to Randall's desk. People were filing in through the back door, making their way to their offices. I didn't care. I grabbed Randall and hugged him tight.

"Thank you for your friendship, Randall," I said to him with a brotherly embrace.

"My friend, it's been an honor to study with you," said Randall.

I slipped the paper into the breast pocket of my pinpoint oxford and grabbed my Bible and my briefcase.

We went our separate ways for the day.

Chapter 36
An Epiphany

March 14th, 1988: Monday Night, 11:30PM

"Wake up! Honey, wake up–"

"What is it?" Jonetta jerked out of sleep.

"I need you to read this," pointing to a passage in my open Bible.

She hurried to prop herself upright against her pillow, hearing the urgency in my voice. She took the Bible from my hands while rubbing her eyes. "What time is it?"

"11:30 p.m.," I answered.

"What do you want me to read?" she asked.

"Randall gave me a couple of references to study. Look here in Acts 22," I said as I scanned my index finger down the page until I found verse 16. "Read verse 16."

She read it to herself then looked up at me and smiled. Why'd she smile?

"Well?" I asked.

"Well," she replied, "be baptized and wash away thy sins."

"You're not surprised?" I was surprised that she *wasn't* surprised.

"I've been studying those tracts that you brought home. I've been reading through them for the last couple of months now. I wondered how long it was going to take you to see it for yourself."

My wife had been reading the Bible behind my back! Of all the nerve. She was a good woman!

"You've read Paul's conversion?" I asked.

"Yeah." She was nonchalant.

"You know he was struck down on the Damascus road by Christ and became a believer on that road? You know that Jesus told him to go to Damascus to find out what to do, and that he prayed for three days without any food or water?"

"Uh huh," she said as she smiled. Tears began to form in her eyes.

"You know that, even though he prayed for three days, he wasn't saved?"

"Yes." Now the tears were streaming down her face.

"Jonetta, Paul had a direct encounter with Jesus Christ. He was a complete believer in Jesus Christ, but he wasn't saved! He prayed for three days, and he still wasn't saved! He still had his sins because Ananias told him to get up and be baptized to wash away his sins!

"Ananias didn't tell him to ask Jesus into his heart, and he didn't tell him to say the Sinner's Prayer! Did you know that?" I was in a state of shock.

"I know that, sweetheart, and I'm so glad that you've finally seen it! I wasn't going to wait on you much longer," she explained. "I've wanted to be baptized for weeks now. I've been worried about my soul, but I've been waiting on you to see it for yourself," she said with joy through tears of happiness.

"Well, do you know what this means?" I asked her as I jumped out of bed and rushed to our closet.

She jumped out of bed, as well. "Yeah. It means that we're going to get baptized!"

At that point we were yanking clothes out of the dresser drawers. I was talking rapidly.

"Jonetta, when I got into that water at the age of 13, I thought that I had no sin. The Baptist preacher told me that I was already saved. He said baptism had nothing to do with salvation. He said it was just an outward show of an inward change."

"Yeah," she said as she pulled on her shoes.

I kept talking.

"And if I got into the water thinking I had no sins, I was not baptized for the remission of sins. I wasn't baptized like those in the Bible were baptized. It was not biblical.

"Jonetta, I was baptized for the wrong reason, and if that's the case, my baptism is no good. I'm still in my sins at this moment. I'm not a true Christian!"

"Michael, I haven't been baptized for the remission of my sins either, but who are we going to get to baptize us at this time of the night?" she asked.

We were definitely on the same page.

"I'm calling Larry. He'll know." I grabbed the phone from our nightstand.

Larry picked up the phone after the fourth ring.

"Hello," he said in a gravelly voice.

"Larry, it's Mike. Listen, I'm sorry to wake you, but Jonetta and I need to be baptized!"

"Right now?" Larry responded with surprise.

"Yeah, right now!"

"Mike, that's fantastic! Hang on just a sec…"

I could hear movement on Larry's end. He was probably trying to find a light.

"Mike," Larry came back on the line, "Randall is the only one that I know I can call. Is it okay if he's the one to–"

"Larry, I wouldn't want anyone else," I interrupted with relief at the thought that my friend Randall might be the one to baptize us.

"Alright," Larry responded. "I'll call Randall right now and get him to meet us at the church building. Just pick me up at my place. I'll be ready." Larry hung up.

We were on our way to obeying the gospel and becoming New Testament Christians!

We grabbed our jackets and the car-keys on the way out the door. The thought hit me again, what would mom and dad think?

But Jesus said:

> *Think not that I am come to send peace on earth: I came not to send peace, but a sword. For I am come to set a man at variance against his father, and the daughter against her mother, and the daughter in law against her mother in law. And a man's foes shall be they of his own household* (Matthew 10:34-36).

I now understood His statement. The sword that Christ sent was the Word. John said in Revelation 1:16:

> *...and out of his* [Christ's] *mouth went a sharp two-edged sword...*

The Hebrew writer wrote, in Hebrews 4:12:

> *For the word of God is quick, and powerful, and sharper than any two-edged sword, piercing even to the dividing asunder of soul and spirit, and of the joints and marrow, and is a discerner of the thoughts and intents of the heart.*

Paul wrote to the church of Christ at Ephesus, in Ephesians 6:17:

> *...and the sword of the Spirit, which is the word of God*:

Jesus came to establish, confirm, and send a sword. That sword was the Word of God, the written New Testament. The Bible would divide members of families, because some would obey it, and some would not.

Those who chose not to obey would question, resent, argue, debate, resist, and hate the decision of their family members who *did* obey.

What would mom and dad think? It did not matter. I had come to the knowledge of the truth. I would follow Jesus Christ at all cost. Maybe God *did* want me after all.

Then I remembered 1 Timothy 2:3-4:

For this is good and acceptable in the sight of God our Saviour; Who will have all men to be saved, and to come unto the knowledge of the truth.

Chapter 37
Digging Down

March 15th, 1988: 12:25AM
(less than an hour later)

Yes, it is easier to believe a lie that one has heard a thousand times than to believe a fact that one has never heard before.

It took months of diligent digging, tenacious and consistent digging, into the Bible. I had to choose to invest time into God's Word, rather than spend time doing the normal things that I did. It took muscle and a shovel.

It took muscle and a shovel to dig down beyond the mud and the sand and the gravel of a lifetime of erroneous religious teachings. I had to dig down beyond the denominational creeds, the religious confusion, the unbiblical practices, and all of the doctrines that opposed the New Testament's plain and simple Truth.

I dug deep down beyond it all. I dug beyond my own personal ideas of how salvation was *supposedly* obtained and beyond all of the ideas taught to me by denominational pastors, beyond what those pastors alleged, and beyond their mistaken beliefs and false teachings. They, too, had been cutting off the end of the ham.

I dug down to the Truth and down to the Bible's teaching for salvation from my sins. I dug down to God's scheme of redemption, his plan of salvation for all of mankind.

I dug down until I found the most precious thing ever available to mankind. It was a stream of soul-saving blood and water. A stream two thousand years old. A stream that still flows generously in great abundance with a current powered by the love of the Savior. It is a current so strong that nothing could ever stop its flow.

I dug down until I found that mysterious stream of blood and water, the source of that precious river of blood and water was the pierced side of Jesus Christ. After one of the soldiers pierced his side with a spear, forthwith came there out blood and water (John 19:34).

Every man and woman can bathe in the precious stream of soul-saving blood. How? Through any water that's used for proper, Bible baptism. Christ's blood is found in those waters.

I could bathe in His blood and be washed of my sins simply by exercising faith in God's instructions. Was I willing to exercise real Bible faith by obeying God's commands, thus receiving His grace through obedience?

> *By faith Abraham, when he was called to go out into a place which he should after receive for an inheritance,* ***obeyed****; and he went out, not knowing whither he went* (Hebrews 11:8).

> *By faith Abel offered unto God a more excellent sacrifice than Cain, by which he obtained witness that he was righteous, God testifying of his gifts: and by it he being dead yet speaketh* (Hebrews 11:4).

> *By faith they passed through the Red sea as by dry land: which the Egyptians assaying to do were drowned. By faith the walls of Jericho fell down, after they were compassed about seven days. By faith the harlot Rahab perished not with them that believed not, when she had received the spies with peace* (Hebrews 11:29-31).

I was escaping the mental conditioning that had held me for so long. My spiritual collar had been removed. Granddad Shank would want me to heed the words of the Bible. He would want that more than anything.

Jonetta and I picked up Larry at his apartment. I looked at the digital clock in the car. 12:45 a.m.

"We're going to the Jackson Street church of Christ," Larry said as he jumped into the back seat of our Grand Am.

"Great! Thanks a lot, Larry."

"Hey, I'm honored to be a part of this event. No, let me say that I'm honored to be a part of the greatest event of your lives!"

"Larry, we're so thankful for your willingness to go with us tonight," Jonetta said.

"How do we get there?" I asked him.

"I'll show you. The Jackson Street congregation is close to Fisk University. It's an all-black congregation," said Larry.

"Larry, I don't care if it's an all-green congregation!" I responded. "But Fisk University? That part of town is a little risky this time of night, isn't it?"

"Don't worry, Mike. All things work together for good to them that love God, to them who are the called according to His purpose," Larry replied.

A few minutes later we had merged onto I-40 east toward the city. "Larry, will Randall be waiting at the church building to baptize us?" I asked.

"Yeah, and he might bring someone with him to witness the event," answered Larry.

"Just pray for our safety, Larry. I don't want anything to happen before we get there."

Larry smiled and offered a prayer.

Chapter 38
Top of the Steps & Into the Water

March 15th, 1988: 1:15AM

It was 1:15 a.m. Jonetta and I stood at the top of the baptistery barefoot, with our hands locked together, and tears streaming down our faces. We were surrounded by the most beautiful singing that we had ever heard. It resonated through the building by a handful of men who had given their lives to Jesus Christ.

We looked at each other about to take the step into the watery grave of baptism to be immersed into God's Son. We knew one thing was certain, our lives would never be the same.

She kissed my cheek, and the word that I had been searching for rushed to the forefront of my mind. The one word that accurately described the men's singing, pure.

The middle-aged black man was already down in the baptistery. He wore hip-waders and had his shirt sleeves rolled up. The water-level was at his sternum.

Repentance. I had made the decision to turn my back on the sins I enjoyed greatly. I thought of the Hebrew writer's words found in 11:24:

> *By faith Moses, when he was come to years, refused to be called the son of Pharaoh's daughter; Choosing rather to suffer affliction with the people of God, than to enjoy the pleasures of sin for a season.*

The pleasures of sin must be sacrificed in order to follow Christ. My smoking, drinking, cursing, lewd jokes, the lust of the flesh, the lust of the eyes, and the pride of life had to be turned away from in order to follow the One that offered eternal life.

The man in the water reached his hand toward Jonetta. She let go of my hand and stepped down into the water. The water rose high upon her five foot frame.

"Jonetta Shank," said the man. The room grew very quiet. "Have you made the decision to repent of your sins as commanded by our Lord Jesus Christ?"

"I have," Jonetta replied.

"And, Jonetta Shank, do you believe that Jesus Christ is Son of the living God?"

"Yes, I do."

"That is the confession that killed our Lord and Savior. By the authority vested in me by Christ Jesus our Lord as a fellow minister and a servant in His kingdom, I now baptize you in the name of the Father, the Son and the Holy Spirit for the remission of sins."

The man immersed Jonetta, pushing her body backward, down into the water toward a horizontal position, then quickly back up. It was a beautiful thing to watch.

She came up with a smile on her face. As soon as she was upright, the men shouted for joy with many "Amens" being shouted throughout the building. Jonetta was born again, and God added her to the church of our Lord at *that* very moment!

"Congratulations, Sister Shank. This is the greatest decision of your life! May you become a faithful servant of Christ. Remain faithful to Him unto death, and He will give you a crown of everlasting life, Revelation 2:10."

Her new brother in Christ hugged her, and tears flowed down his face. She was no longer a member of any denomination. She wore no other name than Christian. The Bible was now her only creed, and she was now a sister to every Christian we read about in the pages of the Bible.

She climbed the steps upward to my side and grabbed me when she reached the top of the steps, hugging me tightly. Then she whispered in my ear, "Hurry so that we can be together again." There were tears running down her cheeks and urgency in her voice.

I knew exactly what she was talking about, because at that very moment we were unequally yoked together. She was now in Christ, and I was not. If Christ returned at that very moment I would have been as those who do not know God and who do not obey the gospel of our Lord Jesus Christ.

The man extended his hand toward me. It was now my turn. Jonetta released her arms from around me, and I walked down the steps into the baptistery. The water was ice cold, but the man's hands were warm. He exuded love and peace.

Being there seemed surreal. Passages flashed through my mind as I thought of the many stories of conversions that I had read in the Bible. I looked out into the auditorium as my foot reached the floor of the baptistery, and my eyes met Randall's eyes. He watched with tears in his eyes and a smile on his face. I had grown to love him so very much. He was my dearest friend, and I was so humbled by all that he had done for me and my wife.

"Michael Shank," the man's voice grabbed my attention. "Have you made the decision to repent of all sin in your life as commanded by Jesus Christ?"

"I have."

"Do you believe that Jesus Christ is the Son of the living God?"

"Yes. I believe that Jesus Christ is the Son of God."

"You have made the good confession of faith in Christ Jesus. It is the public confession that caused Jesus to be nailed to the cross of Calvary. I now baptize you in the name of the Father, the Son, and the Holy Spirit for the remission of sins."

He instructed me to hold my nose with one hand and grasp my wrist with my other hand. He then put his hand at the center of my back and grabbed me by my wrist with his other hand.

Without any hesitation he pushed me backward, forcing my entire body down under the surface of the water. As soon as my body was entirely submerged, my feet came off the floor of the baptistery tank.

In that brief millisecond I was suspended horizontally in the medium of water, held in place by the hands of a Christian. They were the hands of Christ working here on the earth.

It was, at that moment, that the operation of God took place, the circumcision made without hands, contacting the blood of the One who died for me.

In that brief moment time stood still. I was translated out of the world, into Christ, and into the kingdom of His dear Son.

At that split second in time my sins were being washed away. God was the surgeon, and I was on His operating table. One by one my many thousands of sins were being removed, just as cancerous tumors are removed from the sick and dying. The Master Surgeon worked at light speed, within that millisecond of time circumcising my spiritual flesh and washing me in Christ's blood.

My old self died and was now being buried in the grave with the Lord Jesus Christ. The grave covered over with water. The deed was done.

Now, a type of resurrection was about to take place. Time caught again, and I was yanked up from the watery grave raised up in the likeness of the resurrection of Christ Jesus, raised up as a new creature, and raised up to walk in newness of life.

I inhaled a huge breath of air after my body broke the surface of the water. A new life! Completely clean! Free!

Tears shot forth as the building filled with shouts of joy from my new brothers in Christ! God added me to the church of His son, the church of Jesus Christ! My name added to the list of the saved.

I knew at that moment that I was a true Christian. My knowing was not based on temporary, shallow emotions. My knowing did not come from mere feelings or the excitement of the moment. The knowledge came from Randall's teaching and from the knowledge of the living Word of the Almighty God.

John said in John 6:45:

It is written in the prophets, And they shall be all taught of God. Every man therefore that hath heard, and hath learned of the Father, cometh unto me.

I had come to Jesus Christ by the incredible grace of God, and I had now been saved through obedient faith. I was a member of the body of Christ. I was born again. I was a New Testament Christian and a Christian only.

The men rejoiced! My wife rejoiced! The angels in Heaven rejoiced!

Words cannot possibly describe the peace that accompanied obeying the gospel of Jesus Christ. Those Godly Christian men put us into Christ that night, and our lives would never be the same.

And what agreement hath the temple of God with idols? for ye are the temple of the living God; as God hath said, I will dwell in them, and walk in them; and I will be their God, and they shall be my people. Wherefore come out from among them, and be ye separate, saith the Lord (2 Corinthians 6:16-17).

Friend, if you've read this book in its entirety, you have been taught of God. Jesus said:

At that time Jesus answered and said, I thank thee, O Father, Lord of heaven and earth, because thou hast hid these things from the wise and prudent, and hast revealed them unto babes. Even so, Father: for so it seemed good in thy sight. All things are delivered unto me of my Father: and no man knoweth the Son, but the Father; neither knoweth any man the Father, save the Son, and he to whomsoever the Son will reveal him. Come unto me, all ye that labour and are heavy laden, and I will give you rest. Take my yoke upon you, and learn of me; for I am meek and lowly in heart: and ye shall find rest unto your souls. For my yoke is easy, and my burden is light (Matthew 11:25-30).

Someone gave you this book for a reason. They probably gave you this book with reservation and maybe with a little fear. But thanks be to God that their love for you and their concern for your soul far outweighed anything that would have prevented the gospel from reaching your heart.

Jesus talked about four types of soil that represent the human heart. Only one type of soil is the kind of soil that the gospel can grow within (Luke 8:15).

The Adversary will do all that is within his power to prevent you from obeying the gospel of Christ.

There is a question that pierces your heart and mind at this very moment. It is the question of decision.

Will you obey the gospel of Jesus Christ, or will you reject it?

If you believe that Jesus Christ is the Son of God, repent and be baptized for the remission of your sins. Gladly receive his words, and be baptized. God will add you to the church of His Son, the church of Christ.

Even though I do not know you, it is my personal hope and prayer that you will contact the person who gave you this book (regardless of the day or time) and tell them that you want to obey the gospel.

This is **the greatest and most urgent decision** you will ever face in this life. Nothing has ever been this important in your past, and nothing will ever be this important in your future.

> *I call heaven and earth to record this day against you, that I have set before you life and death, blessing and cursing: therefore choose life, that both thou and thy seed may live* (Deuteronomy 30:19).

Will you choose eternal life?

Will ***you*** obey the gospel?

Chapter 39
The Sinner's Prayer
The Greatest Religious
Hoax in the History of Mankind

Fight or run? What is it going to be? I hope you are angry, angry enough to open your Bible and defend your reason for the hope that is within you. Angry enough that you will try to defend your religious positions, beliefs, and practices with the Word of God.

Open your Bible and dig, because the sooner you begin to fight, the sooner your eyes will be opened to the Truth. The sooner your eyes are opened, the sooner you will flee from the dangerous, divisive, destructive, insidious devices of the Adversary – the devices of denominationalism, confusion, false doctrines, erroneous practices, and the spiritual blindness that covers your heart and mind.

Open your Bible, because if you are honest with yourself and with God, you will flee from man-made denominations.

Open your Bible, because truth is not subjective, nor is it complicated.

This is about the hoax that is the Sinner's Prayer. It is a hoax of perversion.

This modern apostasy is a false teaching that prevents men from obeying the new birth spoken of in John 3:1-5. This truth is so clearly demonstrated in Acts 2:36-41. The Bible refutes the Sinner's Prayer in Mark 16:16, John 9:31, Acts 2:38, Acts 22:16, Galatians 3:26-27, Colossians 2:11-13 and 1 Peter 3:21.

The Sinner's Prayer doctrine is less than three hundred years old and was not accepted into main-stream religion until the 1930s. The Sinner's Prayer has many variations; however, the basic skeleton of the prayer is as follows:

> Lord Jesus, I need You. Thank You for dying on the cross for my sins. I open the door of my life and receive You as my Savior and Lord. Thank You for forgiving my sins and giving me eternal life. Take control of my life. Make me the kind of person You want me to be[1].

Another variation of the doctrine put forth by modern denominational preachers is:

> Accept Jesus into your heart through prayer right now and he'll receive you. You will be born again at the moment you receive Jesus into your heart and trust him as your Lord and personal Savior. God loves you and forgives you of all of your sins. Simply accept Christ and ask him to come into your heart. He will save you by praying the following prayer right now... (Shank, 1981).

Bass, Thompson, and Harrub wrote:

> Where exactly in the Scriptures does it teach that in order to be saved one should pray to ask Jesus to come into his heart? Through the years we have asked many within various religious groups this important question. But we have yet to find anyone who could provide a single biblical reference to substantiate such a claim. The salvation that Jesus freely gives is not conditioned on prayer; rather it is conditioned on the obedience of faith (Romans 1:5; 16:26). Truth be told the alien sinner can pray for salvation as long and hard as he wants, but that prayer will not result in such. God has stated in plain, easy-to-understand language exactly what the alien sinner must do to be forgiven. And that cannot be accomplished through prayer. It is fruitless for the alien sinner to pray to God to send Jesus into his heart. God will not respond to such a request and, additionally, salvation is not accomplished via prayer.
>
> Some in the religious world today appeal erroneously to Luke 18:9-14 commonly known as the parable of the Pharisee and the publican to support their idea that God hears the prayer of the alien sinner. In this situation the Lord contrasted the attitudes of two men: one a self-righteous religious leader, a Pharisee, and the other a humble tax collector, a Publican.

> The Pharisee stood up in a prominent area of the temple sanctuary and loudly thanked God that he was not like other men announcing his righteous deeds and attributes. Conversely, the Publican, standing afar off, humbly asked God to be merciful to him a sinner.
>
> As Christ finished the parable He explained to the disciples that it was the lowly Publican who went away justified, not the Pharisee.
>
> Those who advocate the sinner's prayer or the mourner's bench as the way to heaven sometimes use this text to suggest that God will hear and forgive an alien sinner. But when they do, they overlook the Publican's relationship to God. Obviously this man was a Jew, one of God's chosen people (the story takes place in an area, the temple sanctuary, where Gentiles were not allowed). As a Jewish man under the Old Covenant, this man was considered a child of God. He was a child in sin, but still one of God's own, nonetheless.
>
> Additionally, this humble Publican did not pray to God for salvation; instead, like King David before him, he prayed for forgiveness. As a Jew, he had every right to ask God for forgiveness, just as David had done many years earlier. Just as those today who have fallen away and seek to return have the right to do.
>
> This parable cannot be used to justify the so-called Sinner's Prayer[2].

The Sinner's Prayer, also known as The Four Spiritual Laws booklet,[3] is a "twisting of the scriptures." Bright's fourth law, as stated in his booklet, says that Christ is received "through personal invitation."

Modern day denominational preachers promote this doctrine with an attempt to use Revelation 3:20 as proof that we must "ask Jesus into our hearts" for salvation. They, in this way, replace the true Bible doctrine of the new birth that was commanded by Jesus Christ (Mark 16:15-16; John 3:1-5) with the false doctrine that is The Sinner's Prayer (cf: Acts 2:38-41; Galatians 3:26-29). Revelation 3:20 says:

> *Behold, I stand at the door, and knock: if any man hear my voice, and open the door, I will come in to him, and will sup with him, and he with me.*

Their attempt to prove the validity of The Sinner's Prayer with Revelation 3:20 falls apart when the verse *stays in its context* as the Lord intended. What is the context? The Lord was *not* speaking to *lost sinners,* but He was speaking to *Christians* at the church of Christ at Laodicea.

Jesus made His statement regarding those Christians who had developed lukewarm practices (Revelation 3:15-16), due to the growth of their wealth and comfort (v.17). Christ called them to repentance from their sinful, lukewarm attitudes (v.19).

In Revelation 3:20, Jesus once again employs the illustration of the door making a comparable inference to His previous teaching found in John 10:7:

> *Verily, verily, I say unto you, I am the door of the* ***sheep****.*

Revelation 3:20 is a statement to the *sheep* – those who are *already saved*! It is *not* a call to the lost sinner, and it is a great perversion of the Sacred Text by those attempting to support the false and wicked doctrine of The Sinner's Prayer with the verses in Revelation 3.

Honest–hearted men and women who allow the verse to remain *in context* will not be able to subscribe to, adhere to, teach, promote, advocate, or further The Sinner's Prayer doctrine.

It is also important to note that The Sinner's Prayer is also a relatively new invention. The doctrine cannot be found prior to Edward Kimball teaching it to Dwight L. Moody, circa 1855[6]. Supposedly, Edward Kimball taught Dwight L. Moody, who taught Wilbur Chapman, who taught Billy Sunday, who taught Mordecai Ham, who taught Billy Frank, aka. Billy Graham. However, the historical documentation of this story contains conflicts with the characters and timelines."

It is also astonishing to realize that the multitude of false teachers who advocate the Sinner's Prayer fail to recognize, accept, and verbalize the connection link to John 10:1:

> *Verily, verily, I say unto you, He that entereth not by the door into the sheepfold, but climbeth up some other way, the same is a thief and a robber.*

The Sinner's Prayer is an attempt to enter the sheepfold (the church, Acts 2:47; Ephesians 1:22-23; Colossians 1:18; Acts 20:28) by an alternative route rather than by the Door of Jesus Christ and His one method of entrance. The Bible repeatedly proclaims the method of entrance into and through the Door of Christ.

How do men and women enter into the Door, Jesus Christ? Paul said in Romans 6:3:

> *Know ye not, that so many of us as were baptized* ***into*** *Jesus Christ were baptized into his death?*

Paul's statement in Galatians 3:26-29 further defines the passageway into Christ:

> *For ye are all the children of God by faith in Christ Jesus. For as many of you as have been baptized* ***into*** *Christ have* ***put on*** *Christ. There is neither Jew nor Greek, there is neither bond nor free, there is neither male nor female: for ye are* ***all one in*** *Christ Jesus. And if ye be Christ's, then are ye Abraham's seed, and* ***heirs*** *according to the promise.*

Any other method of entrance, such as the Sinner's Prayer, is a false approach spoken of by Christ in His words, *"But climbeth up some* ***other*** *way"* (John 10:1). Those trying to enter the Door using the Sinner's Prayer are, in Christ's words, *"the same is a thief and a robber"* (*Ibid*).

Teaching that one can be saved by repeating the Sinner's Prayer is a doctrine that will condemn numberless good people to the Lake of Fire. Why? Because the Sinner's Prayer puts *no* one into Jesus Christ. The Sinner's Prayer is not the obedient act whereby we put on Christ. The Sinner's Prayer, therefore, does not make all *one* in Christ Jesus. And because the Sinner's Prayer does not make us *heirs* according to the promise. Baptism for remission of sins is the *only* obedient act that accomplishes all of these things (Galatians 3:26-29; Romans 6:3-5).

The Sinner's Prayer is a false doctrine promoted by men and women who are ignorant of God's Word. It is an erroneous approach to salvation which has no root, example, command, or authority of the Holy Scriptures.

Denominationalists refuse to accept the entirety of God's plan of redemption for mankind. They ignore the elements that they simply don't understand, or refuse to accept.

However, when honest, sincere, good-hearted, moral, Truth-seeking people research the entirety of the Scriptures, they consistently and unanimously find God's marvelous plan of redemption and salvation, which is:

Hearing or reading. The Word of God must be preached (taught and heard) or it must be read by the individual.

> *It is written in the prophets, And they shall be all taught of God. Every man therefore that hath heard, and hath learned of the Father, cometh unto me* (John 6:45).

> *And Philip ran thither to him, and heard him read the prophet Esaias, and said, Understandest thou what thou readest? And he said, How can I, except some man should guide me? And he desired Philip that he would come up and sit with him* (Acts 8:30-31).

> *And I said, What shall I do, Lord? And the Lord said unto me, Arise, and go into Damascus; and there it shall be told thee of all things which are appointed for thee to do* (Acts 22:10).

> *How then shall they call on him in whom they have not believed? and how shall they believe in him of whom they have not heard? and how shall they hear without a preacher?* (Romans 10:14).

> *So then faith cometh by hearing, and hearing by the word of God* (Romans 10:17).

Believing. God's Word must be believed with the entirety of the heart and mind.

> *He saith unto them, But whom say ye that I am? And Simon Peter answered and said, Thou art the Christ, the Son of the living God* (Matthew 16:15-16).

> *I said therefore unto you, that ye shall die in your sins: for if ye believe not that I am he, ye shall die in your sins* (John 8:24).

> *And as they went on their way, they came unto a certain water: and the eunuch said, See, here is water; what doth hinder me to be baptized? And Philip said, If thou believest with all thine heart, thou mayest. And he answered and said, I believe that Jesus Christ is the Son of God* (Acts 8:36-37).

Repenting of past sins. The believer who seeks salvation by the grace of God through the blood of Christ must have a true willingness to turn away from all practices of sin.

The method of the Sinner's Prayer may assume repentance, but it does not teach, state, or emphasize the necessity of the action of repentance. This is why so many who say the Sinner's Prayer are later found continuing in their former sins.

> *I tell you, Nay: but, except ye repent, ye shall all likewise perish* (Luke 13:3).

> *What shall we say then? Shall we continue in sin, that grace may abound? God forbid. How shall we, that are dead to sin, live any longer therein* (Romans 6:1-2)*?*

> *Know ye not that the unrighteous shall not inherit the kingdom of God? Be not deceived: neither fornicators, nor idolaters, nor*

adulterers, nor effeminate, nor abusers of themselves with mankind, Nor thieves, nor covetous, nor drunkards, nor revilers, nor extortioners, shall inherit the kingdom of God (1 Corinthians 6:9-10*).*

Now I rejoice, not that ye were made sorry, but that ye sorrowed to repentance: for ye were made sorry after a godly manner, that ye might receive damage by us in nothing. For godly sorrow worketh repentance to salvation not to be repented of: but the sorrow of the world worketh death (2 Corinthians 7:9-10).

Then Peter said unto them, Repent, and be baptized every one of you in the name of Jesus Christ for the remission of sins, and ye shall receive the gift of the Holy Ghost (Acts 2:38).

The Lord is not slack concerning his promise, as some men count slackness; but is longsuffering to us-ward, not willing that any should perish, but that all should come to repentance (2 Peter 3:9).

Verbalizing a public profession of one's belief that Jesus Christ is the Son of God. Every accountable, responsible soul who believes the gospel of Jesus Christ (His death, burial, and resurrection) is commanded by God to confess their belief publically (Matt. 10:32-33).

Again, the method of the Sinner's Prayer does not teach, state, or emphasize the necessity of making a public confession of belief. Many who have repeated the Sinner's Prayer have done so while watching television or listening to their radio, completely alone.

The Sinner's Prayer also perverts the biblical example of the order in which God's plan is to be followed. Denominationalists advocate that the individual repeat the

Sinner's Prayer, then after their prayer is repeated, they are instructed to go and tell someone. But they claim it is not necessary to tell anyone.

> *Whosoever therefore shall confess me before men, him will I confess also before my Father which is in heaven. But whosoever shall deny me before men, him will I also deny before my Father which is in heaven* (Matthew 10:32-33).

> *Nevertheless among the chief rulers also many believed on him; but because of the Pharisees they did not confess him, lest they should be put out of the synagogue: For they loved the praise of men more than the praise of God* (John 12:42-43).

> *And Philip said, If thou believest with all thine heart, thou mayest [be baptized]. And he answered and said, I believe that Jesus Christ is the Son of God* (Acts 8:37).

> *For with the heart man believeth unto righteousness; and with the mouth confession is made unto* [toward; in the direction of] *salvation. For the scripture saith, Whosoever believeth on him shall not be ashamed* (Romans 10:10-11).

Submission to the passive act of being baptized [immersed] into Christ for the remission of sins. Baptism is the only *passive* step in God's salvation process. It is the only step that one cannot perform on themselves, because an individual has to submit themselves into another's hands for the process to be performed.

Those who reject baptism as a work must also reject repentance as a work. The Apostle Paul wrote,

> *For godly sorrow worketh repentance to salvation not to be repented of: but the sorrow of the world worketh death* (2 Corinthians 7:10).

Those who reject baptism by calling it a work of man are either ignorant of or dishonest with God's Word. Colossians 2:11-13 states:

> *In whom also ye are circumcised with the circumcision made without hands, in putting off the body of the sins of the flesh by the circumcision of Christ: Buried with him in baptism, wherein also ye are risen with him through the faith of the operation of God, who hath raised him from the dead. And you, being dead in your sins and the uncircumcision of your flesh, hath he quickened together with him, having forgiven you all trespasses;*

Yes, baptism is certainly a work, but it is a work of God – not of man. Paul called baptism an operation of God.

Those who wish to minimize, ignore, reject, discredit, refute, and disparage the essential act of being baptized must throw out the New Testament completely. No honest individual, after studying the massive volume of scriptural references relating to baptism, could possibly refute its absolute necessity in being saved from sin; nor can anyone refute the fact that men and women are not and cannot be saved before baptism.

In the previously referenced verses (Colossians 2:11-13), Paul teaches us that baptism has *multiple efficacies* and benefits. He taught in these verses that baptism:

- Is a circumcision made without hands (by God Himself)
- Is a putting away of the body of sins of the flesh
- Is a burial with Christ

- Is the place where you rise with Christ through the faith of the operation of God
- Is an operation performed by God
- Is where you are quickened together with Christ
- Is the place where, through being quickened, you are forgiven of all trespasses (sins, offences against God, etc.)

The Sinner's Prayer, or any other so-called salvation method that opposes baptism for remission of sins, does not achieve any of the previously mentioned spiritual imperatives that happen within the realm of water immersion.

According to the Apostle Paul, complete immersion in water is the *only* phase of God's process by which *all* of these things take place.

Paul said that he was baptized to have all of his sins washed away. In Acts 22, Paul was bound and ordered to be taken into the castle (Acts 21:27-36) after Asiatic Jews raised an insurrection against him. They wanted him killed. However, Paul requested the liberty to speak to the crowd and was permitted to do so (Acts 21:37-40). As Acts 22 opens, Paul speaks to the audience and begins to defend his faith in Christ. Paul retells his own conversion story speaking expressly about his own baptism:

> *And one Ananias, a devout man according to the law, having a good report of all the Jews which dwelt there, Came unto me, and stood, and said unto me, Brother Saul, receive thy sight. And the same hour I looked up upon him. And he said, The God of our fathers hath chosen thee, that thou shouldest know his will, and see that Just One, and shouldest hear the voice of his mouth. For thou shalt be his witness unto all men of what thou hast seen and heard. And now why tarriest thou?* ***Arise, and be baptized,***

and wash away thy sins, calling on the name of the Lord (Acts 22:12-16).

Ananias had been a devout Jew, which is why he addressed Saul [Paul] with the Jewish salutation, "Brother." When Ananias came to Saul, Saul was already a complete believer. At that moment, Saul already believed that Jesus Christ was the Son of God. We know this fact from Saul's statements in Acts 22:6-11.

Then, Ananias stated that God had chosen Saul to know His [God's] will. That was to see the Just One [Jesus Christ]. So Saul had a direct, miraculous, first-hand encounter with Jesus Christ, but Saul still was not saved from sin!

How do we know that Saul was not saved, even though he was a repentant believer in Jesus Christ? We know because of Ananias' statement found in verse 16:

> *And now why tarriest thou? Arise, and be baptized, and wash away thy sins, calling on the name of the Lord.*

Ananias was a disciple of Christ and was being directed by God (Acts 9:10-15). With this fact in place, here are the questions you need to seriously consider:

1. If Saul [Paul] was saved ***before*** baptism, why did Ananias, via God's direction, tell Saul to be baptized to ***wash away his sins***?

2. If Saul was saved *before* baptism, wouldn't his sins have been removed (forgiven, washed away) *before* baptism?

3. If baptism has nothing to do with salvation, wouldn't Ananias have declared Saul to have had ***no*** sin when he came to Saul? Wouldn't he have declared Saul to be

in a saved state, due to Saul's previous, direct encounter with Jesus Christ on the Damascus Road, Saul's new-found belief in Jesus Christ, and Saul's action of spending three days in prayer and fasting – all of this before ever meeting Ananias and being immersed? Yet Ananias told him to arise and be baptized and wash away his sins?

4. Why didn't Ananias command Saul to say the Sinner's Prayer and ask Jesus into his heart to have his sins forgiven?

5. Why do men and women *now* teach and preach a Salvation approach called the Sinner's Prayer which is clearly *different* than Saul's salvation approach?

6. How is it possible that men and women are *now* saved by the Sinner's Prayer, a doctrine that did not exist in the first century and didn't exist until some 1700 years after the first century?

7. Doesn't the Bible reveal (specifically in Saul's conversion account) that calling on the name of the Lord is to be baptized?

Peter, an apostle of Christ, said this of baptism:

The like figure [the like figure of the great flood, 1 Peter 3:20] *whereunto even baptism doth also now save us (not the putting away of the filth of the flesh, but the answer of a good conscience toward God,) by the resurrection of Jesus Christ:* (1 Peter 3:21).

According to Peter, baptism now saves us. Peter clarifies that baptism is not taking a bath to wash physical dirt from our body, but it is the obedient action commanded by God for a clear conscience toward God.

Then, Peter provides the reason why baptism saves: by the resurrection of Jesus Christ.

This harmonizes perfectly with Paul's statement:

> *Know ye not, that so many of us as were baptized into Jesus Christ were baptized into his death? Therefore we are buried with him by baptism into death: that like as Christ was raised up from the dead by the glory of the Father, even so we also should walk in newness of life. For if we have been planted together in the likeness of his death* [baptism], *we shall be also in the likeness of his resurrection:* (Romans 6:3-5).

When you are fully immersed for the remission of your sins in the name of the Father, the Son, and the Holy Spirit, God adds you to the church of Christ (Acts 2:47). God demands your worship, and you must worship Him in truth and in Spirit (John 4:24).

New Testament Christians worship together upon the first day of the week (Acts 20:7), singing using only their voices (Eph. 5:19; Col. 3:16-17), giving voluntarily, sacrificially, and freely back to the Lord in a cheerful manner as they have been prospered by God (1 Cor. 16:1-2). They participate in prayer, are edified by preaching, and eat the Lord's Supper (Acts 20:7). They strive for the morals of Jesus Christ, imitate His lifestyle, and embrace His teachings. They use whatever talents they possess to serve the Lord and to expand the kingdom of Christ, His church.

They are Christians only and only Christians. They speak where the Bible speaks, and they are silent where the Bible is silent.

They bring up their children in the admonition and nurturing of the Lord, and they treat their spouses with love, kindness, affection, mercy, and great value.

Christians commit sin, but when they do they have an Advocate with the Father. They repent of their sins and return to walking in the light as He is in the light, having fellowship one with another, and the blood of Jesus Christ continually cleanses the Christian of all sins (1 John 1:7-9).

The Sinner's Prayer when examined in the light of the Scriptures is a false doctrine that must be destroyed along with all of the false doctrines of man.

Won't you yield your will and your life to the love and teachings of Jesus Christ? Won't you become a true Bible Christian? Give your life to the Lord. He will bless you in this life and the life to come.

Won't you obey the gospel before it is eternally too late? Repent and be baptized for the remission of your sins. The Lord will add you to His church.

Friend, if you decide to obey the gospel, a wonderful new life awaits you!

Chapter 40
Friend, It *Is* About *You*
Your Soul is Your Most Priceless Possession

Please let me point out something that I hope is completely apparent. I have used no *personal* interpretation of the Holy Scriptures. I have merely shared my story and revealed the Scriptures of God just as it happened.

Here's the hard part. Will you accept the simple, plain, straight-forward teaching of God's Word?

Peter said:

> *And account that the longsuffering of our Lord is salvation; even as our beloved brother Paul also according to the wisdom given unto him hath written unto you; As also in all his epistles, speaking in them of these things; in which are some things hard to be understood,* ***which they that are unlearned and unstable wrest, as they do also the other scriptures, unto their own destruction.*** 2 Peter 3:15-16

We are living in a world saturated in spiritual confusion. It is a world steeped in unholy, unbiblical traditions. Throughout history men have wrested the Scriptures to their own particular desires and preconceptions. Peter said the result would be their own destruction.

Satan appears as he has throughout time as something other than what he really is. He has deceived countless men and women through his power, through signs that seem heavenly in origin, and by remarkable wonders.

Why have countless souls been, and continue to be deceived? Because they do not love, nor will they receive and obey the Truth.

If you do not develop a love for the Truth, and if you refuse to receive the Truth, God will assist you in your desire to hold on to the lies you refuse to let go of.

Paul said:

> *Even him, whose coming is after the working of Satan with all power and signs and lying wonders, And with all deceivableness of unrighteousness in them that perish; because they received not the love of the truth, that they might be saved. And for this cause* ***God shall send them strong delusion, that they should believe a lie.*** 2 Thessalonians 2:9-11

Why have false doctrines and denominations of men proliferated throughout time? Through three incremental processes:

1. Satan's power of subtle deception
2. Man's rejection of truth
3. God's delivery of those who reject His truth over to the lies that they desire to hang on to

Be honest with yourself. Isn't it remarkable that tens of thousands of so-called preachers proclaim the message, "Ask Jesus into your heart, repeat the Sinner's Prayer, faith only saves, and have a personal relationship with Jesus," yet none of these doctrines are found in God's Word?

Paul wrote of those who teach and follow false teachings:

> *I marvel that ye are so soon removed from him that called you into the grace of Christ unto another gospel: which is not another; but there be some that trouble you, and would pervert the gospel of Christ.* Galatians 1:6-7

How do some pervert the gospel? They teach an *alteration* of the original. What *was* the original? Paul was referring to Peter's first sermon preached on the Day of Pentecost. It was a message that came from the Holy Spirit of God. In other words, it came directly from God. It was the message of Jesus Christ as the

Messiah of God about His death, burial, resurrection and then, the Divine instructions of how to be saved (Acts 2:38-47).

Peter's message was further proof of Paul's statement to Titus:

> *For the grace of God that bringeth salvation hath appeared to all men,* ***teaching*** *us…*Titus 2:11-12

God's grace brings salvation. His grace appeared on the Day of Pentecost instructing men *how* to be saved. His grace appears to you and I in the same way today. His grace appears to us through His Word, instructing us to lovingly obey Him by stepping into his grace.

Unfortunately, many in Peter's audience rejected his words just as people do today. They live in modifications, alterations, or substitutions of the original message and, therefore, are guilty of Paul's warning:

> *But though we, or an angel from heaven, preach any other gospel unto you than that which we have preached unto you, let him be accursed. As we said before, so say I now again, If any man preach any other gospel unto you than that ye have received, let him be accursed.* Galatians 1:8-9

I challenge you to get out your shovel and dig. Read the Word for yourself. See whether or not the things I have shared with you in this book are really so.

Many will hate me for what I have shared with you in this book. Many denominational preachers will seek to purge this book from society, and many who love their respective denominations will work to discredit, silence, and bury this work.

This is why I shared my story with you. Wake from your sleep. Summon an honest heart like the heart described in Luke

8:15. Find the courage to act on God's Truth and act upon it before it is *eternally too late*.

Friend, you have an eternal appointment to keep. The appointment is with God, and the date of your appointment is the Day of Judgment. The Hebrew writer wrote:

> *And as it is appointed unto men once to die, but after this the judgment*: Hebrews 9:27

Won't you give this your most serious and sober consideration?

Someday you will die.

Someday Jesus will return.

What will *He* do with *you*?

If a member of the church of Christ (Romans 16:16) gave you this book, won't you take a moment to share your thoughts with them?

They are praying that you will. Randall is praying you will. The entire Shank family is praying that you will.

Want to know what happened to Michael and Jonetta after their baptism? You'll find it in *When Shovels Break*.

Epilogue:
Randall's "Secret"
Q & A

Many readers have requested the following answers in this *Question and Answer* section:

Who is Randall Edges? While everyone would love to meet Randall in person, his identity was changed to protect his privacy and the privacy of his family.

Randall is, outside of my Dad, the finest man that I have ever known. He is so much more than my limited ability has allowed me to convey with the written word.

Randall has always wanted Jesus Christ to be the only "star" of the story of our lives. His love and humility would never allow him to be put in a "celebrity limelight," but there can be no doubt that Randall's efforts for the Cause of Jesus Christ will impact countless souls for Christ's body, the church (Col. 1:18).

And yes, I am absolutely convinced that you will meet him personally in the eternal life beyond. Maybe then our Lord will tell us how many souls reached Heaven because of Randall!

Some have said this story isn't true, because Randall's identity has been changed. It's hurtful that a few "Christians" have *assumed* that our conversion story is false, simply because of the need to protect someone's privacy.

It begs the question, "What motivates this type of thinking?" I have found, in these rare occasions, that some are authors, themselves. In other cases, some have become angry when I have denied their request to fulfill their own personal curiosity.

The important question to ask is this, who would gain by destroying any faithful work that wins souls to Jesus Christ? You know the answer. The Adversary is always at the origin of jealousy, back-biting, gossip, and malicious behavior. We know by reading the Bible that Satan, in many cases, attacked the church from "within."

Jonetta and I have tried to grow beyond the hurt inflicted by the few previously mentioned. We have been helped greatly by a wonderful piece of advice given to us by our dear friend and brother in Christ, Paul S. (*San Angelo, TX*).

Paul said, "Michael, experience has taught me something very valuable. I have learned not to wrestle a pig. You see," he continued, "there's only two things that ever happen when you wrestle a pig. 1) It amuses the pig. 2) You end up getting the mire all over you!" God bless you, Paul. We no longer wrestle pigs.

How did Michael remember his conversion story with such detail? As Jonetta and I unpacked the moving truck in late October of 2008, I was carrying boxes marked *attic* into the garage of our new home. I stumbled at the bottom of the loading-ramp and dropped some of the boxes onto the garage floor.

One of the boxes burst open and the contents were strewn across the concrete floor. As we began to pick up the items, I found an old spiral bound notebook. On the cover was scribbled:

Conversion Story: 1988

It was the story of our conversion that I had written twenty years before. The notebook had been put into a *keepsake* box marked "Attic" and forgotten until that day.

You see, I documented the entire account, in detail, *as the story happened* and in the days that followed our baptism into Christ.

Why did I document the story as it happened? It began as an effort to refute Randall's biblical arguments, but I continued to write the story as it evolved because of my love for writing. I also wanted an accurate record of our study together, because I thought that it would be useful in the future if I ever encountered someone else from the church of Christ!

After our obedience to the gospel, I threw the story in a box, never considering the idea of sharing it with anyone. Why wouldn't I want to share this story? First, I didn't want anyone to know what kind of person I was prior to my conversion. Second, it seemed like a *testimonial,* and members of the Lord's church did not do testimonials.

When the notebook reappeared, I began reading it and realized how much I had forgotten, but had no desire to put the story into print. It was Jonetta's persistent encouragement over a three year period that finally convinced me to publish the story. Thank God for good women!

Why is the King James Version of the Bible used throughout the story? The KJV continues to be the most prevalent translation used among many contemporary mainstream denominations, as well as within churches of Christ. While there are many "easier to read" versions available today, it seems as though the KJV is one translation many continue to depend on, and most people continue to accept as an accurate, reliable translation.

The KJV is also the version that Randall used in teaching me the Truth, so I have chosen to utilize the KJV in this story for accuracy and consistency.

Why didn't Randall baptize Mike and Jonetta? Randall didn't want us to be like those at Corinth:

> *Now this I say, that every one of you saith, I am of Paul; and I of Apollos; and I of Cephas; and I of Christ. Is Christ divided? Was Paul crucified for you? Or were ye baptized in the name of Paul? I thank God that I baptized none of you, but Crispus and Gaius; Lest any should say that I had baptized in mine own name* (1 Cor. 1:12-15).

He realized the potential for this to happen due to our close relationship and was wise enough to employ prevention at the beginning.

It is also interesting to realize that Randall relinquished all "credit" for his labors to another Christian, and to the Lord.

Why didn't Randall just invite Mike and Jonetta to his church? Great question! Could it be because Randall followed the Lord's command found in Matthew 28:19?

Go ye therefore, and teach all nations, baptizing them…

Inviting the lost to services is not the "approach" that our Lord wanted us to take, is it?

How did Randall recite the Scripture so quickly and accurately without an open Bible? Randall shared the answer with me a few days after Jonetta and I was baptized. It's possibly the most vital question surrounding this story, and it might be one of the most important questions any New Testament Christian can ask after reading this story. I call his answer, "**Randall's Secret**."

Randall explained, "Mr. Mike, you've gotta *work* at internalizing the Lord's Word. Peter said that Jesus had the *words of life*. John 6:68 says, '*Then Simon Peter answered him, Lord, to whom shall we go? Thou hast the words of eternal life*.'"

"But how in the world do you do that?" I asked.

Randall opened his briefcase and pulled out a very worn stack of 3x5 index cards with a couple of rubber-bands around the stack. After pulling off the rubber bands, he started showing me the cards. Each card contained one Bible verse that Randall had written by hand.

"Mr. Mike," Randall began to explain, "you go get you a bunch of these notecards and write *one* Bible verse on *each* one. Memorize one verse from one card every week – just one. At the end of the year, you'll have memorized fifty verses, and that's more Bible than almost anyone you'll find walking around on the street today.

"Do it again the second year and you'll have about a hundred verses memorized. That's more Bible than almost any denominational preacher knows! Brother, keep this up throughout your life, always reviewing the older cards along with the new cards. Just one verse a week!"

It was an incredible revelation! Randall didn't have any magic. He didn't have a photographic memory. He didn't possess supernatural powers! Randall had simply applied the principle of memorizing one verse a week throughout the years of his life.

What were the fruits of his diligence to this simple principle?

Jesus Christ permeated every part of his being. Randall enjoyed a purity of life and a quality of existence beyond anyone else that I had ever met. He possessed the peace that surpassed all human understanding (Philippians 4:7). Randall enjoyed the true happiness and excitement that accompanies a tangible hope in Jesus Christ (Romans 5:5; 8:24; 12:12; Galatians 5:5; Philippians 1:20; Colossians 1:27; 1 Timothy 6:17). He easily identified error and promoted Truth (Romans 12:2). He did not need to be ashamed, but comfortably divided the Word of Truth through his acceptance of Paul's command to study (2 Timothy 2:15). Randall, through his principle of regular memorization of the Bible, put on the armor of God daily (Ephesians 6:10-18), and contended for the faith which was once delivered to the saints (Jude 3). He displayed confidence within humility (Romans 12:3).

Randall, because of his diligence to memorize a verse each week, had the gentle ability to discuss almost any Bible topic without fear (2 Timothy 3:16). He was able to manage his own emotions (2 Peter 1:5-11) and his tongue (James 3:2).

And Randall never boasted, was never arrogant, and never made a big deal about his extensive knowledge of God's Word.

He offered the following passages to affirm his principle of the need and benefits of regular memorization of Scripture:

> ***Thy word have I hid in mine heart****, that I might not sin against thee* (Psa. 119:11).

> *This book of the law shall not depart out of thy mouth; but* ***thou shalt meditate therein day and night****, that thou mayest observe to do according to all that is written therein: for then thou shalt make thy way prosperous, and then thou shalt have good success* (Jos. 1:8).

> *And these words, which I command thee this day,* ***shall be in thine heart****: And thou shalt* ***teach them diligently*** *unto thy children, and shalt talk of them when thou sittest in thine house, and when thou walkest by the way, and when thou liest down, and when thou risest up. And thou shalt* ***bind them*** *for a sign upon thine hand, and they shall be as* ***frontlets between thine eyes****. And thou shalt* ***write them upon the posts of thy house, and on thy gates*** (Deut. 6:6-9).

Therefore ***shall ye lay up these my words in your heart and in your soul****, and bind them for a sign upon your hand, that they may be as frontlets between your eyes* (Deut. 11:18).

Thy words were found, and ***I did eat them****; and thy word was unto me the joy and rejoicing of mine heart: for I am called by thy name, O LORD God of hosts* (Jer. 15:16).

Blessed is the man that walketh not in the counsel of the ungodly, nor standeth in the way of sinners, nor sitteth in the seat of the scornful. But his delight is in the law of the LORD; and ***in his law doth he meditate day and night****. And he shall be like a tree planted by the rivers of water,* ***that bringeth forth his fruit in his season; his leaf also shall not wither; and whatsoever he doeth shall prosper*** (Psa. 1:1-3).
I delight to do thy will, O my God: yea, ***thy law is within my heart*** (Psa. 40:8).

How does the Lord's Law get written on the hearts of men and women today? This is the relevant, practical question. The answer? It cannot and does not happen in any way other than regular, daily memorization.

Look at what happens when we ***don't*** put effort into committing God's Word to memory:

For if any be a hearer of the word, and not a doer, he is like unto a man beholding his natural face in a glass: ***For he beholdeth himself, and goeth his way, and***

> ***straightway forgetteth what manner of man he was****. But whoso looketh into the perfect law of liberty, and continueth therein, he being not a forgetful hearer, but a doer of the work, this man shall be blessed in his deed* (James 1:23-25).

If we just read without taking the time and effort to internalize (memorize) the Word of God, **we go our way and forget**.

I sincerely hope that "Randall's Secret" gives you a renewed sense of excitement and zeal. Why? ***Because if you will take this information and apply it to your daily life, it will make you into a Randall!***

Will ***you*** become a Randall?

ORDERING INFORMATION

Buy paperback, hardback, single or multiple copies on sale. We also offer deep discounts for multiple copies direct from the author at:

michaelshankministries.com

Find us on Facebook at:
https://www.facebook.com/pages/Muscle-and-a-Shovel/225178630892427

You can also order from Amazon.com, Barnes & Noble, Books-a-Million, Ingram Books, The Book Depository, and many Christian bookstores across the nation.

OTHER PUBLICATIONS

Muscle and a Shovel
Muscle and a Shovel eBook & Kindle Version
Muscle and a Shovel 13-Week Student Workbook
Muscle and a Shovel 13-Week Teacher's Manual
Muscle and a Shovel Spanish Version
Muscle and a Shovel Portuguese Version
When Shovels Break
When Shovels Break eBook & Kindle Version
Revel Knox: 7 Times from Hell (Western novel with the gospel and the plan of salvation embedded within the story)
Revel Knox: 7 Times from Hell eBook
Muscle and a Shovel Audio Book

READERS HAVE SAID

"If every Christian would read this book they would strengthened beyond belief. If every Christian gave 10 copies of this book to their friends and family the world could be evangelized in a short period of time!"

Mark A., Oklahoma

"Congregations of the Lord's church should make a commitment to giving 100 copies of Muscle and a Shovel to the lost in their communities. Can you imagine what the Lord could do through this work? We would once again create a Restoration Movement instead of living in a Restoration Standstill."

Janice T., Alabama

Dan Webb (N.B. Hardeman's Nephew) said the following about *Muscle and a Shovel*:

"I have preached the gospel for approximately 60 years. I have read countless volumes of brotherhood and non-brotherhood books throughout my preaching career. I can honestly say that I've never in my 60 year career ever seen anything like this in our brotherhood. This book refutes almost every false doctrine with the Bible in a story format that captivates and holds the reader to the very end.

"This book is something that will not only reach millions of lost souls, but it is a product that will serve to strengthen our brethren all over the world.

"Every Christian should own a copy of this book; every Christian should give a copy to every lost soul that they know. There's little doubt that this is one of the most magnificent evangelism tools in our brotherhood today. Maybe one of the very best ever! If our brethren gave this book to the lost, the Lord's church will grow at a rate not seen since the Restoration Movement. Give this book to a friend and change their life!"

ABOUT THE AUTHOR

Michael Shank lives in rural southern Illinois with his wife, four sons and their chocolate lab. He earned a BS in Management Communication from Southern Christian University. He now serves the church through preaching around the country and writing.

ABOUT THE COVER DESIGNER

Joe Kelly is a bright young man with an incredible creative talent. He discovered a passion for art and creativity at an early age; doodling and sketching anything that came to mind.

Joe is majoring in visual communications and graphic design at Western Kentucky Community & Technical College. He has gained valuable experience through freelance projects, a current internship, and a dedication to continual practice. Joe intends to build a successful career as a designer after graduation, and is seeking any opportunity to advance towards that objective.

We're grateful to God for Joe's design-work on this new cover. If you have an interest in considering Mr. Kelly for design work, you can reach him at:

jkelly.graphicdesign@gmail.com

END NOTES

PREFACE

1. Larry and Andy Wachowski (1999). *The Matrix*. Movie: Executive Producer, Joel Silver. Warner Bros. Pictures: Burbank, CA.

Chapter 1

1. Pontiac and Grand Am are copyright names of GM, P.O. Box 33170, Detroit, MI 48232-5170

2. Darkwoods, Castle Rock Entertainment (1999). *The Green Mile*. Stephen King: Novel (same name). Feature film, drama. 187 minutes. John Coffey played by Michael Clarke Duncan.

3. Mr. Clean is a registered trade-mark owned by Procter & Gamble Corporation.

Chapter 2

1. Peter Gabriel (1986). *Big Time*. From the album "So." Produced by Daniel Lanois, Virgin Records.

2. Krispy Kreme Doughnuts is a registered trademark licensed by Krispy Kreme Doughnuts, Inc., P.O. Box 83, Winston-Salem, N.C. 27102

Chapter 4

1. BMW is a registered, licensed trademark of BMW and its affiliates. BMW of North America, LLC, 300 Chestnut Ridge Road, Woodcliff Lake, NJ 07677-7731

2. Ping is a licensed trademark of Ping Corporation, P.O. Box 82000, Phoenix, Arizona 85071-2000

3. Big Mac is a licensed trademark of McDonald's Corporation and its affiliates. McDonald's Corporation, 2111 McDonald's Dr., Oak Brook, IL 60523

Chapter 9

1. J. E. Tull, *Shapers of Baptist Thought* (1972); L. Davis, *Immigrants, Baptists, and the Protestant Mindin America* (1973); R. G. Torbet, *A History of the Baptists* (4th ed. 1975); W. H. Brachney, *The Baptists* (1988).

Chapter 10

1. Kool-Aid is a licensed trademark of Kraft Foods, Inc., Tree Lakes Drive, Northfield, IL, 60093

2. Marlboro is a licensed trademark of Philip Morris USA, PO Box 18583, Pittsburgh, PA 15236

Chapter 12
1. Old Spice is a licensed trademark of P&G, 1 Procter and Gamble Plaza, Cincinnati, OH 45202

Chapter 18
1. Seiko is a registered trademark of Seiko Corporation and its Affiliates. 8-10,, Toranomon 2-chome, Minato-ku, Tokyo 105-8467, Japan

2. Thayer, J. (1996). Baptidzo (phonetic); Baptizo. Strong's #907.
Definition: To dip, immerse, submerge, overwhelm. Thayer's Greek-English Lexicon of the New Testament. Hendrickson Publishers. ISBN: 1565632095

Chapter 19
1. Skoal is a registered trademark of U.S. Smokeless Tobacco Company, PO Box 18583, Pittsburgh, PA 15236

Chapter 20
1. Palmer, Edwin. (1972). The Five Points of Calvinism. Baker Publishing Group. Ada, MI.

2. Bucher, Dr. Richard P. (nd). Calvinistic Theology. Lexington, KY.
URL: http://www.orlutheran.com/html/calvinisttheology.html

3. Wilson, B. (1942). The Emphatic Diaglott. International Bible Students Association: Watchtower Bible and Tract Society Publishers, Brooklyn, NY.

Chapter 21
1. Cosby Show Television Sitcom Series (1984-1992).
Weinberger, Leeson, Cosby: Creators. Carsey Werner Production Company: Los Angeles.

2. Updated research, 2011. *Greek for 1519: The Meaning of Eis in Acts 2:38*. Obeying The Truth Org.

Chapter 22
1. Unity. (2008). *Merriam-Webster Online Dictionary*. Retrieved April 22, 2008 from
http://www.merriam-webster.com/dictionary/unity
2. Tolerance. (2008). *Merriam-Webster Online Dictionary*. Retrieved April 22, 2008 from
http://www.merriam-webster.com/dictionary/tolerance

Chapter 23
1. NSA. National Security Agency. Ft. Meade, Maryland.

Chapter 24
1. New York Times, 620 8th Avenue, New York, NY, 10018.

2. Rasky, S. (1987). The New York Times: *A Front-Runner for Commerce Post*. NYT Business Day (August 1, 1987).

3. Hitler, Adolf. (1925-26). Mein Kampf. Eher Verlag publisher. Germany.

Chapter 26

1. Hiscox, E.T. (1965). Hiscox Standard Baptist Manual. Judson Press, Valley Forge, PA.

Chapter 27

1. J. Coltrane. *Blue Train: Blue Train Album,* 1957. Produced by Alfred Lion, Van Gelder Studio. Hackensack, NJ

2. Updated from What Did Early Christians Believe About Using Instrumental Music in Worship.
Accessed 2011 from http://www.bible.ca/H-music.htm

3. The Catholic Encyclopedia, (1905). Subsection: Organ. Robert Appleton Publishing Company, NY

4. Proverbs 14:12

Chapter 29

1. Thayer, J. (1996). Poimen. Strong's #4166. Definition: Shepherd; Herdsman; Pastor. Thayer's Greek-English Lexicon of the New Testament. Hendrickson Publishers. ISBN: 1565632095

Chapter 30

1. Exposé. (1987). Album *Exposure: Seasons Change*. Arista label. Written and produced by Lewis Martineé. Genre: Pop, R&B.

2. Thompson, D.M. (1980). *Let Sects and Parties Fall: A Short History of the Association of Churches of Christ in Great Britain and Ireland*, Berean Publishing Trust.

3. Murch, J.D. (1962). *Christians Only*. Cincinnati: Standard Publishing.

4. Campbell, Alexander. (1827). *The Christian Baptist: Volumes I – IV*.

5. Leith, John L. (1983). *Creeds of the Churches: A Reader in Christian Doctrine, From the Bible to the Present* (p.193). Chicago: Aldine Publishing.

Chapter 31

1. Kobe Steaks, 210 25th Ave N # 100, Nashville, TN 37203-1615

Chapter 34

1. She's Having a Baby. (1988). Paramount Pictures and Hughes Entertainment. 106 minutes.

2. Thayer, J. (1996). Hades. Strong's #86. Definition: the place (state) of departed souls - grave, hell. Thayer's Greek-English Lexicon of the New Testament. Hendrickson Publishers. ISBN: 1565632095

Chapter 39

1. McDowell, Josh, *The New Evidence that Demands a Verdict*, Nashville, TN: Nelson (1999).

2. Bass, Thompson, and Harrub (2001). *Does God Hear and Respond to the Prayer of an Alien Sinner?* Montgomery, AL: Apologetics Press. URL: http://www.apologetics press.org/APContent.aspx?category=11 &article=434

3. Bright, B. (1964). *The Four Spiritual Laws*. Nashville, TN: Nelson Word Publishing.

4. McLoughlin Jr., W. (1955). *Billy Sunday Was His Real Name*. Chicago, IL: University of Chicago Press.

5. Kashatus, W. (2010, March 10). *Evangelist Billy Sunday Preaches to More Than 650,000 in W-B*. Citizen's Voice.

6. Chapman, J. (n/a). The Life & Work of Dwight Lyman Moody. www.biblebelievers.com/moody/05

BIBLIOGRAPHY

Bass, Thompson, and Harrub, *Does God Hear and Respond to the Prayer of an Alien Sinner?* Montgomery, AL: Apologetics Press (2001).

Brachney, W. H., *The Baptists*, Santa Barbara: ABC-CLIO (1994).

Bucher, Dr. Richard P., Calvinistic Theology, Lexington. URL: http://www.orlutheran.com/html/calvinisttheology.html

Calvin, J., *Institutes of the Christian Religion*, London: Hatfield and Norton Publishers (1599).

Campbell, A., *The Christian Baptist*, Vol. I-IV (1827).
Catholic Encyclopedia, *Subsection: Organ*. New York: Robert Appleton Publishing (1905).

Davis, Lawrence B., *Immigrants, Baptists, and the Protestant Mind in America*, Urbana: University of Illinois Press (1973).

Herbermann, Pace, Pallen, Shahan, Wynne (editors), *The Catholic Encyclopedia*, New York: Robert Appleton Publishing Company (1905).

Hiscox, E.T., *Hiscox Standard Baptist Manual*, Valley Forge: Judson Press (1965).

Hitler, A., *Mein Kampf*, Germany: Eher Verlag publisher (Vol. I, 1925; Vol. II, 1926).

McDowell, Josh, *The New Evidence that Demands a Verdict*, Nashville, TN: Nelson (1999).

Leith, John L., *Creeds of the churches: A Reader in Christian Doctrine From the Bible to the Present*, Chicago: Aldine Publishing (1983). p.193

Lewis, C.S., *The Christian in Danger: Learning in War-Time*, Oxford: Ashley Sampson Publisher (1939).

Merriam-Webster Dictionary Online, Springfield: John Morse Publisher (2008).

Murch, J.D. *Christians Only*, Eugene: Wipf & Stock Publishers (1962).

Obeying the Truth, *Greek for 1519: The Meaning of Eis in Acts 2:38*, accessed April 16, 2010 from http://www.obeyingthetruth.org/into.htm

Palmer, Edwin., *The Five Points of Calvinism*, Ada: Baker Publishing (1972).

Thayer, J.H., *Thayer's Greek-English Lexicon of the New Testament*, Peabody: Hendrickson Publishers (1996).

Thompson, D.M. *Let Sects and Parties Fall: A Short History of the Association of Churches of Christ in Great Britain and Ireland*, Birmingham, England: Berean Publishing Trust (1980).

Torbet, R.G., *A History of the Baptists*, Valley Forge: Judson Press (1982).

Tull, James. E., *Shapers of Baptist Thought*, Valley Forge: Judson Press (1972).

Wilson, B., *The Emphatic Diaglott*, Brooklyn: Watchtower Bible and Tract Society (1942).

SCRIPTURAL REFERENCES

All Scriptures referenced within this book are from the King James Version of the Holy Bible, due to its common acceptance among a variety of denominations. It was also the version used in teaching me the gospel. Over 1,000 individual verses are referenced.

Chapter 1
Ephesians 5:19
Colossians 3:16
Romans 8:28

Chapter 3

Matthew 24:36
2 Thessalonians 1:6-10
Acts 20:28
2 Thessalonians 1:7-8

Chapter 4
1 Peter 3:21

Chapter 5
1 Peter 3:21
Ephesians 2:8-9
2 Timothy 2:15
Ephesians 2:8
Ephesians 2:15
Ephesians 2:10-22
Ephesians 2:8-9
Galatians 5:4
James 2:17, 19, 24
Ephesians 2:8-9
2 Peter 3:16
1 Peter 4:11
Ephesians 2:8-9

Chapter 6
Acts 20:28

Chapter 8
Matthew 3
2 Peter 2:3
Chapter 9
Matthew 3
Matthew 3:6
Matthew 5:23-24
Matthew 16:13-18
Acts 20:28
Colossians 1:18
Matthew 16:18
Matthew 16:16
Matthew 14:10
Acts 2
John 8:32
Matthew 22:29

Chapter 10
John 3:16
John 15:5

Chapter 11
2 Timothy 3:16-17
John 3:16
John 3:1-5
1 Peter 3:15
Romans 12:18
John 3:5
1 Peter 3:21

Chapter 13
Proverbs 14:12
Jeremiah 17:9
2 Thessalonians 1:7-8

Chapter 14
Acts 10:34
John 14:15
Matthew 7:23
Matthew 15:9
Romans 6:17
Acts 2

Chapter 15
Luke 23:42-43
Hebrews 9:16-17
Galatians 6:2
Hebrews 9
Ephesians 2:14-16
Romans 6:3-5
Matthew 27:51
John 8:24
Mark 16:16
Numbers 21:4-9
John 12:42
Acts 2:36
Acts 2:38
John 3:5

Chapter 16
Acts 2:38

Chapter 17
1 Peter 3:15
John 12:48
Matthew 7:21

Matthew 15:13-14

Chapter 18
Mark 16:16
Matthew 7:21-23

Chapter 19
Acts 8:26-40
Isaiah 53
Acts 8:36
Romans 10:17
Acts 8:27
Luke 13:3
Acts 8:37
Acts 8:38
Mark 16:16
Acts 8:26, 29
John 16:13
John 6:45

Chapter 20
Matthew 15:9
John 15
1 Timothy 4:1-3
Matthew 23:9
Deuteronomy 30:19
Ezekiel 18:20
Deuteronomy 12:31
Jeremiah 32:35
Ezekiel 18:23
2 Peter 3:9
Philippians 2:12
Galatians 5:4
Hebrews 12:15
Revelation 2:10
1 John 2:2
Titus 2:11-12a
Hebrews 6:4-6
1 Corinthians 9:27
Mark 16:17-20
James 1:25
1 Corinthians 13:8-10
John 16:13-14
Matthew 24:35
John 17:17
Acts 2

John 16:13
Matthew-John
Acts
Romans-Jude
Revelation
Mark 16:17-20
2 Timothy 3:16-17
Galatians 1:8-9
John 16:13
Galatians 1:8
2 Timothy 4:3-4
Ephesians 5:21-33
2 John 1:9-10
2 Timothy 4:3-4

Chapter 21
Acts 2:38
Matthew 26:28
Mark 1:4
Luke 3:3
John 6:68

Chapter 22
John 17:21
Acts 2:46
Philippians 2:2
1 Peter 3:8
Matthew 7:14
John 15:5-10
John 15:6
John 15:5
1 Corinthians 1:10-13

Chapter 23
Matthew 3

Chapter 24
John 15:5-10
1 Corinthians 1:10-13
James 2:24
John 3:1-5
Galatians 1:8-9
Luke 8:15
Acts 17:11
2 Corinthians 11:13-15
Matthew 22:29

Matthew 15:9
Genesis 3:2-4
Matthew 7:21-23

Chapter 25
Matthew 16:18
Acts 2:38, 41, 36, 41, 47
Colossians 1:18
Ephesians 4:4
1 Peter 5:8
Ephesians 5:23-25
Romans 16:16
Acts 2
1 Timothy 3:1-7
Titus 1:5-9
1 Timothy 3:8-12
Acts 2:33
Colossians 1:18
Ephesians 1:20-23
Ephesians 4:3-6

Chapter 26
John 4:24
Matthew 15:9
Matthew 7:21
John 16:13
Acts 20:7
Exodus 20:8
Acts 20:7
Matthew 28:19
Colossians 3:16
Galatians 3:24
Exodus 31:12-15
Leviticus 27:30
Deuteronomy 14:23
2 Chronicles 31:5
Galatians 5:4
1 Corinthians 16:1-2

Chapter 27
Ephesians 5:18-19
2 Peter 1:20-21
Colossians 3:16
John 16:13
Genesis 6:14
Leviticus 10:1-2

1 Corinthians 14:16
1 Corinthians 14:15
Psalms 42
Matthew 22:29
Ephesians 5:19
Colossians 3:16
John 4:24

Chapter 28
Psalms 111:9
John 12:42-43
Matthew 23:9
Acts 10:26

Chapter 29
Ephesians 4:11
Acts 11:30
Acts 14:23
Acts 15:2, 4, 6, 22, 23
Acts 16:4
Acts 20:17-18
Titus 1:5
James 5:14
1 Peter 5:1, 5
Acts 10:25-26
1 Peter 2:9
1 Timothy 3:1-7

Chapter 30
Romans 1:16
2 Thessalonians 1:6-10
1 Corinthians 15:1-4
Romans 6:3-5
Galatians 3:26-27
Acts 2:47
Colossians 1:18
Romans 6:3-5
2 Thessalonians 1:6-10
Acts 22:16
Ephesians 5:23-25
Acts 2:47
John 3:3-5
Acts 2:38
Mark 16:16
Ephesians 4:5
1 Peter 3:21

2 Peter 2:1-2
Acts 5:41
Matthew 18:20
Romans 6
Genesis 3:2-4
Mark 16:16

Chapter 32
Matthew 7:14
Ephesians 4:4
Colossians 1:18
Acts 2:36-47
Colossians 1:18
Ephesians 5:23-25
Acts 20:28
Romans 1:16
1 Corinthians 15:1-4
2 Thessalonians 1:8
Romans 6:3-5
2 Thessalonians 1:6-10
Galatians 1:8-9
Acts 2:38
Acts 22:16
Colossians 2:11-13
Titus 2:11-12
Hebrews 11
Acts 2:41
Acts 2:47
Ephesians 4:4
Romans 16:16
Acts 2:41
Acts 2:42-46
Acts 2:42
Acts 20:7
Ephesians 5:19
Colossians 3:16
1 Corinthians 16:1-2
Acts 20:7
Ephesians 5:19
Colossians 3:16
1 Corinthians 16:2
2 Corinthians 9:7
1 Corinthians 16:2
Galatians 5:1-4
Ephesians 2:13-16
Colossians 2:14-15

Matthew 5:20
1 Timothy 3:1-7
Acts 14:23
1 Timothy 5:17
Titus 1:5
Ephesians 1:22-23
Acts 2:32-36
Acts 20:28
1 Timothy 3:15
Acts 2:47
Acts 8:36-38
Matthew 15:9
Proverbs 14:12
James 1:25
James 2:12
Ephesians 1:22-23
Romans 16:16

Chapter 34
Luke 16:19-31
1 John 4:7

Chapter 35
1 John 4:4
Acts 2:38
Romans 6:22-23
Acts 2:38-39
1 Corinthians 14:33
Ephesians 1:3
Galatians 3:26-27
Colossians 1:13
Colossians 2:11-13
Acts 8
1 Peter 3:21
John 16:13
Ephesians 2:8
Colossians 2:12
John 9:31
Acts 22:16

Chapter 36
Acts 22:16
Matthew 10:34-36
Revelation 1:16
Hebrews 4:12
Ephesians 6:17

1 Timothy 2:3-4

Chapter 37
John 19:34
Hebrews 11:8
Hebrews 11:4
Hebrews 11:29-31

Chapter 38
Hebrews 11:24
Revelation 2:10
John 6:45
2 Corinthians 6:16-17
Matthew 11:25-30
Luke 8:15
Deuteronomy 30:19

Chapter 39
John 3:1-5
Acts 2:36-41
Mark 16:16
John 9:31
Acts 2:38
Acts 22:16
Galatians 3:26-27
Colossians 2:11-13
1 Peter 3:21
Romans 1:5
Romans 16:26
Luke 18:9-14
Mark 16:16
John 3:1-5
Acts 2:38-41
Galatians 3:26-29
Revelation 3:20
Revelation 3:14-17, 19, 20
John 10:7
Revelation 3:20
John 10:1
Acts 2:47
Ephesians 1:22-23
Colossians 1:18
Acts 20:28
Romans 6:3
Galatians 3:26-29
John 10:1

Galatians 3:26-29
Romans 6:3-5
John 6:45
Acts 8:30-31
Acts 22:10
Romans 10:14
Romans 10:17
Matthew 16:15-16
John 8:24
Acts 8:36-37
Romans 6:1-2
1 Corinthians 6:9-10
Luke 13:3
2 Corinthians 7:9-10
Acts 2:38
2 Peter 3:9
Matthew 10:32-33
John 12:42-43
Acts 8:37
Romans 10:10-11
2 Corinthians 7:10
Colossians 2:11-13
Acts 22
Acts 21:27-36
Acts 21:37-40
Acts 22:12-16
Acts 22:6-11, 16
Acts 9:10-15
1 Peter 3:21
Romans 6:3-5
John 4:24
Acts 20:7
Ephesians 5:19
Colossians 3:16-17
1 Corinthians 16:1-2
Acts 20:7

Chapter 40
2 Peter 3:15-16
2 Thessalonians 2:9-11
Galatians 1:6-7
Acts 2:38-47
Titus 2:11-12
Galatians 1:8-9
Luke 8:15
Hebrews 9:27

Romans 16:16

Epilogue
Colossians 1:18
1 Corinthians 1:12-15
Matthew 28:19
John 6:68
Philippians 4:7
Romans 5:5
Romans 8:24
Romans 12:12
Galatians 5:5
Philippians 1:20
Colossians 1:27
1 Timothy 6:17
Romans 12:2
2 Timothy 2:15
Ephesians 6:10-18
Jude 1:3
Romans 12:3
2 Timothy 3:16
2 Peter 1:5-11
James 3:2
Psalm 119:11
Joshua 1:8
Deuteronomy 6:6-9
Deuteronomy 11:18
Jeremiah 15:16
Psalms 1:1-3
Psalms 40:8
James 1:23-25